THE COUNTRY MUSIC ALMANAC

Tom Biracree

PRENTICE HALL GENERAL REFERENCE

NEW YORK • LONDON • TORONTO • SYDNEY • TOKYO • SINGAPORE

To my beloved wife, Nancy, for bearing so much of the burden, and to my son Ryan, who is the music in our lives.

ACKNOWLEDGMENTS

Tony Seidl, a good ole country boy, sparked the project, and Gerry Helferich had the vision to quickly hop aboard the train and the strength of character to hold on when the going got rough. Karen Jahne's name should be on the title page; without her talent and hard work, this book wouldn't exist. Pat Reshen and the entire staff of Pink Coyote Designs Inc. literally worked around the clock to produce this book—it's a joy to work with talented professionals who really care.

We wish to thank the following organizations for the use of their photographs:

p. 12 Republic Pictures; p. 19 CBS Television; p. 23 United Artists; p. 28 Flatt & Scruggs; p. 37 MGM Records; p. 40 RCA Records; p. 44 Republic Pictures; p. 49 Columbia Records; p. 52 Decca Records; p. 58 CBS Television; p. 64 NBC Television; p. 67 United Artists; p. 78 RCA Victor Records; p. 80 Capitol Records; p. 94 Decca Records; p. 110 RCA Records; p. 112 Epic Records; p. 116 RCA Records; p. 122 Republic Pictures; p. 130 RCA Records; p. 133 Capitol Records; p. 138 Capitol Records; p. 141 Warner Bros.; p. 143 RCA Records; p. 145 RCA Records; p. 147 Arista Records; p. 149 MCA; p. 156 RCA Records; p. 158 RCA Records; p. 160 RCA Records; p. 167 MGM Records; p. 169 Curb/Warner Bros.; p. 171 CBS Television; p. 181 Decca Records; p. 186 RCA Records; p. 187 Capitol Records; p. 190 Capitol Nashville/SBK; p. 194 Monument Records; p. 194 Decca Records; p. 195 MCA Records; p. 196 Columbia Records; p. 198 RCA Records; p. 200 (top) CBS Television; p. 200 (bottom) Epic Records; p. 201 MCA Records; p. 202 (top) CBS Television; p. 202 (middle) Warner Bros.; p. 202 (bottom) Warner Bros.; p. 203 Curb/Warner Bros. All other photos are from the author's collection.

PRENTICE HALL GENERAL REFERENCE
15 Columbus Circle
New York, New York, 10023

Library of Congress Cataloging-in-Publication Data
Biracree, Tom
 The Country Music Almanac / Tom Biracree.
  p. cm.
 Includes Index
 ISBN 0-671-79761-1
 1. Country Music—Miscellanea. I. Title.
ML3524.B57 1993
781.642—dc20

Designed by Eduardo Andino,
Pink Coyote Designs Inc.

Manufactured in the United States of America

10 9 8 7 6 5 4 3 2 1

First Edition

CONTENTS

WHO'S WHO IN COUNTRY MUSIC

COUNTRY SONGS

INTRODUCTION

If you're looking for evidence that country music is America's music, all you need is one statistic—the average yearly ratings for the Nashville Network are nearly three times higher than the ratings for MTV. Rock and roll—that "Johnny-come-lately" sound that sprang up in the 1950s—may garner more headlines, but in the 1990s, it's country music that sets the cash registers ringing. Sales of country albums reached $700 million in 1992, and two-thirds of American record store owners named country as the hottest-selling format.

Why is country enjoying such a boom? John J. O'Connor wrote in the *New York Times*, "There has always been something warmly reassuring about country music. The scene is infused with a sense of tradition." Although today's new country stars such as Garth Brooks, Vince Gill, and Alan Jackson have an image more upscale suburban than cowboy, their music is built upon the work of the classic country music stars of decades ago, from Jimmie Rodgers to Ernest Tubb to Hank Williams to George Jones. The Grand Ole Opry—broadcast on Saturday nights continuously since 1924—today puts on shows in which Brooks and Gill perform with Minnie Pearl, Porter Wagoner, or bluegrass pioneer Bill Monroe. Although the issues in the songs have changed, country music still focuses on emotional truth and spiritual nourishment. The sentimentality and civility stressed in country music fit a country recoiling from the greed and selfishness of the 1970s and 1980s. Country's fresh, talented stars singing ballads with touching, comprehensible lyrics seem light-years away from the heavy metal and rap that dominate the rock scene today.

This book is a celebration of country music past and present. Packed into these pages are fun facts about more than 1,000 past and present country musicians and country groups. You can find out when Roy Acuff was born, how Gene Autry became a movie star, what songs have reached Number One on the country charts since 1941, which artists have grabbed Grammy and Country Music Association Awards, and a whole lot more. The fun facts, interspersed with pictures, will make listening to your favorite music a lot more fun.

Roy Rogers

THE COUNTRY TRADITION:
A RICH HISTORY

WHERE DID COUNTRY MUSIC COME FROM?

Country music is grassroots American music, having its origins not in the bustling cities, but in rural America where working people tilled and mined the soil. Although the formal history of country music dates back only to the early 1920s, its seeds were the ballads and folk songs brought over to this country by the first immigrants who scattered into the wilderness. These old songs, which were soon forgotten in big cities, were passed down from generation to generation in locations as scattered as the mountains of West Virginia, the cotton fields of Georgia, and the vast cattle ranches of Texas. This Anglo-Saxon musical heritage was influenced by the musical heritage of African-Americans. The result was true folk music that provided the primary entertainment at dances, fairs, and other local events.

In the early 1920s, the booming popularity of two relatively new technologies brought about the emergence of this rural music: the phonograph and the radio. Until the mid-1920s, record companies concentrated on producing music that appealed to urban audiences, with whose tastes they were familiar. When a few bold pioneers, such as Ralph Peer, ventured into rural America to record what came to be known as "hillbilly" music, they discovered this music had a vast, untapped audience.

Radio was an even more revolutionary technology that brought free entertainment into the smallest, most remote communities. Small radio stations sprang up to serve this market. The least expensive and easiest way for these stations to fill air time was live entertainment by local musicians. Again, audience response was enthusiastic. By the end of the 1920s, powerful 50,000-watt radio stations reached enormous areas of the country with shows such as the "Grand Ole Opry" and the "National Barn Dance" that featured "hillbilly" musicians. Some of these musicians, such as Jimmie Rodgers and Uncle Dave Macon, became stars.

When the Depression settled on America in the 1930s, country musicians struggled to make a living by constantly touring. Despite the strain on the musicians, live concerts brought them in contact with an audience eager for diversion. At the same time, another invention, the talking motion picture, created a new kind of hero — the singing cowboy. Gene Autry and others cowboys helped spread the popularity of a kind of music that was now called country-western.

By the 1940s, more than 300,000 jukeboxes had been installed in bars and restaurants. Because the noise of a bar crowd made it hard to hear music, some country musicians used electric guitars to create a hard-driving sound called "honky-tonk." Country music also created its equivalent of the "big band" sound called "western swing." Yet a third style that evolved from the old-time country string bands was a lively, banjo-driven sound called "bluegrass." Because the Armed Services in World War II were a huge melting pot, all types of country music reached vast new audiences.

Rock-and-roll, which had strong country roots, dominated popular music in the 1950s and 1960s. To compete, many country musicians incorporated some pop elements into their music to create what came to be called the "Nashville sound," or "country-pop."

Beginning in the late 1960s, country music was rejuvenated. The "outlaw" movement led by Johnny Cash and Waylon Jennings reintroduced the hard-driving honky-tonk style. Innovators like Gram Parsons pioneered "country-rock," a style that inspired such groups as Alabama. Country stars like Dolly Parton crossed over to produce pop hits. Male vocalists like George Strait revived the country ballad singing that had been the staple of such pioneers as Roy Acuff and Ernest Tubb.

In the 1990s, country music was attracting talented men and women that would have turned to rock a decade earlier. In 1992, Garth Brooks was the Number One musical performer across all categories, while Billy Ray Cyrus's "Achy Breaky" dominated American dance floors. The music that began in the most remote reaches of this land had truly become the American sound.

The men and women who produce that sound tend to be different from other musicians. Perhaps because so many come from rural families, they tend to have a rich sense of tradition and a deep appreciation of those artists who have come before them. Every country fan should share their love for the legendary stars and their knowledge of important events in the evolution of the music.

TEST YOUR COUNTRY I.Q.

If country is your favorite sound, you've probably absorbed a lot of facts about the music you've heard and the people who make that music. Test your country I.Q. by taking this tough quiz—if you answer more than 40 questions correctly, you're a country genius.

1. Q: Which American singer was named Country Music Star of the Decade *in England* in 1980?
   A: Texan Don Williams

2. Q: Who was the first female country singer to perform at West Point Academy?
   A: Sunday Sharpe (her real name) with her 1974 hit, "I'm Having Your Baby."

3. Q: One of 11 children, she first recorded as Ann Fowler, but took over the slot and name of another singer sponsored by Page Milk. Who was she?
   A: Patti Page.

4. Q: Whose brothers are Jay Lee Webb and Ernest Ray, and sister is named Peggy Sue?
   A: Loretta Lynn.

5. Q: What superstar has given only one hit to the country fans who love him most? What was the song title?
   A: Burt Reynolds, with "Let's Do Something Cheap and Superficial."

6. Q: Which three country singers were also A & R Directors for which recording companies?
   A: Owen Bradley for Decca; Bonnie Guitar for Dot and ABC/Paramount; and Fred Carter, Jr., for ABC Records.

7. Q: Which country singer besides rodeo queen Lynn Anderson is an accomplished California equestrian?
   A: Juice Newton.

8. Q: How often and when did Ernest Tubb put "Blue

Christmas" on the charts?

A: Three times: Number one in 1949, number five in 1950, and number five in 1952.

9. Q: Which country singer is in the *Guinness Book of World Records*, holding the record for being buried underground for 140 days?

A: Elvis—NOT. Bill White, Jim Mundy's brother.

10.Q: Which country singer besides Rita Coolidge is part Native American and what song put her on the charts?

A: Dixie Harrison with "Yes Ma'am, He Found Me in a Honky Tonk."

11. Q: What Canadian group is comprised entirely of Native Americans?

A: Billy Thunderkloud & the Chieftones.

12. Q: This Hispanic star appears in *The Milagro Beanfield War*. What are his names, by birth and on stage?

A: Freddy Fender, born Baldemar G. Huerta.

13. Q: Name three scruffy, long-haired singers credited with the Outlaw Movement in country music.

A: Willie Nelson, Waylon Jennings, Tompall Glaser.

14. Q: In the movie *Coal Miner's Daughter*, Sissy Spacek is standing on the porch with a baby on her hip. Who's the kid?

A: Crystal Gayle.

15. Q: OK, everybody knows Trigger. What was the name of Hank Snow's horse?

A: Shawnee.

16. Q: An English rocker came to Nashville to pick up its sound and married into its royal family. Who was he?

A: Nick Lowe, who married Carlene Carter.

17. Q: Which country star chaired the Family Farm Defense Fund and organized its successful benefits?

A: John Conlee.

18. Q: Two albums of country classics were recorded by this group in disco style.

A: Albert Coleman's Atlanta Pops.

19. Q: Lynn Anderson recorded "Even Cowgirls Get the Blues" in l980. Who is the popular author of a 1976 book by the same name?

A: Tom Robbins.

20. Q: Roy Drusky sang "(From Now on All My Friends Are Gonna Be) Strangers" in 1965. What Texas author wrote a book by the same title?

A: Larry McMurtry.

21. Q: Where did the group Dr. Hook get its name?

A: Band leader Ray Sawyer has an eye patch.

22. Q: Which came first, Nashville's Country Music Association Awards or L.A.'s Academy of Country Music Awards?

A: The ACM Awards, in 1965, preceded the CMA Awards by two years.

23. Q: Who made a Number One hit of "I Will Always Love You" ten years before Whitney Houston sang it?

A: Dolly Parton in *The Best Little Whorehouse in Texas*.

24. Q: Which U.S. Senator made it on the country charts without singing a word?

A: Everett Dirksen with his spoken "Gallant Men."

25. Q: What country singer sang jingles for McDonalds, Miller and Budweiser?

A: T. Graham Brown.

26. Q: Which country superstar also sells a clothing line?

A: Jimmy Buffett.

27. Q: Jim Reeves and Patsy Cline had two hit singles, although they never recorded together. How?

A: Their voices were electronically spliced in 1981.

28. Q: Bing Crosby and the Andrews Sisters invaded country music with a Number One hit in 1944. What was it?

A: "Pistol Packin' Mama."

29. Q: Who wrote and recorded "Born to Lose," taking it to number three on the charts a full 18 years before Ray Charles?

A: Ted Daffan in 1944.

30. Q: Which great session musician gave Bob Dylan's
   Nashville Skyline an authentic country sound?
   A: Charlie Daniels, founder of the Charlie Daniels Band.

31. Q: Which country singer starred in *North Dallas 40*?
   A: Mac Davis.

32. Q: Who wrote "Flowers on the Wall"?
   A: Lew Dewitt, founding member of the Statler Brothers.

33. Q: What was the name of Hank Williams' backup band?
   A: The Drifting Cowboys.

34. Q: Morton Downey, Jr., once hit the country charts. How?
   A: As Sean Morton Downey, he sang "Green Eyed Girl"
   in 1981.

35. Q: Which country singer has been most honored by
   organized labor?
   A: Dave Dudley, who was given a gold card by the
   Nashville Truck Drivers Union.

36. Q: Jimmy Driftwood's "The Battle of New Orleans" is
   based on what melody?
   A: Square dance tune "The Eighth of January."

37. Q: Steve Earle sang "Six Days on the Road" for what
   movie?
   A: *Planes, Trains & Automobiles* in 1988.

38. Q: Who is credited with inventing the twangy guitar
   sound of country music?
   A: Duane Eddy.

39. Q: What country lyric gave Ethel and the Shameless
   Hussies a name for their trio?
   A: Ray Stevens's "The Streak."

40. Q: When was the theme music for the 1968 movie *Bonnie
   and Clyde* recorded?
   A: In 1949 as "Foggy Mountain Breakdown," by Flatt &
   Scruggs and the Foggy Mountain Boys.

41. Q: Who was the recording artist and the artist manager for
   Slim Whitman, Webb Pierce, David Houston and
   Johnny Horton, with whom he died in a car crash?
   A: Tillman Franks.

42. Q: What Texas band leader served in the Peace in Corps Borneo?
    A: Kinky Friedman, founder of The Texas Jewboys.

43. Q: Which two country stars are cousins of the Reverend Jimmy Swaggart?
    A: Mickey Gilley and Jerry Lee Lewis.

44. Q: Johnny Cash recorded an album at San Quentin prison. What country star served time there?
    A: Merle Haggard.

45. Q: Who owns "Opryland," the program transmitted from the Grand Ole Opry?
    A: Gaylord Entertainment, likewise owner of The Nashville Network, Country Music Television, and a new cable network in Europe.

46. Q: What was the sister act that opened for and recorded with brother acts?
    A: The Forester Sisters, who opened for the Gatlin Brothers and had a Number One single with The Bellamy Brothers.

47. Q: Mickey Gilley's "Here Comes the Hurt Again" was written by songwriters with 60 ASCAP awards. Who?
    A: Jerry Foster and Bill Rice, who also wrote "39 and Holding" for Jerry Lee Lewis.

48. Q: What famous country singer played in Buddy Holly's Crickets?
    A: Waylon Jennings.

49. Q: Although it had been used in pop and jazz songs, what was the first country song with Honky Tonk in the title?
    A: Al Dexter's "Honky Tonk Blues."

50. Q: Who pioneered the way for female country singers with her 1936 hit "I Wanna Be a Cowboy's Sweetheart?"
    A: Patsy Montana, born Ruby Blevins and daughter of rodeo impressario Monte Montana.

CHRONOLOGY OF COUNTRY MUSIC

It's hard to keep events straight that occurred in the past without linking them to important dates. In our personal lives, those dates are often weddings, birth dates of children, the passing of loved ones, or an important promotion. In recent American history, such landmark events as the assassination of President Kennedy, the bombing of Pearl Harbor, and the landing on the moon trigger many memories.

The history of country music, too, is a succession of dates that stretches back more than 200 years. Which dates are particularly important depend on everyone's own experience—they could include the birthday of favorite singer, the release date of a memorable song, a tragedy such as the death of Patsy Cline, or any one of the other 700 events listed in this chronology.

1736

First American fiddling contest held in Hanover County, Virginia.

1781

Thomas Jefferson, in his writings, refers to a new musical instrument called the "banjo."

1830

The five-string banjo is invented by Joel (Joe) Sweeney, a minstrel entertainer from Virginia.

1839

The Tyrolese Rainer Family, an alpine Swiss singing group, tours the U.S.A., inspiring the formation of harmony singing groups in rural areas.

1848

Uncle Jimmy Thompson born.

1868

March 23: Fiddlin' John Carson born.

1870

About this time, rural folk musicians combine fiddles and banjos in the first string bands.
October 7: Uncle Dave Macon born.

1887

November 20: Eck Robertson born.

1890

March 11: W. Lee O'Daniel born.

1891

April 15: A. P. Carter born.

1892

March 22: Charlie Poole born.
April 6: Henry Whittier born.

1893

April 6: Vernon Dahlhart born.
May 25: Ernest "Pop" Stoneman born.

1894

May 1: Sam McGee born.

1895

July 13: Bradley Kincaid born.
July 21: Ken Maynard born.
November 9: George D. Hay born.

1896

August 23: Wendell Hall born.

1897

September 8: Jimmie Rodgers born.

1898

July 20: J. E. Mainer born.

1899

January 26: Doc Hopkins born.
September 13: Kelly Harrell born.
November 4: Kirk McGee born.

1900

August 9: Buell Kazee born.
September 21: Dickey Lee born.

1901

November 1: Lew Childre born.
December 5: Ray Whitley born.

1902

May 4: Al Dexter born.

1903

September 8: Milton Brown born.
September 27: A fast mail train on the Southern Railroad crashes, killing 12 people. The event sparks the song "The Wreck of the Old 97," the first country hit.

1904

May 6: Cliff Carlisle born.

1905

January 12: Tex Ritter born.
March 6: Bob Wills born.
April 11: Hartford Taylor born.
August 5: Frank Luther born.
December 17: Karl Davis born.

1907

April 21: Wade Mainer born.
September 29: Gene Autry born.

1908

July 10: Paul Howard born.
October 20: Stuart Hamblin born.
December 19: Bill Carlisle born.
December 25: Alton Delmore born.

1909

March 29: Moon Mullican born.
May 10: Maybelle Addington Carter born.
November 8: Scotty born.

1910

January 27: Walter Callahan born.
February 22: Spade Cooley born.

Roy Rogers and Trigger

    June 4: Texas Ruby born.
    November 9: Curly Fox born.
    December 3: Rabon Delmore born.

1911

    September 9: Zeke Clements born.
    September 13: Bill Monroe born.
    November 5: Roy Rogers born.

1912

    March 27: Homer Callahan born.
    August 8: Rex Griffin born.
    September 21: Ted Daffan born.
    October 25: Minnie Pearl born.
    October 31: Dale Evans born.
    November 29: Robert Lunn born.

1913

March 17: Andy Parker born.
July 15: Cowboy Copas born.
October 20: Grandpa Jones born.
December 24: Lulu Belle born.

1914

About this time, guitars are first played in rural areas.
February 9: Ernest Tubb born.
February 16: Jimmy Wakely born.
February 18: Pee Wee King born.
May 11: Bob Atcher born.
May 13: Johnny Wright born.
June 26: Doc Williams born.
October 30: Patsy Montana born.
November 17: Archie Campbell born.
December 8: Floyd Tillman born.
December 14: Cousin Jody born.
December 15: "Red River" Dave McEnery born.

1915

April 25: Cliff Bruner born.
June 1: Johnny Bond born.
June 15: A. P. Carter marries Sara Dougherty.
June 17: Stringbean born.
July 15: Guy Willis born.
October 10: Owen Bradley born.
December 11: Dolly Good born.

1916

June 20: T. Texas Tyler born.

1917

January 3: Leon McAuliffe born.
February: Wally Fowler born.
March 1: Cliffie Stone born.
June 20: Jimmie Driftwood born.
June 27: Elton Britt born.
July 7: John (Lonzo) Sullivan born.
July 29: Henry "Homer" Haynes born.
August 23: Tex Williams born.
November 11: Yodeling Slim Clark born.
November 29: Merle Travis born.
December 20: Skeeter Willis born.

1918

February 15: Hank Locklin born.

May 15: Eddy Arnold born.

July 17: Red Sovine born.

August 18: Hank Penny born.

August 30: Kitty Wells born.

October 16: Stoney Cooper born.

1919

Lloyd Loar designs an easy-to-hold mandolin for the Gibson Company that soon becomes very popular in rural America.

January 19: Rollin (Oscar) Sullivan born.

1920

February 13: Boudleaux Bryant born.

February 22: Del Wood born.

1921

February 7: Wilma Lee born.

April 10: Sheb Wooley born.

May 27: Redd Stewart born.

December 22: Harold "Hawkshaw" Hawkins born.

1922

March 16: Radio station WSB in Nashville goes on the air for the first time.

May 31: Vic Willis born.

June 30: Fiddlers Eck Robertson and Henry Gilliland cut the first country records for Victor in New York.

1923

January 4: Radio station WBAP in Fort Worth airs the first live "barn dance" broadcast.

March 2: Doc Watson born.

March 10: Kenneth "Jethro" Burns born.

March 29: Eck Robertson performs two previously recorded songs on WSB, becoming the first musician to use radio to promote a record.

June 14: Fiddlin' John Carson records "Little Old Cabin in the Lane" for Ralph Peer, a single that proves there is an audience for country music.

July 9: Molly O'Day born.

August 20: Jim Reeves born.

September 17: Hank Williams born.

1924

January 20: Slim Whitman born.

April 19: Chicago radio station WLS airs its first live show featuring rural music, a program that soon becomes the "WLS Barn Dance."

April 21: Ira Louvin born.

June 6: Rosalie Allen born.

June 20: Chet Atkins born.

August 29: The Jenkins Family becomes the first country music family to be recorded.

October 27: Bonnie Lou born.

November 1: Edison Records releases Vernon Dalhart's "Wreck of the Old '97," which becomes country music's first massive hit.

December 31: Rex Allen born.

1925

January 15: A group of mountain musicians led by Al Hopkins call themselves "The Hill Billies," giving a name to American rural music.

April 7: Felice Bryant born.

April 29: Danny Davis born.

April 30: Johnny Horton born.

May 23: Mac Wiseman born.

June 28: George Morgan born.

July 2: Marvin Rainwater born.

August 27: Carter Stanley born.

August 28: Billy Grammer born.

September 3: Hank Thompson born.

September 26: Marty Robbins born.

October 5: Radio station WSM in Nashville begins broadcasting.

November 28: Radio station WSM airs its first "Barn Dance."

December 19: "Little" Jimmy Dickens born.

1926

Uncle Dave Macon joins the WSM "Barn Dance," becoming its first star.

January 12: Ray Price born.

August 8: Webb Pierce born.

September 28: Jerry Clower born.

November 2: Charlie Walker born.

November 15: National Broadcasting Company launches the NBC Radio Network.

December 15: Rose Maddox born.

1927

February 13: Jim McReynolds born.
February 25: Ralph Stanley born.
March 15: Carl Smith born.
June 2: Carl Butler born.
July 7: Charlie Loudermilk born.
August 1-4: Jimmie Rodgers and the Carter Family cut their first recordings for Victor Records in Bristol, Tennessee.
August 16: Fess Parker born.
August 27: Jimmy Newman born.
December 3: Ferlin Husky born.

1928

Jerry Wallace born
April 3: Don Gibson born.
April 25: Vassar Clements born.
May 3: Dave Dudley born.
November 15: C. W. McCall born.
December 8: George Hay renames the WSM "Barn Dance" the "Grand Ole Opry."
December 15: Ernie Ashworth born.

1929

January 14: Billy Walker born.
April 3: Johnny Horton born.
May 1: Sonny James born.
July 9: Jesse McReynolds born.
August 12: Buck Owens born.
September 8: Harlan Howard born.

1930

January 7: Jack Green born.
March 13: Liz Anderson born.
April 29: Eddie Noack born.
July 7: Doyle Wilburn born.
August 12: Porter Wagoner born.
August 22: Rex Griffin born.
September 28: Tommy Collins born.

1931

February 17: Uncle Jimmy Thompson dies at age 83.
April 5: Jack "Cowboy" Clement born.
May 27: Kenny Price born.
September 1: Boxcar Willie born.
September 12: George Jones born.

November 30: Teddy Wilburn born.
December 7: Bob Osborne born.
December 30: Skeeter Davis born.

1932

The "WLS Barn Dance" moves to Chicago's Eighth Street
  Theater, becoming the first show aired before
  a large audience.
The "Iowa Barn Frolic" starts on WHO in Des Moines.
January 26: Claude Gray born.
February 25: Faron Young born.
February 26: Johnny Cash born.
March 13: Jan Howard born.
March 17: Dick Curliss born.
April 7: Cal Smith born.
April 9: Carl Perkins born.
August 8: Mel Tillis born.
September 8: Patsy Cline born.
October 1: Bonnie Owens born.
October 8: Pete Drake born.
October 11: Dottie West born.
November 6: Stonewall Jackson born.
December 14: Charlie Rich born.

1933

A half-hour of the "WLS Barn Dance" is broadcast
  nationally on the NBC radio network and is renamed the
  "National Barn Dance."
January 7: "Wheeling Jamboree" is first aired on radio
  station WWVA in Wheeling, West Virginia.
January 11: Goldie Hill born.
February 5: Claude King born.
April 15: Roy Clark born.
April 30: Willie Nelson born.
May 26: Jimmie Rodgers dies at age 35.
August 15: Bobby Helms born.
September 1: Conway Twitty born.
September 3: Tompall Glaser born.
October 21: Mel Street born.
November 21: Jean Sheppard born.
December 15: Jerry Wallace born.
December 21: Freddie Hart born.

1934

American Decca, a new company, sells records for 35 cents
  instead of the standard 75 cents, touching off a price war

that rejuvenates record sales.

The "Crazy Barn Dance" first airs on WBT in Charlotte.

March 1: Jim Ed Brown born.

March 31: John Loudermilk born.

June 7: Wynn Stewart born.

July 14: Del Reeves born.

September 8: Merle Kilgore born.

September 25: Royce Kendall born.

October 27: Grand Ole Opry moves from the National Life and Accident Insurance building to the Hillsboro Theater.

1935

January 8: Elvis Presley born.

January 10: Ronnie Hawkins born.

February 17: Johnny Bush born.

April 7: Bobby Bare born.

April 14: Loretta Lynn born.

August 20: Justin Tubb born.

September 8: Hank Cochran born.

September 29: Jerry Lee Lewis born.

1936

Grand Ole Opry moves from the Hillsboro Theater to the Dixie Tabernacle.

January 2: Roger Miller born.

January 24: Doug Kershaw born.

January 28: Bill Phillips born.

February 3: Chuck Glaser born.

March 9: Mickey Gilley born.

April 12: Judy Lynn born.

April 22: Glen Campbell born.

April 23: Roy Orbison born.

May 25: Tom T. Hall born.

June 22: Kris Kristofferson born.

June 30: Doyle Holly born.

September 7: Buddy Holly born.

1937

January 27: Buddy Emmons born.

January 30: Jeanne Pruett born.

February 1: Don Everly born.

March 20: Jerry Reed born.

April 15: Bob Luman born.

June 4 Freddie Fender born.

June 6: Pee Wee King and the Golden West Cowboys

debut at the Grand Ole Opry.

June 15: Waylon Jennings born.

July 4: Ray Pillow born.

July 19: George Hamilton IV born.

September 6: Merle Haggard born.

October: Roy Acuff makes his Grand Ole Opry debut.

Minnie Pearl

October 4: Lloyd Green born.

October 20: Wanda Jackson born.

October 29: Sonny Osbourne born.

November 1: Bill Anderson born.

December 16: James Glaser born.

December 17: Nat Stuckey born.

December 24: Stoney Edwards born.

December 26: Ronnie Prophet born.

December 30: John Hartford born.

1938

The "Boone County Jamboree" airs on WLW in Cincinnati, Ohio.

Bill Monroe forms the Blue Grass Boys, leading to the use of the term "bluegrass" for the style of music he is instrumental in creating.

February 26: Roy Acuff's band becomes The Smokey Mountain Boys.

March 18: Charley Pride born.

April 2: Warner Mack born.

April 13: Milton Brown dies at age 34.

August 21: Kenny Rogers born.

October 9: Bill Monroe and the Blue Grass Boys first perform at the Grand Ole Opry.

October 5: Johnny Duncan born.

October 14: Melba Montgomery born.

November 11: Narvel Felts born.

November 16: Troy Seals born.

December 9: David Houston born.

1939

January 19: Phil Everly born.

February 9: Red Lane born.

March 6: Jerry Naylor born.

March 11: Flaco Jimenez born.

May 27: Don Williams born.

June 16: Billy "Crash" Craddock born.

July: Grand Ole Opry moves from the Dixie Tabernacle to the War Memorial Auditorium.

August 18: Molly Bee born.

September 5: John Stewart born.

September 6: David Allan Coe born.

October 14: One-half hour of "Grand Ole Opry" premieres on the NBC Radio network as "The Prince Albert Show."

1940

January 8: Cristy Lane born.

March 8: Rick Nelson born.

May 19: Mickey Newbury born.

June 23: Diana Trask born.

June 28: The movie *Grand Ole Opry* premiers in Nashville.

July 16: Jeannie Sealy born.

November: Minnie Pearl makes her debut on "Grand Ole Opry."

December 24: Johnny Carver born.

1941

March 28: Charlie McCoy born.

May 31: Augie Meyers born. Johnny Paycheck born.

June 8: Vernon Oxford born.

August 14: Connie Smith born.

September 26: David Frizzell born.

November 6: Guy Clark born.

November 29: Jody Miller born.

December 7: The Japanese attack Pearl Harbor, bringing the United States into World War II. Soon Southern musicians in the Armed Service will introduce country music to soldiers from all parts of the country.

1942

January 21: Mac Davis born.

March 13: Bobby Wright born.

March 16: Jerry Jeff Walker born.

May: Elton Britt's patriotic song "There's a Star Spangled Banner Waving Somewhere" becomes country music's first crossover hit.

May 5: Tammy Wynette born.

May 8: Jack Blanchard born.

May 12: Billy Swan born.

May 18: Rodney Dillard born.

May 28: Obie McClinton born.

August 27: B. J. Thomas born.

October 13: Roy Acuff and songwriter Fred Rose form Acuff-Rose Publication, Nashville's first and most influential music publishing company.

November 6: Doug Sahm born.

December: Ernest Tubb debuts at the Grand Ole Opry.

December 30: Michael Nesmith born.

1943

The Grand Ole Opry moves to the Ryman Auditorium,

which will be its home for 31 years.

January 7: Leona Williams born.

January 9: Roy Head born.

June 6: Joe Stampley born.

August 5: Sammi Smith born.

October 11: Gene Watson born.

December 31: John Denver born.

1944

January 16: Jim Stafford born. Ronnie Milsap born.

February 12: Moe Bandy born.

May 1: Rita Coolidge born.

May 15: K. T. Oslin born.

June 7: Clarence White born.

July 11: Bobby G. Rice born.

July 15: Roy Brasfield debuts on the Grand Ole Opry.

July 20 T. G. Sheppard born.

July 27: Bobby Gentry born.

October 31: Kinky Friedman born.

November 27: Eddie Rabbitt born.

December 4: Chris Hillman born.

December 11: Brenda Lee born.

1945

Paul Cohen and the Decca Company record Red Foley in Nashville, the first step in a sequence of events making that city a major recording center.

May 23: Misty Morgan born.

May 28: Gary Stewart born.

June 8: Steve Fromholz born.

October 19: Jeannie C. Riley born.

1946

Spade Cooley is nicknamed "The King of Western Swing," giving a name to the style of music pioneered by Bill Wills and Milton Brown.

January 11: Naomi Judd born.

January 19: Dolly Parton born.

February 2: Howard Bellamy born.

June 20: Anne Murray born.

July 3: Johnny Lee born.

August 11: John Conlee born.

December 25: Jimmy Buffett born.

1947

February 9: Joe Ely born.

March 15: Ry Cooder born.

April 2: Emmylou Harris born.

May 24: Mike Reid born.

May 25: Jessi Colter born.

September 9: Freddy Weller born.

September 26: Lynn Anderson born.

October: The first country music show is staged at New York's Carnegie Hall, a show starring Ernest Tubb.

December 27: Tracy Nelson born.

1948

April 3: "Louisiana Hayride" first airs on KWKH in Shreveport, Louisiana.

May 17: Penny DeHaven born.

May 28: Larry Gatlin born.

September 14: Vernon Dalhart dies at age 65.

December 25: Barbara Mandrell born.

1949

May 4: Stella Parton born.

May 26: Hank Williams, Jr., born.

June 11: Hank Williams, Sr., sings "Lonesome Blues" for his "Grand Ole Opry" debut.

Crystal Gayle

August 10: Gene Jackson born.
August 27: Jeff Cook born.
November 10: Donna Fargo born.
December 13: Randy Owen born.

1950

Maybelle Carter and her three daughters, Helen, June, and Anita, join "Grand Ole Opry" as "The Carter Family."
January 7: Hank Snow and Tennessee Ernie Ford make their "Grand Ole Opry" debuts.
March 1: Connie Eaton born.
August 7: Rodney Crowell born.
September 16: David Bellamy born.
November 12: Barbara Fairchild born.
December 6: Helen Cornelius born.

1951

January 9: Crystal Gayle born.
April 6: LaCosta born.

1952

January 12: Ricky Van Shelton born.
January 22: Teddy Gentry born.
March 1: Uncle Dave Macon plays the Grand Ole Opry for the last time.
March 22 Uncle Dave Macon dies at age 82.
May 18: George Strait born.
December 10: Johnny Rodriguez born.

1953

January 1: Hank Williams, Sr., dies at age 29.
March 31: Greg Martin born.
April 9: Hank Ketchum born.
June 1: Ronnie Dunn born.
September 21: Kenny Star born.
October 8: Ricky Lee Phelps born.
December 19: Janie Frickie born.

1954

March 28: Reba McEntire born.
April 8: John Schneider born.
July 18: Ricky Skaggs born.
July 13: Louise Mandrell born.
November 30: Jeannie Kendall born.
December 25: Steve Wariner born.

1955

Four different recordings of "The Ballad of Davy Crockett" hit the pop charts: by Bill Hayes, Tennessee Ernie Ford, Fess Parker, and the Voices of Walter Schumann.

May 11: Mark Herndon born.

May 24: Rosanne Cash born.

September 26: Carlene Carter born.

November 12: Tennessee Ernie Ford's "Sixteen Tons," the 15th-best-selling single of the past 40 years, hits the charts.

December 4: Brian Prout born.

December 12: John Anderson born.

1956

January 17: Steve Earle born.

March 26: Charly McClain born.

June 19: Doug Stone born.

August 29: Dan Truman born.

October: Johnny Cash's first big hit, "I Walk the Line," is released.

October 23: Dwight Yoakem born.

December 9: Sylvia born.

1957

Country-pop, a melding of the two styles, reaches a period of peak popularity.

Porter Wagoner joins "Grand Ole Opry."

January 4: Patty Loveless born.

April 12: Vince Gill born.

July 24: Pam Tillis born.

November 1: Lyle Lovett born.

1958

February 3: Buddy Holly, Richie Valens, and the Big Bopper die in a plane crash.

February 21: Mary-Chapin Carpenter born.

May 12: Kix Brooks born.

May 23: Shelly West born.

July 5: Fred Young born.

September 30: Marty Stuart born.

October 10: Tanya Tucker born.

October 17: Alan Jackson born.

1959

January 27: Richard Young born.

April 27: Johnny Horton's "The Battle of New Orleans" hits the pop charts on its way to Number One.

May 4: Randy Travis born.

June 21: Kathy Mattea born.

June 27: Lorrie Morgan born.

November 30: Marty Robbins' best-selling single, "El Paso," hits the pop charts on its way to Number One.

1960

Patsy Cline, Hank Locklin, Bobby Lord, and Billy Walker join "Grand Ole Opry."

January 11: Jim Reeves's "He'll Have to Go" hits the pop charts on its way to Number Two.

November 5: Johnny Horton dies at age 45.

November 7: A. P. Carter dies at age 69.

November 13: Patsy Cline's "Crazy," her best-selling single, is released.

December 15: Doug Phelps born.

December 28: Joe Diffie born. Marty Roe born.

1961

Bill Anderson joins "Grand Ole Opry."

May 22: Dana Williams born.

August 26: Jimmy Olender born.

November 3: Country Music Association announces the founding of its Country Music Hall of Fame, with the first honorees being Jimmie Rodgers, Hank Williams, and Fred Rose.

1962

Sonny James, Leroy Van Dyke, and Carl and Pearl Butler join the roster of "Grand Ole Opry."

After 38 years in country music, the Stoneman Family make their "Grand Ole Opry" debut.

February 4: Clint Black born.

February 7: Garth Brooks born.

April 2: Billy Dean born.

1963

The Browns, Marion Worth and Dottie West join "Grand Ole Opry."

February 9: Travis Tritt born

March 3: Patsy Cline, Hawkshaw Hawkins, and the Cowboy Copas are killed in a plane crash.

March 8: Jack Anglin dies in a car crash on the way to

Patsy Cline's funeral.

March 29: Texas Ruby is killed in a fire at age 52.

September 6: Mark Chestnut born.

1964

Jimmy Dean features country music on his prime time show on ABC-TV.

May 30: Wynonna Judd born.

July 31: Jim Reeves is killed in an airplane crash.

November 11: "Bonanza" star Lorne Greene hits Number One on the charts with his cowboy song "Ringo."

November 28: Willie Nelson joins the "Grand Ole Opry."

December 6: Twelve artists are dropped from the "Grand Ole Opry" roster: George Morgan, Don Gibson, Billy Grammer, Johnny Wright, Kitty Wells, the Jordanaires, Faron Young, Ferlin Husky, Chet Atkins, Justin Tubb, Stonewall Jackson, and Ray Price.

December 19: Trisha Yearwood born.

1965

Waylon Jennings signs with RCA records and begins recording hard-driving music that will be called the outlaw movement.

The Academy of Country Music in Los Angeles presents its first annual awards.

Bobby Bare, Norma Jean, Connie Smith, and Bob Luman join Grand Ole Opry.

June 12: Tex Ritter joins the roster of the "Grand Ole Opry," becoming one of its elder statesmen.

1966

Ray Pillow joins "Grand Ole Opry."

December 25: Jack Greene's "There Goes My Everything" hits Number One on the charts, launching his solo career.

1967

Stu Phillips, Del Reeves, Jeannie Seely join "Grand Ole Opry."

January: Charley Pride makes his "Grand Ole Opry" debut.

February 6: Roger Miller's biggest crossover hit, "King of the Road," hits the charts.

August 12: Bobby Gentry's "Ode to Billy Joe" hits the pop charts on its way to Number One.

October: The Country Music Association in Nashville begins its annual awards program.

Flatt and Scruggs

1968

June 14: Pop Stoneman dies at age 75.

August 31: Jeannie C. Riley rockets to Number One with "Harper Valley P. T. A."

November 16: Glen Campbell's "Wichita Lineman" hits the charts.

December 28: Tammy Wynette's best-selling single, "Stand By Your Man," hits the charts.

1969

Bob Dylan records his *Nashville Skyline* album in Nashville, an event that gives new respectability to country music and triggers the development of country-rock.

Johnny Cash began hosting his own network television show.

Flatt and Scruggs dissolve their partnership.

February 16: George Jones and Tammy Wynette marry.

March 15: Glen Campbell's "Galveston" hits the charts.

June: "Hee Haw" airs for the first time.

August 2: Johnny Cash's best-selling single "A Boy Named Sue" hits the charts.

November 23: Spade Cooley dies at age 59.

1970

Lester Flatt and the Nashville Grass and Tom T. Hall join "Grand Ole Opry."

June 30: Ground is broken for the new Opryland amusement park.

1971

Jan Howard joins "Grand Ole Opry."

February: Loretta Lynn and Conway Twitty make their "Grand Ole Opry" debut as a duet.

June 26: John Denver hit the charts with his first big hit, "Take Me Home, Country Roads."

August 7: Henry "Homer" Haynes dies at age 54.

1972

David Houston and Barbara Mandrell join "Grand Ole Opry."

Opryland amusement park opens.

June 23: Elton Britt dies at 54.

August 5: Mac Davis's "Baby Don't Get Hooked On Me" crosses over to the pop charts on its way to Number One.

1974

The film *Nashville* shoots on location in Nashville, stirring controversy in the music community.

January 2: Tex Ritter dies at age 68.

March 16: The new Grand Ole Opry House opens with President Richard Nixon in attendance.

1975

Don Gibson rejoins "Grand Ole Opry."

March 13: George Jones and Tammy Wynette divorce.

April 5: John Denver's "Thank God I'm a Country Boy" hits the pop charts on its way to Number One.

May 13: Bob Wills dies at age 70.

June 21: Glen Campbell's "Rhinestone Cowboy" hits the pop charts on its way to Number One.

July 7: George Morgan dies.

1976

George Hamilton IV joins "Grand Ole Opry."

March 6: The Bellemy Brothers' "Let Your Love Flow" hits the pop charts on its way to Number One.

1977

March 8: Glen Campbell's "Southern Nights" hits the pop charts on its way to Number One.

March 22: Stoney Cooper dies at age 68.

May 7: Jimmy Buffett's "Margaritaville" hits the pop and

country charts.

September 24: Crystal Gayle crosses over to the pop charts with "Don't It Make My Brown Eyes Blue."

1978

June 12: Johnny Bond dies at age 63.

June 24: Foy Willing dies at age 63.

October 23: Maybelle Carter dies at age 69.

1979

Larry Gatlin and the Gatlin Brothers joins "Grand Ole Opry."

July 21: The Charlie Daniels Band's "The Devil Went Down to Georgia" crosses over to the pop charts.

1980

January: Comedian George Burns makes the country charts with "I Wish I Was Eighteen Again."

March 4: Movie *Coal Miner's Daughter* premiers in Nashville.

April 4: Red Slovine dies in an auto accident in Nashville at age 61.

June 19: Boxcar Willie makes his "Grand Ole Opry" debut at 60 years of age.

October 4: Kenny Rogers's "Lady" hits the pop charts on its way to Number One.

1981

John Conlee joins "Grand Ole Opry."

June 6: The Oak Ridge Boy's "Elvira" crosses over to the pop charts.

July 25: Alabama crosses over to the pop charts with "Feels So Right."

1982

May: Ricky Skaggs joins "Grand Ole Opry."

June 19: Riders in the Sky joins "Grand Ole Opry."

July 2: DeFord Bailey dies at age 82.

1983

March 7: The Nashville Network airs its first broadcast.

October 20: Merle Travis dies at age 65.

1984

Lorrie Morgan and the Whites join "Grand Ole Opry."
June 18: Paul Howard dies at age 75.
September 6: Ernest Tubb dies at age 70.
November 28: Al Dexter dies at age 82.

1985

August: John Russell joins "Grand Ole Opry."
November: Reba McEntire joins "Grand Ole Opry."
November 14: CBS broadcasts a two-hour tribute to the
   60th Anniversary of "Grand Ole Opry."
December 31: Rick Nelson dies in a plane crash.

1986

February: Mel McDaniel joins "Grand Ole Opry."
November: Randy Travis joins "Grand Ole Opry."

1987

August 22: Roy Clark joins "Grand Ole Opry."
August 29: Archie Campbell dies at age 72.

1988

June 10: Herman Crook, the last surviving member of the
   original 1926 "Grand Ole Opry" cast, dies at age 89.
   Ricky Van Shelton joins "Grand Ole Opry."
June 11: Patti Loveless joins "Grand Ole Opry."

1990

October: Garth Brooks joins "Grand Ole Opry" in the
   same week that his first two albums, *Garth Brooks* and
   No Fences both reach Gold Record status.
December 4: The Judds give their final performance.

1991

Clint Black, Vince Gill and Alan Jackson join "Grand
   Ole Opry."
February 24: Webb Pierce dies at age 69.
October 17: Tennessee Ernie Ford dies at age 72.

1992

Travis Tritt and Emmylou Harris join "Grand Ole Opry."
October 25: Roger Miller dies at age 56.
November 23: Roy Acuff dies at age 89.

COUNTRY MUSIC FIRSTS

In history, hindsight is always much clearer than foresight. Many significant events and turning points in country music history went unrecorded because no one knew they were significant at the time. Many other important milestones are known.

FIRST COUNTRY MUSIC RADIO STATION

WSB in Atlanta, Georgia, went on the air as a 100-watt station on March 16, 1922. On September 9, 1922, the station aired a live performance by Fiddlin' John Carson and soon featured many more musicians performing rural music.

FIRST MUSICIAN TO WEAR WESTERN REGALIA WHILE PERFORMING

Texas fiddle player A. C. "Eck" Robertson donned cowboy regalia in 1922.

FIRST BROADCAST BARN DANCE

Radio station WBAP in Fort Worth, Texas, aired the first "Barn Dance" program on January 4, 1923.

FIRST COUNTRY MUSICIAN TO MAKE A RECORD

In June, 1922, "Eck" Robertson and a friend, fiddler Henry Gilliland, were in Virginia for a Confederate reunion when they got the idea to go to New York to make a record. They managed to persuade Victor Records to cut six songs.

FIRST COUNTRY MUSICIAN TO PROMOTE HIS RECORDS ON RADIO

Eck Robertson played "Sally Goodin" and "Arkansas Traveler," another of his releases, on radio station WBAP in Fort Worth in March, 1923.

FIRST COUNTRY RECORD RELEASED

Victor Records released Eck Robertson's version of "Sally Goodin" in April, 1923.

FIRST COUNTRY MUSICIAN RECRUITED TO MAKE RECORDS

On June 14, 1923, Fiddlin' John Carson cut "Little Old Log Cabin in the Lane" and "That Old Hen Cackled and the Rooster's Goin' To Crow." Ralph Peer of Okeh Records had set up a portable recording studio in Atlanta, Georgia, and after hearing about Carson's reputation, had sought him out.

FIRST MILLION-SELLING COUNTRY SINGLE

"The Wreck of the Old '97," recorded by Vernon Dalhart for Victor Records in 1924 achieved an unprecedented sales figure.

FIRST COUNTRY MUSIC FAMILY TO BE RECORDED

The Jenkins Family had their first recording session on August 29, 1924.

FIRST IMPORTANT COUNTRY MUSIC GROUP

In 1925, Victor Records recorded a North Carolina string band, who described themselves as "hillbillies" in the big city. Peer named the group the "Al Hopkins and the Hill Billies," a name which served to catagorize the new music genre.

FIRST COWBOY BALLAD TO SELL A MILLION COPIES

Carl T. Sprague, who billed himself as "The Original Singing Cowboy," recorded the million-copy hit "When the Work's All Done" in 1925.

FIRST MUSICIAN TO PLAY ON THE WSM "BARN DANCE"

The first (and only) musician to play on the first WSM "Barn Dance," which aired on November 28, 1925, was 78-year-old fiddler Jimmy Thompson.

FIRST BAND TO PERFORM ON THE WSM "BARN DANCE"

The first group to play on the WSM Barn Dance was the Possum Hunters, led by Dr. Humphrey Bate, a physician who graduated from Vanderbilt School of Medicine.

FIRST COUNTRY GROUP TO PERFORM FOR A PRESIDENT

Al Hopkins and the Hill Billies played for Calvin Coolidge in 1927.

FIRST COUNTRY GROUP TO PERFORM IN A MOVIE
Al Hopkins and the Hill Billies performed in a 15-minute short released by Warner Brothers in 1927.

FIRST "GRAND OLE OPRY" BROADCAST
Radio station WSR in Nashville aired the first "Grand Ole Opry" broadcast on December 10, 1927.

FIRST PERFORMER ON THE "GRAND OLE OPRY"
Immediately after George Hay told the WSM listening audience that the new name of the show was the "Grand Ole Opry," he introduced DeFord Bailey, a black harmonica player. Bailey, who had been crippled after contracting polio as a child, played "Pan American Blues."

FIRST RECORDING SESSION IN NASHVILLE
In 1928, Victor Records brought its portable equipment to Nashville to record several string bands, including Sam and Kirk McGee.

FIRST JUKEBOXES
Wurlitzer introduced the first commercial jukeboxes in 1928.

FIRST COWBOY TO SING ON FILM
Ken Maynard sang a cowboy song in "The Wagon Masters," one of the first cowboy "talkies."

FIRST WESTERN SONG USED AS A FILM TITLE
Ken Maynard used "The Strawberry Roan" as the title of his 1933 cowboy film.

FIRST ELECTRIC GUITAR IN A COUNTRY BAND
Bob Dunn introduced an electric guitar when he joined Milton Brown and his Musical Brownies in 1934.

FIRST MILLION-SELLING COUNTRY SINGLE BY A FEMALE
"I Wanna Be a Cowboy's Sweetheart," recorded by Patsy Montana for ARC in 1935, made her the first female star of country music.

FIRST DRUMMER IN A MAJOR COUNTRY BAND
Smokey Dacus, who joined Bob Wills and His Texas
Playboys in 1935, made that country band the first with a
rhythm section.

FIRST MAJOR HONKY-TONK SONG
Hundreds of bars featuring country music sprang up after
the repeal of Prohibition in 1934. The first major hit to
use the term "honky-tonk" was Al Dexter's "Honky Tonk
Blues" in 1937.

FIRST TRUCKING SONG
Ted Daffan wrote "Truck Driver's Blues," the first trucking
song, in 1939.

FIRST ELECTRIC GUITAR ON THE "GRAND OLE OPRY"
Sam Gill played an electric guitar on the "Grand Ole Opry"
in 1939. George Hay told him not to do it again, so it was
several years before another electric guitar was heard on
that stage.

FIRST MUSICIAN TO PLAY A DOBRO ON THE "GRAND OLE OPRY"
Clell Summey, a member of the Crazy Tennesseans, played
the dobro for the first time on the "Grand Old Opry" during Roy Acuff's sensational second appearance on
February 5, 1938.

FIRST COUNTRY MUSIC STAR TO HOST A NETWORK RADIO PROGRAM
Red Foley co-starred with comedian Red Skelton on
"Avalon Time," a national program first broadcast in 1939.

FIRST MAJOR RECORDING SESSION IN NASHVILLE
In March or April of 1945, Paul Cohen of Decca Records
rented WSM's Studio B, one of the early homes of the
Grand Ole Opry, for a recording session with Red Foley
that included "Tennessee Saturday Night" and "Blues in
the Heart."

FIRST ALL-COUNTRY MUSIC RADIO STATION
In 1949, KXLA in Pasadena, California became the first
radio station to program predominently country music at

the exclusion of other kinds.

FIRST COUNTRY STAR TO RECORD IN HI-FI AND IN STEREO

Hank Thompson and the Brazos Valley Boys, a western swing band, were the first to use these advanced recording techniques in the 1950s.

FIRST GUITAR-SHAPED SWIMMING POOL BUILT IN NASHVILLE

Webb Pierce constructed Nashville's first guitar-shaped swimming pool in the 1950s.

FIRST MILLION-SELLING COUNTRY ALBUM

Tennessee Ernie Ford's *Hymns* went platinum in 1963, the first country album certified for sales exceeding one million copies.

FIRST U.S. PRESIDENT TO VISIT THE GRAND OLE OPRY

President Richard Nixon attended the opening of the new Grand Ole Opry House at Opryland on March 16, 1974. Nixon went on stage, received some informal yo-yo lessons from Roy Acuff, then played the piano himself while the company sang "God Bless America."

FIRST NASHVILLE ALBUM TO GO PLATINUM

The first album produced in Nashville to sell more than one million copies was *Wanted: The Outlaws*, which featured Waylon Jennings, Jessi Colter, Willie Nelson, and Tompall Glaser and was released in 1975.

FIRST ALBUM BY A FEMALE COUNTRY SINGER TO GO PLATINUM

Crystal Gayle's album *We Must Believe in Magic* was released in June 1977, went gold on November 14, 1977, and was certified platinum on February 15, 1978.

FIRST FEMALE COUNTRY SINGER TO ENTERTAIN TROOPS IN VIETNAM

Penny DeHaven headlined a country music tour of Vietnam.

FIRST COUNTRY ARTIST TO TOUR CHINA

Crystal Gayle toured China in 1979.

COUNTRY MUSIC HALL OF FAME

The Country Music Hall of Fame was established by the Country Music Association in 1961 to honor a select group of performers and professionals who have made extraordinary contributions to the field. In 32 years, just 64 people have been chosen for country music's highest honor. (An asterisk indicates those who are still living.)

1961   Jimmie Rodgers, Fred Rose, Hank Williams
1962   Roy Acuff
1964   Tex Ritter
1965   Ernest Tubb
1966   Eddy Arnold*, James R. Denny, George D. Hay, Uncle Dave Macon

Hank Williams

1967	Red Foley, J. L. Frank, Jim Reeves, Stephen H. Sholes
1968	Bob Wills
1969	Gene Autry*
1970	Bill Monroe*, Original Carter Family (A.P. Carter, Maybelle Carter, Sara Carter)
1971	Arthur Edward Satherley
1972	Jimmie Davis*
1973	Chet Atkins*, Patsy Cline
1974	Owen Bradley*, Frank "Pee Wee" King*
1975	Minnie Pearl*
1976	Kitty Wells*, Paul Cohen
1977	Merle Travis
1978	Grandpa Jones*
1979	Hubert Long, Hank Snow*
1980	Connie B. Gay, Original Sons of the Pioneers (Hugh Farr, Karl Farr, Bob Nolan, Lloyd Perryman, Roy Rogers, Tim Spencer), Johnny Cash*
1981	Vernon Dalhart, Grant Turner
1982	Lefty Frizzell, Marty Robbins, Roy Horton*
1983	"Little" Jimmy Dickens*
1984	Floyd Tillman*, Ralph Peer
1985	Lester Flatt & Earl Scruggs
1986	Wesley Rose, the Duke of Paducah
1987	Rod Brasfield
1988	Roy Rogers*, Loretta Lynn*
1989	Hank Thompson*, Cliffie Stone*, Jack Stapp
1990	Tennessee Ernie Ford
1991	Felice* & Boudleaux Bryant
1992	George Jones*, Frances Williams Preston*

INSIDE LOOK AT THE
COUNTRY MUSIC HALL OF FAME

Number of Men: 56
Number of Women: 8
Number of Living: 23
Number of Deceased: 41
Performers: 47
Others: 17
Group members: 8

Duets: 2
Oldest Living: Jimmie Davis (born 1902)
Oldest (deceased): Arther Edward Satherley (born 1889)
Youngest: Loretta Lynn (born 1935)
Youngest (deceased): Hank Williams (died at age 29)

COUNTRY PIONEERS: PERFORMERS IN THE HALL OF FAME

ROY ACUFF

NICKNAME: "King of Country Music"

INSTRUMENT: Fiddle

BORN: February 19, 1938
   Maynardsville, Tennessee

DIED: November 23, 1992

The man who would eventually become the most famous country singer in America was born and raised, along with two brothers and two sisters, in a three-room shack in a small Tennessee town. Roy Acuff was a superb athlete who earned 13 letters in high school, then went on to play minor-league baseball. Just before he was to travel to New York for a tryout with the Yankees, he suffered such severe sunstroke that he was confined to bed for two years, ending his promising baseball career. Subsequently, he took a job as a callboy on the L&N Railroad, but his heart was in music. In 1932, Acuff joined a traveling medicine show. The next year, he formed a group called the Tennessee Crackerjacks and got a regular job at Knoxville radio station WROL. Then he moved to rival station KNOX, where he and his band members earned 50 cents each per show. When he was refused a raise, he renamed his band the Crazy Tennesseans and went back to WROL.

Acuff's big break came after he recorded "The Great Speckled Bird" and "The Wabash Cannonball" for ARC Records in 1936. Both songs were hits, and he began to tour. His first Grand Ole Opry appearance was on February 19, 1938. Two weeks later, he was invited to join the Opry company if he changed the name of his band to the Smoky Mountain Boys.

Roy Acuff reached the peak of his success in the early 1940s, when "Wabash Cannonball" went gold. With songwriter Fred Rose, he founded Acuff-Rose in 1942, a music publishing company that became one of the most powerful in the business. Acuff was earning so much money ($200,000 per year) that he turned his attention to politics. He ran unsuccessfully as Republican candidate for governor of Tennessee in 1944, 1946, and 1948.

Acuff's record sales began to decline in the 1950s. In 1957, he founded Hickory Records, yet another successful business. He also remained the emcee of the Grand Ole Opry into the 1990s.

GREATEST HITS
"The Great Speckled Bird"
"Wabash Cannonball"
"Ida Red"

Eddy Arnold

"When I Lay My Burden Down"
"Wreck on the Highway"
"Fireball Mail"
"Night Train to Memphis"
"Pins and Needles, Low and Lonely"
"So Many Times"

CAREER HIGHLIGHTS
- He was elected as first living member of the Country Music Hall of Fame in 1962.
- Acuff celebrated 50th anniversary at the Grand Ole Opry in 1988.
- He was named by President Bush as a Kennedy Center honoree in 1991.

COWLICKS
- Acuff was an expert on the yo-yo. He gave President Nixon yo-yo lessons at the opening of the new Nashville Opryhouse in 1974.
- As they charged American marines at Okinawa, Japanese troops reportedly yelled, "To hell with Roosevelt, to hell with Babe Ruth, to hell with Roy Acuff."
- Acuff appeared in six movies, including *Grand Ole Opry, My Darling Clementine*, and *Night Train to Memphis*.

EDDY ARNOLD

REAL NAME: Richard Edward Arnold

NICKNAME: "The Tennessee Plowboy"

INSTRUMENT: Guitar

BORN: May 15, 1918
Henderson, Tennessee

Arnold was born on a farm and, like many country stars, was introduced to music by his father, an old-time fiddler. He dropped out of high school to help work the family farm during the Depression, but played at local barn dances at night. In 1936, he was invited to play on a small radio station in Jackson,

Tennessee, but it took him six more years to land a regular job.

During that period, Arnold perfected his characteristic vocal style, so smooth that it had no trace of hillbilly or honky-tonk in it. This very commercial voice attracted the attention of Pee Wee King, who hired Arnold to join his Golden West Cowboys at the Grand Ole Opry in the early 1940s. The exposure led to an RCA Records contract for Arnold as a solo act.

Within two years, Arnold had recorded his first number-one hit and went on to an incredible string of successful records. "Billboard" ranked him as the most successful country recording artist in the 1940s and the second-most-successful artist in the 1950s. Because his voice appealed to a broad spectrum of listeners, not just country music devotees, Arnold was courted by the television networks and hosted four different television variety shows in the 1950s. Later he had his own syndicated television program and went on to host more than 20 specials. Two of his songs made the Top Ten charts in 1980, giving him the unprecedented distinction of having recorded hits in five consecutive decades. He continued to perform 50 years after joining Pee Wee King's band.

GREATEST HITS

"Each Minute Seems Like a Million Years"
"I'll Hold You in My Heart"
"It's a Sin"
"Bouquet of Roses"
"Anytime"
"I Wanna Play House With You"
"Cattle Call"
"I Really Don't Want to Know"
"Make The World Go Away"
"Somebody Like Me"
"Then You Can Tell Me Goodbye"
"Cowboy"
"That's What I Get for Loving You"

CAREER HIGHLIGHTS

- "Bouquet of Roses" spent 54 weeks on the Top 40 charts, an all-time record for a country tune.
- Arnold is the best-selling country singles artist of all time.

- Arnold was elected to the Country Music Hall of Fame in 1966.

COWLICKS
- As a teenager, Arnold played at barn dances, often arriving on the family's mule.
- In 1945, Arnold hired Colonel Tom Parker as his manager, a man who would himself become famous managing Elvis Presley.

CHET ATKINS

INSTRUMENTS: Guitar, fiddle

BORN: June 20, 1924
       Luttrell, Tennessee

Chet Atkins was born on a 50-acre farm, but his father earned much of his living as a voice and piano teacher. His first instrument was the fiddle, before picking up the guitar at age nine. By the 1940s, his skill with both instruments allowed him to play with Archie Campbell, Bill Carlisle, and Red Foley. In 1950, he came to Nashville as a fiddler with The Carter Sisters and Mother Maybelle, but he soon became known as that city's top session guitarist. In addition to recording on his own, he moved into record production. He was named manager of RCA's Nashville studio in 1960 and a vice president of RCA Records in 1968, producing hits for Hank Snow, Waylon Jennings, Perry Como, Al Hirt, and others.

He demonstrated unprecedented versatility as a performer with the Atlanta Symphony, with Arthur Fiedler and the Boston Pops, with jazz guitarist George Benson, with Indian sitarist Ravi Shankar, and with several rock groups. Although he retired from RCA, he continued to record. He has released more than 100 albums selling more than 30 million copies.

GREATEST HITS
"Country Gentlemen"
"Gallopin' Guitar"
"Main Street Breakdown"
"Poor People of Paris"

"Boo Boo Stick Beat Beat"
"One Mint Julep"
"Teensville"
"Yakety Axe"
"Snowbird"
"Fiddlin' Around"

CAREER HIGHLIGHTS
- Atkins has won 10 Grammy Awards and nine Country Music Association Awards.
- He was elected to the Country Music Hall of Fame in 1973.
- For 14 consecutive years, he was voted "Best Instrumentalist" in the *Cashbox* poll.

COWLICKS
- More than any other single person, Atkins was responsible for the development of the "Nashville Sound," the blending of country and pop to produce a more commercial style of music.
- Atkins taught himself to play guitar by listening to Merle Travis on the radio. He didn't realize Travis was playing with only two fingers, so he developed his own three-finger style.

Gene Autry

GENE AUTRY

REAL NAME: Orvin Gene Autry

INSTRUMENT: Guitar

BORN: September 29, 1907
Tioga, Texas

Autry was born on a Texas ranch, where his mother taught him to play the guitar. His family moved to Oklahoma in his teenage years, and Autry took a job as a railroad telegrapher. He was an admirer of Jimmie Rodgers, whose yodeling style he emulated. With encouragement by famous humorist Will Rogers, he landed a job on a Tulsa radio station as "Oklahoma's Singing Cowboy." After some success in New York as a hillbilly singer, he moved to Chicago to appear on radio station WLS's "National Barn Dance." His numerous recordings included "Silver Haired Daddy of Mine," his first major hit.

Autry is most remembered for what happened when he moved to Hollywood in 1934. After a bit part in a western starring Ken Maynard, the first singing movie cowboy, Autry starred in a bizarre 12-part science fiction movie called *The Phantom Empire*. He went on to star in his first western, *Tumbling Tumbleweeds*, which was followed by nearly 100 additional westerns, almost always appearing with his horse Champion and his sidekick (a friend from his Chicago days) Smiley Burnette. Autry's singing style changed from hillybilly to western, and he became the epitome of the singing cowboy, a man as comfortable with a guitar as with a gun. From 1939 to 1956, he was also a star on the radio program "Melody Ranch". In the 1930s and 1940s he recorded a string of memorable hits such as "Yellow Rose of Texas" and "Tumbling Tumbleweeds."

Already a wealthy man, Autry became a shrewd businessman. He invested in a chain of radio and television stations, a record company, a hotel chain, a music publishing company, and owned the California Angels baseball team. Accordingly, he became one of the wealthiest people in the country.

GREATEST HITS
"Silver Haired Daddy of Mine"
"Yellow Rose of Texas"
"Tumbling Tumbleweeds"
"Mexicali Rose"
"Back in The Saddle Again"
"South of the Border"
"You Are My Sunshine"
"It Makes No Difference Now"
"Be Honest With Me"
"At Mail Call Today"
"Here Comes Santa Claus"
"Peter Cottontail"
"Rudolph the Red-Nosed Reindeer"

CAREER HIGHLIGHTS
- Autry was elected to the Country Music Hall of Fame in 1969.
- Autry's "Rudolph the Red-Nosed Reindeer" sold over 10 million copies.
- Autry, Oklahoma, was named after the famous cowboy star.

COWLICKS
- Autry's early records were released on the Sears label and were sold in the Sears, Roebuck catalog along with Gene Autry "Round-up" guitars and Gene Autry songbooks.
- Republic Pictures hired Autry as their singing cowboy after John Wayne refused to sing in future pictures.
- Autry had a distinguished military record flying cargo planes in World War II.

ROY BRASFIELD

BORN: 1910
Smithville, Mississippi

DIED: September 12, 1958
Nashville, Tennessee

Roy Brasfield was the son of a rural mail carrier who also farmed. Neither career appealed to him, so he left home at age 16 to join his older brother Lawrence "Boob" Brasfield, who was working in a traveling tent show. After a few years, the brothers were hired by Brisbee's Comedians, a well-known touring vaudeville show. Roy was a straight man; his brother was one of the comedians. His brother failed to show for a performance one day, so Roy put on his red wig and played the other role. He showed such a gift for comedy that he remained with the Brisbee show until it was disbanded at the start of World War II.

Brasfield enlisted in the Army Air Corps, but a bad back led to his discharge in 1943. In 1944, he was hired by the Grand Ole Opry, making his first appearance on July 15. In 1948, Brasfield and Minnie Pearl were teamed on the portion of the Grand Ole Opry show that was broadcast nationally on the NBC radio network. The two immediately established a chemistry that made them the most famous comedians in country music. They performed together and toured for the next decade.

In 1956, Brasfield was offered a film role by Elia Kazan, who was about to direct *A Face in the Crowd.* He accepted a dramatic part as the right-hand man to Andy Griffith, who starred as a country musician made into a national political figure. Brasfield was extremely proud of the critical praise he received. Just two years later, he died of a heart attack at age 48.

CAREER HIGHLIGHTS
- Roy Brasfield was elected to the Country Music Hall of Fame in 1987.

COWLICKS
- Despite his financial success, Brasfield lived in a modest house trailer until his death.
- Although he was never anything but cheerful in his public appearances, Brasfield continually battled a drinking problem that may have contributed to his early death.

CARTER FAMILY

FOUNDED: 1925

ORIGINAL MEMBERS: Alvin Pleasant (A. P.) Carter

Sara Carter
Maybelle Carter

LATER MEMBERS: June Carter, Anita Carter, Helen Carter, Janette Carter, Joe Carter

A. P. Carter, born in a log cabin in Maces Springs, Virginia, in April 1891, married 16-year-old Sara Dougherty on June 18, 1915. Nine years later, in 1925, A.P.'s brother Ezra married 16-year-old Maybelle Addington. With Sara on autoharp and Maybelle on guitar accompanying A.P.'s voice, the Carter Family began entertaining local residents with their traditional folk songs. In 1927, Ralph Peer of Victor Records heard the group on a talent scouting tour and recorded them on August 1, the same day he recorded Jimmie Rodgers. Soon thereafter, the Carter Family recorded "Wildwood Flower" and "Keep on the Sunny Side," and both became hits.

Although the Carters became well known throughout the south, they continued to work the family farm until 1938, when they moved to Del Rio, Texas, to perform on 50,000-watt radio station XERA. Although A.P. and Sara divorced that same year, they continued to perform together. Sara's daughter Janette and Maybelle's daughters Helen, June, and Anita joined the group in the early 1940s.

In 1943, Sara and A.P. retired. Maybelle and her daughters continued as the Carter Sisters and Mother Maybelle. They became regulars at the Grand Ole Opry in 1948. After A.P.'s death in 1960, they changed their name to the Carter Family. June Carter joined the Johnny Cash road show in 1961 (she later married Cash), and the rest of the family became regulars on Cash's TV show in 1966. Anita's daughter Lori, Helen's son David, and June's daughter Carlene occasionally joined the family in road shows throughout the 1970s. Maybelle died on October 23, 1978. The three sisters and Carlene made only a few appearances in the 1980s.

GREATEST HITS
"Wildwood Flower"

"Keep on the Sunny Side"
"Wabash Cannonball"
"Lonesome Valley"
"I'm Thinking Tonight of My Blue Eyes"
"The Worried Man Blues"
"Will the Circle Be Unbroken"
"Hello Stranger"

CAREER HIGHLIGHTS
- The Carter Family recorded more than 250 songs between 1927 and 1943.
- The Carter Family was elected to the Country Music Hall of Fame in 1970.

COWLICKS
- Many of the Carter Family songs were re-recorded by folk singers in the 1960s, including Joan Baez.
- When the Carters joined the Grand Ole Opry, they brought with them to Nashville a talented guitar player—Chet Atkins.

Johnny Cash

JOHNNY CASH

NICKNAME: The Man in Black

INSTRUMENT: Guitar

BORN: February 26, 1932
Kingsland, Arkansas

Cash was born into a very poor family and experienced tragedies when he was young, including a devastating 1937 Mississippi River flood and the accidental death of his brother, Jack. The family entertained themselves with music, and one of his brothers played local radio stations with a country band. Cash joined the Air Force and taught himself to play the guitar. After his discharge, he married and settled in Memphis, working as an appliance salesman. He met guitarist Luther Perkins and bassist Marshall Grant, and the three gained exposure on a local radio station before auditioning for Sun Records. In 1955, Sun released two of Cash's own songs, "Hey Porter" and "Cry, Cry, Cry" under the name Johnny Cash and the Tennessee Two. Both sold well, and with the release of "Folsom Prison Blues" and "I Walk the Line" the next year, Cash became a star. He joined the Louisiana Hayride, then soon moved on to the Grand Ole Opry. His rich, baritone voice and commanding presence made him a huge star.

Cash and his group (which became the Tennessee Three with the addition of drummer W. S. Holland) became one of the busiest acts in country music. Cash slipped into drug and alcohol abuse. In 1961, Cash's marriage was crumbling when June Carter joined his tour and tried to help him get his life together. But in 1965, he was arrested for possession of narcotics and in 1966, he served one night in jail after a disorderly conduct arrest. He married Carter in 1968, and the next year had his biggest crossover hit, "A Boy Named Sue." He also had his own television show, "The Johnny Cash Show," on ABC-TV from 1969 to 1971. In 1983, a relapse of his drug problem nearly killed him, but he recovered and continues to record and tour.

GREATEST HITS
"Hey Porter"
"Cry, Cry, Cry"
"Folsom Prison Blues"
"I Walk the Line"
"All Over Again"
"Don't Take Your Guns to Town"
"Ring of Fire"
"Understand Your Man"
"It Ain't Me, Babe"
"Orange Blossom Special"
"Daddy Sang Bass"
"A Boy Named Sue"
"Jackson"

CAREER HIGHLIGHTS
- Cash has won seven Grammy awards and 23 songwriting citations from Broadcast Music, Inc (BMI).
- He has placed 43 songs on the pop charts, more than 130 on the country charts, and has sold nearly 55 million records.
- In 1980, he was the youngest person ever elected to the Country Music Hall of Fame.

COWLICKS
- Cash's autobiography, *The Man in Black*, sold over one million copies and his novel about the apostle St. Paul, *Man in White*, was also a best-seller.
- He received critical praise for his performance in the 1970 Kirk Douglas film, *The Gunfight*.
- A born-again Christian, Cash has made appearances with the Reverand Billy Graham.

PATSY CLINE

REAL NAME: Virginia Patterson Hensley

BORN: September 8, 1932
    Winchester, Virginia

DIED: March 5, 1963
    Camden, Texas

Virginia Hensley was born in the beautiful

Patsy Cline

Shenandoah Valley in the midst of the Depression. She was something of a child prodigy, winning a tap-dancing competition at age four and learning to play the piano at age eight. Her family encouraged her ambitions to entertain because they needed the money she earned, singing everywhere from churches to street corners. She quit school as a teenager, clerking in a drug store during the day and performing in clubs at night. At 16, she impressed some touring musicians from Nashville, who arranged an audition with Roy Acuff. He offered her a job, but not enough money to quit her day job, so she returned to Winchester. She kept singing with a local group, and when she married Gerald Cline in 1953, she changed her professional name as well to Patsy Cline, because it sounded "more country." She gradually gained more exposure, appearing on the "Louisiana Hayride," the "Old Dominion Barn Dance," the "Ozark Jubilee," and Jimmy Dean's TV show. She also signed a contract with Four Star Records and recorded two songs.

Her big break, however, came when she won on "Arthur Godfrey Talent Scouts," a nationwide network television show, singing "Walkin' After Midnight." Her record company immediately released the song, which climbed to number three on the charts. Further releases sold decently, but not spectacularly. About the same time, she divorced Cline and married Charlie Dick. After the birth of her daughter Julia in 1958, she went into semi-retirement for two years.

In 1960, her husband persuaded her to take a spot on the Grand Ole Opry. She changed record companies and her first release, "I Fall to Pieces," was her first number-one hit. She soon became one of the dominant stars of country music, challenging Kitty Wells for the title "Queen of Country Music."

On March 3, 1963, Patsy flew to Kansas City for a benefit concert for the widow of country disc jockey Cactus Jack McCall. Afterward, Patsy, Cowboy Copas, and Hawkshaw Hawkins boarded a plane piloted by Copas' son-in-law to return to Nashville. The plane ran into a storm and crashed in such a remote area that it wasn't found until March 6. All aboard perished.

GREATEST HITS
"Walkin' After Midnight"
"I Fall to Pieces"
"Crazy"
"When I Get Through with You"
"Imagine That"
"So Wrong"

"Leavin' On Your Mind"
"Sweet Dreams"

CAREER HIGHLIGHTS
- Cline was elected to the Country Music Hall of Fame in 1973, the first female solo performer to be inducted.
- She was named to the Recording Academy Hall of Fame in 1992.
- Her "Greatest Hits" album went triple-platinum in 1991, 28 years after her death.

COWLICKS
- When Cline traveled to Nashville for her first audition, she was so poor that she had to sleep on a concrete park bench.
- Her hobbies were collecting salt-and-pepper shakers and pictures of country music stars.

VERNON DALHART

REAL NAME: Marion Try Slaughter

BORN: April 6, 1883
Jefferson, Texas

DIED: September 14, 1948
Bridgeport, Connecticut

Dalhart, the son of a ranch owner, moved to Dallas while still a teenager. Working as a piano salesman, he began attending the Dallas Conservatory of Music. After demonstrating some talent, he moved to New York and devoted tremendous energy to his career. His jobs ranged from vaudeville to light opera companies; his recordings ranged from black-faced minstrel songs ("Can't Yo' Heah Me Callin' Caroline") to popular songs and even operatic arias. Then, in May 1924, he record-ed mountain musician Henry Whittier's "The Wreck of the Old '97" for Victor Records. It became country music's first massive hit.

Dalhart recorded prolifically over the decade, concen-trating mostly on country music. But his career faltered in the mid-1930s; toward the end of the decade, he took a job as a night watchman in Bridgeport, Connecticut, and at the time of his death he was a night clerk in a hotel.

GREATEST HITS
"The Wreck of the Old '97"
"The Prisoner's Song"
"The Death of John Collins"
"The John T. Scopes Trial"

CAREER HIGHLIGHTS
- Dalhart recorded more than 5,000 songs under more than 100 pseudonyms that sold nearly 75 million copies.
- He was elected to the Country Music Hall of Fame in 1981.

COWLICKS
- Dalhart recorded "The Wreck of the Old '97" for more than 50 different record companies; his Victor Records edition alone sold 6 million copies.

JIMMIE DAVIS

INSTRUMENT: Guitar

BORN: September 11, 1902
Quitman, Louisiana

Davis, the son of a dirt-poor sharecropper, was born in a cabin in a tiny Louisiana town. From an early age, he proved to be a prodigy in both music and academics. After high school, he earned a Bachelor of Arts degree from Louisiana College and a Master of Arts degree from Louisiana State University while playing at barn dances and parties. In the late 1920s, he was a history professor at Dodd College while singing regularly on a Shreveport radio station, making records, and appearing at regional concerts. The wide exposure he received from several Decca recordings led to his appointment as Public Service Commissioner for the state of Louisiana.

In the mid-1930s, Davis abandoned his country blues style in favor of gospel music. His popularity contributed greatly to his election as Governor of Louisiana in 1944. After his term expired, he returned to gospel music. He was elected governor again in 1960 and, during his term, had a hit record, "Where the Old Red River Flows." After leaving office in 1964, he recorded several more hits in the 1970s and he made appearances through the 1980s.

GREATEST HITS
"Where the Old Red River Flows"
"Down at the Old Country Church"
"Tom Cat and Pussy Blues"
"High Behind Blues"
"At the Crossing"
"Still I Believe"
"Christ Is Sunshine"

CAREER HIGHLIGHTS
- Davis appeared in the films *Louisiana* and *Frontier Fury*.
- Davis was elected to the Country Music Hall of Fame in 1972.

COWLICKS
- Davis wrote "You Are My Sunshine," one of the most popular songs of all time, and used the song as his campaign theme.
- In 1993, Davis was the oldest living member of the Country Music Hall of Fame at age 90.

DELMORE BROTHERS

MEMBERS: Alton Delmore
Rabon Delmore

Alton (born December 25, 1908) and Delmore (born December 3, 1910) were raised on a farm in Elkmont, Alabama. Their mother taught them to play the fiddle, and their career as a brother duo began when they won an old-time fiddle contest in Athens, Alabama, in 1930. Both brothers also played the guitar and were signed to a record contract by Columbia in 1931. In 1932, they became one of the first vocal acts signed as regulars by the Grand Ole Opry.

The Delmore Brothers left the Opry in 1938 to tour and perform on many radio stations. Prolific song writers, the brothers continued to record. Their 1949 single "Blues Stay Away From Me" was their all-time best selling record. The Delmores also recorded with Grandpa Jones and Merle Travis as the Brown's Ferry Four. Alton retired in 1950 after a heart attack (he died on June 8, 1964), and Rabon died of lung cancer on December 4, 1952.

GREATEST HITS
"Brown's Ferry Blues"
"I've Got the Big River Blues"
"Beautiful Brown Eyes"
"Midnight Special"
"Hillbilly Boogie"
"Freight Train Boogie"
"Nashville Blues"
"When It's Time for the Whipperwill to Sing"
"Blues Stay Away From Me"

CAREER HIGHLIGHTS
- Alton Delmore wrote more than 1,000 songs.
- The Delmore Brothers were elected to the Songwriters Hall of Fame in October 1971.

"LITTLE" JIMMY DICKENS

NICKNAME: "Tater"

BORN: December 19, 1925
      Bold, West Virginia

Dickens was a coal miner's son and the youngest of 13 children. Because he didn't want to go into the mines himself, he turned to singing. He first appeared on an early-morning radio show with his uncle and two other musicians, where his job was to crow like a rooster to open the show. He later worked with John Bailes and His Happy Valley Boys and Molly O'Day on that same Beckley, West Virginia station. For ten years he struggled to earn a living, playing on numerous radio stations and performing at coal-mining camps, small theaters, and high school auditoriums. Finally, in Saginaw, Michigan, in 1942, Dickens met Roy Acuff, who invited

"Little" Jimmy Dickens

him to play the Grand Ole Opry. Two weeks later, he was invited to join the Opry.

The Opry broadcasts led to a record contract with Columbia Records. His first release, "Take an Old Cold Tater and Wait," was a Top 10 hit. He followed that with a series of hits and became one of the Opry's most popular performers. In 1957, Dickens was offered the opportunity to star in a major road show sponsored by Philip Morris Tobacco Company. Because the Grand Ole Opry was sponsored by a competitor, R.J. Reynolds, Dickens had to resign. However, it gave him the opportunity to become the first country music performer to complete a round-the-world tour.

In 1965, Dickens recorded his biggest hit, "May the Bird of Paradise Fly Up Your Nose." He was a popular touring act, although he had no hit singles afterward. In 1975, after 18 years, he returned to the Opry company on February 8, 1975.

GREATEST HITS
"Take an Old Cold Tater and Wait"

"Country Boy"
"Pennies for Papa"
"A-Sleeping at the Foot of the Bed"
"Hillbilly Fever"
"The Violet and the Rose"
"May the Bird of Paradise Fly Up Your Nose"

CAREER HIGHLIGHTS
- "Little" Jimmy Dickens was elected to the Country Music Hall of Fame in 1983.

COWLICKS
- Dickens was called "Little" Jimmy because he was only 4'10" tall.
- "Little" Jimmy Dickens was scheduled to be on the same bill with Hank Williams, Sr., in Canton, Ohio, on New Years Day, 1953, but Williams died of a drug and alcohol overdose in the back seat of his Cadillac on his way to Canton.
- Dickens discovered Marty Robbins and persuaded Columbia Records to sign him to his first contract.

FLATT & SCRUGGS

LESTER FLATT

INSTRUMENT: Guitar

BORN: June 19, 1914
        Overton County, Tennessee

DIED: May 11, 1979

EARL SCRUGGS

INSTRUMENT: Banjo

BORN: January 24, 1924
        Flint Hill, North Carolina

Lester Flatt came from a musical family and, as a boy, played guitar and banjo and sang in the church choir. When he was a young man, he earned a living working in a textile mill while playing at a number of local groups. In 1939, playing on a Roanoke, Virginia, radio station led to his joining the Happy Go-Lucky Boys, one of whom had played with "Bluegrass" pioneer Bill Monroe. In 1943, Flatt began to play with Charlie Monroe, Bill's brother. In 1945, he was invited to join Monroe to play for the Grand Ole Opry.

Earl Scruggs' father and older brothers played the banjo in a three-finger style he would later perfect. He first played in public at age six and, by 15, was performing on radio stations. Scruggs, like Flatt, worked in a textile mill to earn a living in the early 1940s, but he eventually ended up playing in Nashville. In 1945, he was also hired by Bill Monroe to play with his Bluegrass Boys for the Grand Ole Opry.

Flatt and Scruggs both made an immediate impact. Flatt's tenor voice made him an ideal choice to sing lead; Scruggs was the first serious banjo player capable of playing lead on any song in a major country band. They become such an integral part of the Bluegrass Boys that Bill Monroe featured their names on some of his album covers. In 1948, tired of Monroe's constant touring, Flatt and Scruggs quit the Bluegrass Boys. They decided to form their own group called the Foggy Mountain Boys. In 1949, they recorded "Foggy Mountain Breakdown," their first major hit.

Over the next two decades, they became one of the best-known acts in country music and one of the major forces in Bluegrass. They had their own syndicated TV show and rejoined the Grand Ole Opry. The peak of their popularity came in 1962 when their theme for the television show "The Beverly Hillbillies," titled "The Ballad of Jed Clampett," was Number One on the country charts for five months.

In the late 1960s, Earl Scruggs become more interested in modernizing his music. Lester Flatt resisted, and the two parted in 1969, with Lester forming the Nashville Grass and Earl forming the Earl Scruggs Revue. Lester Flatt died in 1979, and Earl Scruggs began cutting back his performances in the 1980s.

GREATEST HITS
"Blue Grass Breakdown"
"Foggy Mountain Breakdown"

"My Little Girl in Tennessee"
"Roll in My Sweet Baby's Arms"
"Old Salty Dog Blues"
"The Ballad of Jed Clampett"

CAREER HIGHLIGHTS
- Flatt and Scruggs were elected to the Country Music Hall of Fame in 1985.
- Flatt and Scruggs' "Foggy Mountain Breakdown" was used as the theme for the movie *Bonnie and Clyde*.

COWLICKS
- Prior to Earl Scruggs, banjo players were normally used in country bands to provide comedy relief.
- The Foggy Mountain Boys included the first dobro player in "Bluegrass" music.

RED FOLEY

REAL NAME: Clyde Julian Foley

INSTRUMENT: Guitar

BORN: June 17, 1910
Blue Lick, Kentucky

DIED: September 19, 1968
Fort Wayne, Indiana

Clyde "Red" Foley was the son of a storekeeper who taught him to play the guitar even before he began his schooling. He decided on a career in music after finishing third in a statewide talent contest at age 17. In 1930, Foley was recruited by the WLS "National Barn Dance," where he became a member of John Lair's Cumberland Ridge Ramblers. In 1937, Foley and Lair went to Kentucky to start the "Renfro Valley Barn Dance," an influential new program. Three years later, he returned to the "National Barn Dance" as a star. He also became the first country music star to have a network radio show when he co-hosted "Avalon Time" with comedian Red Skelton.

In 1944, Red Foley finally had his first hit record, "Smoke on the Water," a wartime song that promised victory for the Allied forces. Foley, along with Ernest Tubb, was one of the first stars to insist on recording in Nashville, and he joined the Grand Ole Opry in 1946. He reached the pinnacle of his recording career when he had five Top 10 songs in 1949 and twelve in 1950.

In 1954, Foley left the Grand Ole Opry and moved to Springfield, Missouri, where he hosted ABC-TV's "Ozark Jubilee" from 1955 to 1961. In 1962, he co-starred with Fess Parker in the ABC-TV series "Mr. Smith Goes to Washington." His radio and television appearances continued until his death in 1968.

GREATEST HITS
"Smoke on the Water"
"Tennessee Saturday Night"
"Chattanoogie Shoe Shine Boy"
"Just a Closer Walk With Thee"
"Candy Kisses"
"Tennessee Polka"
"Peace in the Valley for Me"
"Birmingham Bounce"
"Don't Let the Stars Get in Your Eyes"
"Alabama Jubilee"
"Midnight"

CAREER HIGHLIGHTS
- Foley was elected to the Country Music Hall of Fame in 1967.
- His records sold 24 million copies over his career.

COWLICKS
- Red Foley was a star basketball player and track and field competitor in high school.
- Some of his songs came from personal tragedy; his first wife died in childbirth in 1930.

BEN FORD: "THE DUKE OF PADUCAH"

REAL NAME: Benjamin Francis "Whitey" Ford

INSTRUMENT: Banjo

BORN: May 12, 1901
De Soto, Missouri

DIED: June 20, 1986
Nashville, Tennessee

Ben Ford was raised by his grandmother in Little Rock, Arkansas, and in 1918, he went off to join the Navy. After his discharge, he got his first job playing the banjo in a dance hall in the oil fields of Arkansas. Over the next ten years, he performed in medicine shows, burlesque halls, stage shows, and in vaudeville. In the early 1930s, he moved to Chicago and became the master of ceremonies on Gene Autry's WLS radio show. He became an accomplished comedian, perfecting his "Duke of Paducah" character. He left WLS with Red Foley and John Lair to found the "Renfro Valley Barn Dance." When World War II broke out, he toured numerous bases entertaining troops.

In 1942, the management of WSM in Nashville felt the Grand Ole Opry needed more comedy, so they hired the Duke of Paducah. He was an instant hit, convulsing audiences with his closing line, "I'm going to the wagon, these shoes are killin' me." He left the Opry company in 1959 but was a frequent visitor. He continued to tour into his eighties and was a frequent guest on television until he died of cancer in 1986.

CAREER HIGHLIGHTS
- The Duke was elected to the Country Music Hall of Fame in 1986.

COWLICKS
- The Duke kept an indexed and cross-indexed file of jokes that included more than 500,000 entries in 500 categories.
- After leaving the Grand Ole Opry, he had a thriving second career as a motivational speaker, lecturing college students and business people on the subject "You Can Lead a Happy Life."

Tennessee Ernie Ford

TENNESSEE ERNIE FORD

BORN: February 13, 1919
Bristol, Tennessee

DIED: October 17, 1991
Los Angeles, California

As a boy, Ford sang in the church choir and played the trombone in his school band. In 1937, he used his voice to get his first job on a radio station—as an announcer, not as a singer. After working at numerous stations, Ford enlisted in the Air Force in World War II. After his discharge, he was an announcer on a Pasadena, California, station. He met Cliffie Stone, who recruited him to sing on the "Hometown Jamboree" show. When Stone joined Capital Records, he signed Ford. His first singles, "Mule Train" and "Smokey Mountain Boogie," were hits.

Ford continued to work as an announcer in Pasadena until 1951, when his "Shotgun Boogie" became a smash hit. In 1955, he recorded Merle Travis' song, "Sixteen Tons," which became one of the best-selling singles of all-time. Ford had hosted radio shows on CBS and ABC and was soon hosting his own television show on NBC, which ran from 1955 to 1961. He left the show to spend more time with his family, but he continued to record, concentrating increasingly on religious albums. He died of liver disease in 1991.

GREATEST HITS
"Mule Train"
"Smokey Mountain Boogie"
"Anticipation Blues"
"I'll Never Be Free"
"Shotgun Boogie"
"Sixteen Tons"
"Ballad of Davy Crockett"
"Hicktown"
"Honey-eyed Girl"

CAREER HIGHLIGHTS
- Ford's religious album, *Hymns*, was the first country album to sell more than one million copies, going platinum in 1963.
- Tennessee Ernie Ford was elected to the Country Music Hall of Fame in 1990.

COWLICKS
- Ford was a bombardier during World War II.
- When Ford's first son was born while he was flying from California to Nashville for his Grand Ole Opry debut, he celebrated by throwing cigars from the Opry stage.

LEFTY FRIZZELL

REAL NAME: William Orville Frizzell

INSTRUMENT: Guitar

BORN: March 31, 1928
    Corsicana, Texas

DIED: July 19, 1975
    Nashville, Tennessee

Frizzell was the son of an itinerant oil rigger, who

moved his family from job site to job site throughout the Southwest. His one constant was music, and he learned to play the guitar by listening to Jimmie Rodgers. While still in elementary school, he got his first job singing on a children's radio show; at age 16, he was playing in honky-tonks all over Texas. In 1950, Columbia Records signed Frizzell and released his first single, with "If You've Got the Money, I've Got the Time" on one side and "A Love You a Thousand Ways" on the other. Both became Number Oone country records, making Frizzell a star.

In 1951, Frizzell had an unprecedented four songs in the Top 10 at one time. His style was so influential that such stars as George Jones, George Strait, and Merle Haggard cite Frizzell as their major influence. His career tailed off briefly in the mid-1950s due to personal problems—he was a heavy drinker, and his marriage was turbulent. In 1959, he returned to the charts and stayed there until 1964. He continued to tour through the rest of the decade and into the 1970s, influencing youngsters such as John Anderson, Randy Travis, Clint Black, and Alan Jackson. In the mid-1970s, he was making a comeback for ABC Records when he suffered a stroke and died.

GREATEST HITS
"If You've Got the Money, I've Got the Time"
"I Love You a Thousand Ways"
"I Want to Be with You Always"
"Always Late"
"Mom and Dad's Waltz"
"Travelin' Blues"
"Long Black Veil"
"Saginaw, Michigan"

CAREER HIGHLIGHTS
- Frizzell was elected to the Country Music Hall of Fame in 1982.

COWLICKS
- Frizzell's nickname reportedly resulted from a wicked left punch he used on schoolyard bullies.
- Lefty and Hank Williams, Sr., who shared a love of hard drinking and honky-tonks, became good friends.
- Frizzell's album *Lefty Frizzell Sings the Songs of Jimmie Rodgers* is considered the finest tribute to the country music legend.

George Jones

GEORGE JONES

NICKNAME: "The Rolls-Royce of Country Music"

INSTRUMENT: Guitar

BORN: September 12, 1931
Saratoga, Texas

Jones was born to a religious mother and a hard-drinking, truck-driving father. He learned to play guitar in church and began to play at local events. At age 19, he was thrilled to play guitar during a local appearance by Hank Williams. After a stint in the Marines, Jones resumed playing local parties and clubs. In 1954, he was signed by Starday, a Houston recording company. He had his first hit, "Why Baby Why," the next year. He recorded both country and rockabilly songs until devoting himself totally to country music.

In the early 1960s, Jones had a string of hits, but his personal life deteriorated as he began to indulge in his father's weaknesses for drinking and carousing. In 1967, he met and fell in love with Tammy Wynette, whom he married in early 1969. They produced both a daughter (Georgette) and several hit singles as a duet. The marriage grew stormy, however, and they divorced in 1975. From that point, the ups and downs in his career followed ups and downs in his personal life. After great success from 1974 to 1976, he began to miss so many concerts that he was named "Mr. No-Show." In 1979, he filed for bankruptcy and entered a treatment program. In 1980, he had a Number One hit, "He Stopped Loving Her Today," that he had initially declined to record because he found it too sentimental. But the problems started again, as Jones ironically sang in his 1982 release, "Same Old Me," until, in 1986, with the help of his fourth wife, he gave up drinking and poured renewed energy into his career.

GREATEST HITS
"Why Baby Why"
"White Lightning"
"She Thinks I Still Care"
"We Must Have Been Out of Our Minds"
(with Melba Montgomery)
"The Race Is On"
"I'll Share My World With You"
"Take Me" (with Tammy Wynette)
"If Not For You"
"The Grand Tour"
"Bartender's Blues"
"He Stopped Loving Her Today"

CAREER HIGHLIGHTS
- Jones was named Country Music Association Male Vocalist of the year in 1963, 1964, 1980, and 1981.
- He won a Grammy in 1980 for "He Stopped Loving Her Today."
- Jones was elected to the Country Music Hall of Fame in 1992.

COWLICKS
- Early in his career, Jones recorded the rock songs "Rock It" and "Jailhouse Rock" under the pseudonym Thumper Jones.
- In 1983, Jones was arrested in Mississippi for cocaine possession and public intoxication. His weight had dropped from 160 to 105 pounds.
- In 1983, Jones opened his "Jones Country Music Park" in Beaumont, Texas. He sold the park in 1988.

GRANDPA JONES

REAL NAME: Louis Marshall Jones

INSTRUMENT: Guitar

BORN: October 20, 1913
Niagra, Kentucky

Jones was the youngest of ten children born to a share-cropper who frequently moved his large family from farm to farm. In 1928, the Joneses moved to Akron, Ohio, so the father could try to get a job in a rubber factory. Marshall (he never used Louis) had learned to play a guitar his brother had picked up in a junkyard for 75 cents, and he played at local dances and parties. In 1930, he entered an amateur contest with 450 people vying for the $50 first prize and, after a week of eliminations, he won. The next day he was given his own radio show on WJW in Akron, billed as "The Young Singer of Old Songs." He shortly hooked up with harmonica player Joe Troyan and moved first to Cleveland, then to Boston. They had an early-morning radio show and toured New England doing evenings shows, a brutal schedule. Because Jones had a distinctive voice and because he was usually exhausted, people thought he was much older than he was. That led to an idea that changed Jones' career—he would perform as an "old man."

Jones was given an old pair of mountain boots, lines were drawn on his face to suggest wrinkles, and he applied a false mustache. After 1935, he was known as "Grandpa" Jones. In 1937, he toured with a group known as Grandpa Jones & His Grandchildren while appearing as a regular on radio stations in West Virginia and Cincinatti. In 1942, he joined the Delmore Brothers and Merle Travis to make recordings as the Brown's Ferry Four.

A stint in the Army interrupted his career, but after the war he went to Nashville and played with Pee Wee King. He soon became a member of the Grand Ole Opry, where he was a beloved figure. He even recorded several moderately successful songs. Since 1969, he has performed primarily as a comedian on the syndicated

TV show "Hee Haw." In 1984, he published an autobiography covering his 50 years in country music.

GREATEST HITS
"All American Boy"
"T For Texas"
"Old Rattler"
"Old Rattler's Pup"
"Mountain Dew"
"Tragic Romance"
"Eight More Miles to Louisville"

CAREER HIGHLIGHTS
- Grandpa Jones was elected to the Country Music Hall of Fame in 1978.

COWLICKS
- Before he became "Grandpa," Jones played in the house band on the "Lum and Abner" radio show.
- While stationed in Europe during World War II, he organized a band called the Munich Mountaineers, which broadcast on Armed Forces Radio and did much to popularize country music among U.S. troops and abroad.

PEE WEE KING

REAL NAME: Julius Frank Kuczynski

INSTRUMENT: Accordian

BORN: February 18, 1914
Milwaukee, Wisconsin

Frank (he was never called Julius) Kuczynski's family moved to a farm in northern Wisconsin when he was young. His father played the violin and concertina in a local band, so Frank learned those instruments from him. At age 14, he had saved enough money from a newspaper route to purchase a used accordian, and he taught himself to play it. While still in high school, he played with a dance band, calling himself "Frankie King," because he admired the music of waltz musician Wayne King. After graduating, he moved back to Milwaukee, where he played in bands and on local radio stations. In 1934, he was recruited to play in Gene Autry's band on tour and on the WLS "National Barn Dance."

When Autry moved to Hollywood to make cowboy movies, King took over the band, renaming it the Golden West Cowboys. In June 1937, King and the band made their first appearance at the Grand Ole Opry and were invited to become regulars. At various times, Eddy Arnold, Ernest Tubb, and Redd Stewart were members of the Golden West Cowboys. King toured extensively during World War II to entertain the troops. After the war, he moved to Louisville to host a regular radio show for ten years. In 1948, he achieved his first major success as a composer when "Tennessee Waltz" became a smash hit for Cowboy Copas. He also began recording a series of his own hits, and the Golden West Cowboys were voted the top country band in from 1951 to 1955.

Financial pressures forced King to disband the Cowboys in 1959, but he continued to tour and perform with a variety of groups. He appeared on the Grand Ole Opry's 60th anniversary show in 1986.

GREATEST HITS
"Tennessee Tears"
"Slow Poke"
"Silver and Gold"
"Bimbo"

CAREER HIGHLIGHTS
- Pee Wee King was inducted into the Country Music Hall of Fame in 1974.

COWLICKS
- Because there were two other men named Frank in Gene Autry's band, the manager decided King should have a nickname. He was only 5' 6" tall, so he was called "Pee Wee."
- King and the Golden West Cowboys spent World War II as part of the "Camel Caravan," making hundreds of appearances throughout the country.

LORETTA LYNN

REAL NAME: Loretta Webb

NICKNAME: "Coal Miner's Daughter"

BORN: April 19, 1935
        Butcher's Hollow, Kentucky

Her best-selling autobiography, *Coal Miner's Daughter*, and Sissy Spacek's Oscar-winning portrayal of her in the 1980 film of the same name have made Loretta Lynn's life the best known of any country star. Lynn was born in a small coal-mining town. When she was just 14, she married Oliver "Moonshine" Lynn, known as "Moonie." Moonie hitchhiked to Washington to find a job, and Loretta, who had four children in six years, followed in 1952. Her husband bought her a guitar for her 18th birthday. Somehow, after teaching herself to play, she found the time and energy to form a band that included her brother Jay, and sang in local clubs at night. In 1960, Lynn recorded a song called "Honky Tonk Girl" for Zero Records, a company so small that she and Moonie barnstormed from radio station to radio station promoting the record until it hit the country charts.

The Lynns moved to Nashville, where Moonie took a job as an auto mechanic while Loretta competed for and won a job appearing on the Wilburn Brothers' television show. In 1962, Decca Records signed her and released her first major hit, appropriately named "Success." She went on to record a striking series of hits through the 1960s and 1970s. Many of her songs, which she wrote herself, served as strong endorsements of a woman's right to assert and control her own life. Lynn wrote that she saw herself as "a spokesperson for every woman who had gotten married too early, gotten pregnant too often, and felt trapped by the tedium and drudgery of her life." In addition to recording on her own, Lynn recorded with Conway Twitty a series of Number One songs.

Lynn had a total of six children and she was a grandmother at age 32. She became a successful business woman as well as recording artist and actively sought opportunities to express her opinions on women's rights, which she continues to do.

GREATEST HITS
"Honky Tonk Girl"
"Success"
"Before I'm Over You"
"Don't Come Home A-Drinkin' With Lovin' on Your Mind"
"You Ain't Woman Enough"
"Fist City"
"Woman of the World"
"Your Squaw Is on the Warpath"
"Coal Miner's Daughter"
"One's on the Way"
"Rated X"
"Somebody, Somewhere"
"She's Got You"
"After the Fire Is Gone, Lead Me On" (with Twitty)
"Louisiana Woman, Mississippi Man" (with Twitty)
"As Soon As I Hang Up the Phone" (with Twitty)
"Feelin's" (with Twitty)

CAREER HIGHLIGHTS
- In 1972, Loretta Lynn was the first woman to win the Country Music Association's Entertainer of the Year Award.
- She has won more Country Music Association Awards than any other female performer.
- In 1988, Loretta Lynn was elected to the Country Music Hall of Fame.

COWLICKS
- When Loretta Lynn came to Nashville, Patsy Cline took her under her wing. Their friendship ended with Cline's death in 1963.
- Lynn's strongest feminist statement was her 1975 hit "The Pill," about a woman freed by birth control. Lynn once said, "If they'd had the pill when I was having babies, I'd be eating them like popcorn."
- Her deepest personal tragedy was the death by drowning of her oldest son, Jack Benny Lynn, who died at age 34 in 1984.

UNCLE DAVE MACON

NICKNAMES: "The Dixie Dewdrop"
"King of the Hillbillies"
"King of the Banjo Players"

INSTRUMENT: Banjo

BORN: October 7, 1870
Smart Station, Tennessee

DIED: March 22, 1952
Readyville, Tennessee

When Dave Macon was thirteen, his father, a former captain in the Confederate Army, moved the family to Nashville to manage a boarding house that catered to touring theatrical people. Macon became enthralled by a visiting banjo player, got his mother to buy him an instrument, and learned to play. When his father died, Macon moved to a farm in Readyville, Tennessee, where he started a mule and wagon transport company. For over 20 years, Macon entertained the countryside by playing his banjo while sitting on the wagon. By the end of World War II, trucks had eliminated the need to haul freight by mule, and Macon, who was nearly 50 years old, was forced to look for another line of work. For the first time, he asked for $15 when he was invited to play at a local party. To his surprise, the fee was paid. At the party, a scout for the Loews theater chain offered him an engagement at a theater in Birmingham, Alabama, and Macon became a professional entertainer.

In 1923, while playing in Nashville, he met fiddler and guitarist Sid Harkreader. The two toured for two years, then they went to New York in 1925 to make 14 recordings. In December of that year, Macon became the first professional entertainer to play on the fledgling "WSM Barn Dance," the Nashville radio show that was to become the Grand Ole Opry. Macon, who had a vast repertoire of songs and great showmanship, soon became the Opry's first star, and he continued to be one of the most popular regular performers for decades. His last Opry appearance came just three months before his death in 1952.

GREATEST HITS
"The Bible's True"
"Turkey In The Straw"
"The Death of John Henry"
"Whoop 'em Up Cindy"

CAREER HIGHLIGHTS
- Uncle Dave Macon was inducted into the Country Music Hall of Fame in 1966.

COWLICKS
- Macon appeared and stole the show in the 1940 film *Grand Ole Opry*.
- Macon never learned to drive a car. He said in one of his songs, "I'd rather ride a wagon to heaven than to hell in an automobile."

BILL MONROE

NICKNAME: "The Father of Bluegrass Music"

INSTRUMENT: Mandolin, fiddle, guitar

BORN: September 13, 1911
Rosine, Kentucky

Bill Monroe was born the youngest of eight children on a farm in western Kentucky. He had very poor eyesight and was shy, almost reclusive by nature; both qualities led him to devote his energies to music at a very early age. By age 13 he was playing barn dances with his uncle and brothers; at age 18, he joined his brothers Charlie and Birch in Chicago, where they were pursuing music careers. Monroe worked in a refinery by day and played at dances and parties at night. In 1934, Bill and Charlie were offered full-time employment on Chicago radio station WLS.

For the next four years, the Monroe brothers worked on a number of radio stations, toured, and did some recording. In 1938, Bill and Charlie split. Charlie formed the Kentucky Pardners; Bill formed a group he called the Blue Grass Boys.

Monroe and the Blue Grass Boys (who included Earl Scruggs on banjo and Lester Flatt on guitar) developed a hard-driving form of music in which the mandolin, banjo, and fiddle had frequent solos. The music was a blend of traditional white and African-American traditional music and more popular modern forms. In 1939, Monroe and the Blue Grass Boys debuted on the "Grand Ole Opry" with his first famous song, "New Mule Skinner Blues." The sound became so popular that it was given its own name—"Bluegrass" music, after the name of the band. It is the only genre of country music that can be traced to a particular source.

Flatt and Scruggs left the Blue Grass Boys in 1948, a parting so bitter that Monroe refused to continue recording for the label that signed them to a contract. Monroe had little recording success after that, but he continued to play the kind of music that inspired countless new groups and musicians. He had a revival of popularity when folk music became popular in the 1960s and he performed at many college campuses. He was still active into his eighties.

GREATEST HITS
"New Mule Skinner Blues"
"Orange Blossom Special"
"Blue Moon of Kentucky"
"Kentucky Waltz"
"Will You Be Loving Another Man"
"Uncle Pen"
"Walk Softly on This Heart of Mine"
"My Little Georgia Rose"

CAREER HIGHLIGHTS
- Monroe was elected to the Country Music Hall of Fame in 1981.
- He won a Grammy Award for the Best Bluegrass Recording in 1988.

COWLICKS
- Bill Monroe stole Lester Flatt (of Flatt & Scruggs) from his brother Charlie Monroe's band, the Kentucky Pardners, in 1944.

MINNIE PEARL

REAL NAME: Sara Colley

BORN: October 25, 1912
Centerville, Tennessee

Sara Colley was the youngest daughter of a wealthy lumberman. As a girl, she took an interest in vaudeville and after graduating from high school, she majored in stage technique at Ward-Belmont College, an elite "finishing school" for girls in Nashville. She taught for a while, then toured with an Atlanta-based theater company as a drama coach. In 1936, the tour stopped at Brenlea Mountain in Baileyton, Alabama. Sara stayed in a mountain cabin for ten days and spent all of her spare time listening to the funny stories of an eccentric old mountain woman. When the tour moved on, Sara had an idea for the character that was to become "Minnie Pearl."

By 1940, she felt she had developed the character enough to audition for the Grand Ole Opry. The first reaction was lukewarm, but Roy Acuff gave her the chance to refine her character by hiring her to tour with him. When she returned to Nashville, she soon became a beloved fixture on the show. Decked out in her trademark silly hat with the price tag dangling, she seemed the perfect country bumpkin. In 1948, she teamed up with fellow comic Rod Brasfield in a long-term relationship that kept several generations of listeners laughing. Although she recorded some songs, she's known primarily for her comedy.

CAREER HIGHLIGHTS
- Minnie Pearl was named Nashville Woman of the Year in 1965.
- She was elected to the Country Music Hall of Fame in 1978.

COWLICKS
- Grinder's Switch, Minnie Pearl's "hometown," was the name of a tiny two-house town near Sara Colley's home town of Centerville, Tennessee.
- She was married to Henry Cannon, a commercial pilot who flew her to many of her engagements. She often joked, "I married my transportation."

Jim Reeves

JIM REEVES

INSTRUMENT: Guitar

BORN: August 20, 1924
        Panola County, Texas

Jim Reeves, the youngest of nine children, was just ten months old when his father died. His mother supported the family by working in the fields. He was given an old guitar at age five, and by age ten he had his own fifteen-minute radio show on a station in Shreveport, Louisiana, just across the state line from his home. But he soon became more interested in baseball. He won a baseball scholarship to the University of Texas, and after graduation, he played professionally. However, an injury ended his athletic career and he returned to Texas to take a job as a disc jockey. In 1953, he moved to Shreveport to become master of ceremonies of the "Louisiana Hayride." That year he also recorded "Mexican Joe," which was released by a tiny regional record company. Amazingly, it was a hit, and he followed it with another one, "Bimbo."

Reeves took a leave of absence from the "Hayride" and went on tour. He soon signed with RCA Victor Records, substituted for Red Foley on the TV show "Ozark Jubilee," and, in 1955, joined the Grand Ole Opry. In Nashville, Chet Atkins encouraged him to lower his voice, and he went on to record an amazing 33 Top 10 hits in the next nine years. But in July, 1964, Reeves' career was tragically cut short when his private plane crashed in a thunderstorm outside Nashville. He was so popular, however, that 17 of his previously recorded songs became Top 10 hits after his death.

GREATEST HITS
"Mexican Joe"
"Bimbo"
"Yonder Comes a Sucker"
"Four Walls"
"Billy Bayou"
"He'll Have to Go"
"Losing Your Love"
"Adios Amigo"
"Is This Me?"
"I Guess I'm Crazy"
"Is It Really Over?"

CAREER HIGHLIGHTS
- Reeves was elected to the Country Music Hall of Fame in 1967.
- He had 52 Top 10 hits between 1953 and 1982.

COWLICKS
- Reeves' first record contract resulted when Hank Williams failed to show up for a "Louisiana Hayride" broadcast. Reeves went on, impressed the head of Abbott Records, and was signed to a contract.
- He made his only film—*Kimberly Jones*, the story of a con man in the diamond fields—in South Africa in 1963.

TEX RITTER

REAL NAME: Woodward Maurice Ritter

BORN: January 12, 1905
        Murval, Texas

INSTRUMENT: Guitar

Ritter's boyhood dream was to become a lawyer, and after graduating from the University of Texas, he enrolled in law school at Northwestern University. Lack of money, however, forced him to drop out and return to Texas. He soon gained regional popularity singing cowboy songs on his own Houston radio program. In 1930, he moved to New York and snared a starring role in the hit Broadway play "Green Grow the Lilacs." At the same time, he recorded several songs for ARC, including the hit "Get Along, Little Dogies." After roles in several plays and in the popular radio drama "Cowboy Tom's Round-up," he was recruited by Grand National Pictures to become a cowboy movie star in the tradition of Gene Autry, who was under contract to a rival studio.

Arriving in Hollywood in 1936, Ritter starred in more than 85 westerns until 1945. His film career declined after World War II, but Ritter's tours kept him in the

Tex Ritter

public eye. He signed with Capital Records in 1942 and recorded a number of hit songs. In 1965, he joined the Grand Ole Opry. He died of a heart attack on January 2, 1973, while arranging bail for a member of his band.

GREATEST HITS
"Jingle, Jangle, Jingle"
"Jealous Heart"
"There's a New Moon Over My Shoulder"
"Boll Weevil Song"
"I'm Wasting My Tears on You"
"You Two-Timed Me Once Too Often"
"Blood on the Saddle"
"Rye Whiskey"
"High Noon"
"The Wayward Wind"
"I Dreamed of Hillbilly Heaven"

CAREER HIGHLIGHTS
- Ritter recorded the 1953 Academy–Award winning theme from the movie *High Noon.*
- He was a founder of the Country Music Foundation and the Country Music Hall of Fame.
- Ritter was elected to the Country Music Hall of Fame in 1964.

COWLICKS
- Ritter unsuccessfully ran for the U.S. Senate from Tennessee in 1970.
- Ritter's son, John Ritter, appears in the syndicated television series "Three's Company" and "Hooperman," plus many films.

MARTY ROBBINS

REAL NAME: Martin David Robinson

BORN: September 26, 1925
        Glendale, Arizona

DIED: December 8, 1982
        Nashville, Tennessee

Robbins' father played the harmonica and his grandfather, Texas Bob Heckle, was a storyteller and barker with a medicine show who collected old cowboy songs. Growing up in the Phoenix area, Robbins' ambition was to emulate his hero, Gene Autry, by becoming a singing cowboy. After three years in the Navy, he began appearing at clubs in the Phoenix area. After appearances on a local radio station, he was hired to host a local TV show called "Western Caravan." One of his guests, Opry star "Little" Jimmy Dickens, was so enthusiastic about Robbins that he recommended him to Columbia Records.

Robbins began recording for Columbia in 1952, but his first success was his third single, "I'll Go On Alone," which hit number one on the charts for two weeks in 1953. Robbins joined the Grand Ole Opry, but he also paid attention to the brand-new sound called rock-and-roll. In 1954, he recorded "That's All Right," the song which first gained attention for Elvis Presley. Over the next few years, he had several "crossover" hits such as "White Sport Coat" that were strongly influenced by rock or pop.

His heart, however, remained with the country music he'd heard since boyhood. He returned to the pure country fold in 1959 with his smash hit "El Paso." After 1962, he concentrated solely on country music. He also appeared in 18 movies, the most memorable of which was *"Ballad of a Gunfighter."* Ironically, his last Top 10 hit, "Some Memories Just Won't Die," had just finished its run on the charts when he died of a heart attack in December 1982.

GREATEST HITS
"I'll Go On Alone"
"That's All Right"
"Singing the Blues"
"Knee Deep in the Blues"
"The Story of My Life"
"White Sport Coat"
"Teenage Dreams"
"El Paso"
"Don't Worry"
"Devil Woman"
"My Woman, My Woman, My Wife"
"El Paso City"
"Among My Souvenirs"

CAREER HIGHLIGHTS
- Robbins was inducted into the Country Music Hall of Fame in October 1982, just two months before his death.
- He won two Grammy awards for Best Country Vocal, Male—1959 and 1970.

COWLICKS
- Robbins loved stock car racing, and he became skilled enough to win a berth in the NASCAR circuit.
- Robbins had his first heart attack in 1969 and was only the fifteenth person to undergo bypass surgery, a common operation today.

JIMMIE RODGERS

NICKNAMES: "Father of Country Music"
"The Singing Brakeman"
"The Yodeling Cowboy"
"The Blue Yodeler"

INSTRUMENT: Guitar, banjo

BORN: September 8, 1897
Last Gap, Mississippi

The son of a section foreman on the Mobile and Ohio Railroad, Rodgers was a sickly child whose mother died of tuberculosis while he was young. At age 14, he took the first of a series of railroad jobs that culminated in a promotion to brakeman. He became fascinated with the spirituals and old slave songs of his many black co-workers; at the same time, he whiled away the hours imitating the plaintive train whistles, developing his distinctive style of yodeling.

When poor health made physical labor impossible, he became a black-face artist in a traveling medicine show. In 1926, he moved to Ashville, North Carolina, and formed the Jimmie Rodgers Entertainers, a hillbilly band that performed regularly on a local radio station. In 1927, Rodgers traveled to a portable recording studio set up by Victor Records in Bristol, Tennessee. After a dispute with his band, he recorded two songs as solos, "The Soldier's Sweetheart" and "Sleep, Baby, Sleep." Both became instant successes upon their release in October 1927. In 1928, Rodger's first "Blue Yodel" (later retitled "T For Texas") became his first million copy seller and led to his nickname "The Blue Yodeler."

By 1930, Rodgers had become one of the most famous musicians in the country. Even the Depression failed to slow sales of his records. But by 1931, he began to waste away from tuberculosis. He recorded his final song "Fifteen Years Ago Today" just two days before his death on May 26, 1933.

GREATEST HITS
"The Soldier's Sweetheart"
"Mother Was a Lady"
"In the Jailhouse Now"
"Waiting for a Train"
"My Rough and Rowdy Ways"
"Pistol Packin' Papa"
"Blue Yodel Number 8 (Muleskinner Blues)"
"Tuck Away My Lonesome Blues"
"Brakeman's Blues"
"TB Blues"

CAREER HIGHLIGHTS
- Rodgers sold more than 20 million records in six years.
- He was elected one of the first three members of the Country Music Hall of Fame (with Hank Williams and Fred Rose) in 1961.
- Rodgers was elected to the Rock and Roll Hall of Fame in 1986.

COWLICKS
- Rodgers loved fast cars and owned several.
- In Hollywood, Rodgers recorded with Louie Armstrong.
- In 1931, he toured the south with humorist Will Rogers to raise money for Dustbowl victims.

ROY ROGERS

REAL NAME: Leonard Slye

NICKNAME: "King of the Cowboys"

BORN: November 5, 1911
Cincinnati, Ohio

INSTRUMENT: Guitar

Leonard Slye was raised on a farm in Portsmouth, Ohio, where his father taught him how to play the mandolin and the guitar. In 1930, he hitched a ride to California, where he worked as a peach picker and truck driver while playing with a number of bands. In late 1933, he joined with Bob Nolan and Tim Spencer to form the Pioneer Trio, which later became the Sons of the Pioneers. The group performed on a Los Angeles radio station and recorded many hits.

Slye, however, had greater ambitions. He took bit parts in numerous motion pictures under the name Dick Weston before taking the name Roy Rogers. His first starring role was in "Under the Western Skies," which made him a big star. He went on to star in 91 movies and 101 episodes of his own television show, often with his horse Trigger and female companion Dale Evans, whom he married in 1947. He continued to occasionally perform and record, sometimes with the Sons of the Pioneers. His business investments, including a restaurant chain that bears his name, made him a fortune outside the entertainment field.

GREATEST HIT (AS A SOLO PERFORMER)
"Hoppy, Gene and Me"

NOTABLE MOVIES
Under Western Skies
Carson City Kid
Robin Hood of the Pecos
The Man from Music Mountain
The Navajo Trail
Son of Paleface
Pals of the Golden West
Mackintosh and TJ
TV SHOW: "Roy Rogers & Dale Evans"

CAREER HIGHLIGHTS

- As a member of the Sons of the Pioneers, Rodgers received the 1971 Western Heritage Award.
- Rogers was twice elected to the Country Music Hall of Fame: as a member of the Sons of the Pioneers in 1980 and as an individual in 1989.
- His personal fortune is estimated to be in excess of $100 million.

HANK SNOW

REAL NAME: Clarence Eugene Snow
NICKNAME: "The Yodeling Ranger"
"The Singing Ranger"

BORN: May 9, 1914
Liverpool, Nova Scotia, Canada

Snow had an unhappy childhood after his parents divorced, and he ran away from home at age 12 to join the Merchant Marine as a cabin boy. At sea, he learned to play the harmonic and the guitar. After his discharge, he began playing in Nova Scotia clubs. At age 20, he got his first regular radio show and at 22 signed a contract with RCA Canada. For the next thirteen years, he made numerous unsuccessful attempts to gain a foothold in American country music.

His luck changed in 1949. He persuaded RCA Records to release his songs in the U.S. He also met Ernest Tubb, who arranged for Snow to debut on the Grand Ole Opry. His first appearance, on January 7, 1950, did not go well. But after his first U.S. RCA release "Marriage Vows" hit the Top 10, he was invited to join the Opry. His next single "I'm Movin' On" soared to Number One on the charts and became one of the biggest hits of the 1950s. Two decades of additional hits followed. Snow became one of the most popular ambassadors of country music, making appearances all over the world. He continued to appear on the "Grand Ole Opry" through the 1980s.

GREATEST HITS

"I'm Movin' On"
"Marriage Vows"
"The Golden Rocket"
"Rhumba Boogie"
"(Now and Then There's) A Fool Such as Me"
"I Don't Hurt Anymore"
"I've Been Everywhere"
"Ninety Miles an Hour (Down a Dead End Street)"

CAREER HIGHLIGHTS

- "I'm Movin' On" was Number One for an incredible 49 consecutive weeks.
- Snow had 36 Top 10 hits from 1950 to 1974.
- Elected to the Country Music Hall of Fame in 1979.

COWLICKS

- Snow purchased his first guitar with the money he received for unloading an entire freighter load of salt.
- Snow was a skilled guitarist and the first musician to record a duet with Chet Atkins.
- Snow established the Hank Snow Child Abuse Foundation to help children escape the violence he had suffered as a youth.

SONS OF THE PIONEERS

FORMED: 1933

MEMBERS: Roy Rogers
Bob Nolan
Tim Spencer

This famous country music group formed as the Pioneer Trio in Los Angeles in late 1933, after each of the three founders had played in several bands. They changed their name to the Sons of the Pioneers the next year, adding instrumentalists Hugh and Karl Farr. That same year, they recorded their first hit single, "Tumbling Tumbleweeds."

The Sons of the Pioneers recorded many additional hits throughout the 1930s and 1940s, even as Rogers moved on to become a major movie star. They appeared in several Roy Rogers movies. Although Tim Spencer died on April 26, 1974, and Bob Nolan died on June 15,

1980, the Sons of the Pioneers continued to perform with numerous personnel changes into the 1990s.

GREATEST HITS
"Tumbling Tumbleweeds"
"Cool Water"
"Dust"
"Stars and Stripes on Iwo Jima"
"Teardrops in My Heart"
"Baby Doll"
"Room Full of Roses"
"Ride, Concrete Cowboy, Ride"

NOTABLE MOVIES
Rhythm on the Ranges
Hollywood Canteen
Gay Rancheros
Melody Time
Sons of the Pioneers

CAREER HIGHLIGHTS
- The Sons of the Pioneers received the 1971 Western Heritage Award.
- The original members were inducted into the Country Music Hall of Fame in 1980.

COWLICKS
- One former member, Ken Curtis, played Festus on TV's hit western "Gunsmoke."
- The Sons of the Pioneers reunited with Roy Rogers in 1979 to hit the Top 20 with "Ride, Concrete Cowboy, Ride" from the sound track of the movie *Smokey and the Bandit II*.

HANK THOMPSON

INSTRUMENT: Guitar

BORN: September 3, 1925
    Waco, Texas

Hank Thompson's first instrument was the harmonica, with which he won several local talent contests. When he was a teenager, he used four dollars of his win-

Hank Thompson

nings to purchase a used guitar and soon mastered it. Growing up in Texas in the late 1930s, he was influenced by the western swing bands, such as Bob Wills and His Texas Playboys. Thompson played local clubs and parties, and appeared on a local radio station before entering the Navy in 1943, when he turned 18. Upon his discharge, he returned to Waco and formed his own western swing band, the Brazos Valley Boys. Thompson and his band recorded "Whoa Sailor" with a small record company. This song, a hit in Texas, came to the attention of Tex Ritter, who recommended Thompson to Capital Records.

Beginning in 1948, Thompson and the Brazos Valley Boys recorded numerous hits over an 18-year period. Thompson spent more time on the West Coast than he did in Nashville. He was the first country singer to record in hi-fi and in stereo. He and his band continued to tour both in the U.S.A. and abroad into the 1980s.

GREATEST HITS
"Whoa Sailor"
"Humpty Dumpty Heart"
"Today"
"Green Light"
"The Wild Side of Life"
"She's a Whole Lot Like You"
"Oklahoma Hills"
"Hangover Tavern"
"In the Can or in the Bottle"
"Smokey the Bar"
"Who Left the Door to Heaven Open?"

CAREER HIGHLIGHTS
- The Brazos Valley Boys were the most popular western band in every magazine poll from 1953 to 1965.
- Hank Thompson was elected to the Country Music Hall of Fame in 1989.

COWLICKS
- On his first radio show, Thompson was sponsored by a local flour company and dubbed "Hank the Hired Hand."
- Thompson's early exposure to country music came from a neighbor, a woman bootlegger with enough money to purchase a huge record collection.
- His biggest hit, "The Wild Side of Life," put the blame on women for leading men astray; Kitty Wells' response, "It Wasn't God Who Made Honky Tonk Angels," made her a star.

FLOYD TILLMAN

INSTRUMENT: Guitar

BORN: December 8, 1914
      Ryan, Oklahoma

Born in Oklahoma but raised in Texas, Tillman taught himself the guitar at an early age and backed up fiddlers at local barn dances and parties. In 1933, he moved to

San Antonio to play in a honky-tonk. Three years later, he joined a new Houston band called the Blue Ridge Playboys, which featured Ted Daffan and Moon Mullican, who would both become major figures in country music in the 1940s. Tillman was already known as an accomplished guitarist and became a highly respected songwriter with "I'll Keep On Loving You," "They Took the Stars Out of Heaven," "Each Night At Nine," and "It Makes No Difference Now." Tillman recorded the last song in 1939, after it had already been a hit for Dickie McBride of Cliff Bruner's Texas Wanderers.

Tillman finally achieved success as a vocalist in 1948, recording several of his own compositions. These songs were more commercially successful, however, when later recorded by big band vocalist Jimmy Wakely. Tillman's last successful commercial hit was released in 1960, but his influence as a songwriter continued into the 1980s.

GREATEST HITS
"It Makes No Difference Now"
"I Love You So Much It Hurts"
"Slipping Around"
"I'll Never Slip Around Again"
"It Just Tore Me Up"

CAREER HIGHLIGHTS
- Floyd Tillman was elected to the Country Music Hall of Fame in 1984.
- Tillman was one of the first country musicians to use an electric guitar.

COWLICKS
- Tillman went to work as a Western Union messenger at age 13.
- His composition "Slipping Around" triggered a long list of "cheating songs" in country music.

MERLE TRAVIS

INSTRUMENT: Guitar

BORN: November 29, 1917
Rosewood, Kentucky

DIED: October 20, 1983
Tahlequah, Oklahoma

Travis was born in coal-mining country, but even as a youngster he showed a talent for picking a guitar instead of digging coal. As a teenager, he was tutored by Mose Rager, who in turn had been taught by legendary black railroad worker and guitarist Arnold Shultz. He went on to develop a unique style of picking in which the thumb is used to play rhythm on the bass strings and the index finger to play melody on the treble strings, a style that became known as "Travis picking."

His skill won him places in a number of bands, including the Tennessee Tomcats and the Georgia Wildcats. In the early 1940s, he played with the Delmore Brothers and Grandpa Jones in a group called the Brown's Ferry Four. After a stint in the Marine Corps, he moved to California, where he combined songwriting, recording, and movie acting. Many of his songs became huge hits for others, for example, "Sixteen Tons" for Tennessee Ernie Ford and "Smoke, Smoke, Smoke" for Tex Williams. After signing with Capitol Records, he recorded such number-one hits as "Divorce Me C.O.D." and "So Round, So Firm, So Fully Packed." Except for a short stay in Nashville, he continued to live and perform in California until shortly before his death from cancer in 1983.

GREATEST HITS
"Cincinnati Lou"
"Divorce Me C.O.D."
"So Round, So Firm, So Fully Packed"
"Steel Guitar Rag"
"Three Times Seven"
"Dark As a Dungeon"
"Fat Gal"
"Merle's Boogie Woogie"
"John Henry"
"I Am a Pilgrim"
"Re-Enlistment Blues"

CAREER HIGHLIGHTS
- Travis was elected to the Nashville Songwriters Hall of Fame in 1970.

- He was elected to the Country Music Hall of Fame in 1977.

COWLICKS
- Travis' guitar tutor, Mose Rager, also taught Ike Everly, father of the Everly Brothers.
- His most famous movie appearance was as a guitar-strumming sailor in *From Here to Eternity*.
- His last film appearance was with Clint Eastwood in *Honky Tonk Man*.

ERNEST TUBB

NICKNAME: "The Texas Troubadour"

INSTRUMENT: Guitar

BORN: February 9, 1914
        Crisp, Texas

DIED: September 6, 1984
        Nashville, Tennessee

Tubb was born on a Texas farm, but he lived with several different relatives after his parents were divorced. Hearing Jimmie Rodgers made him obsessive about music. He bought every Rodgers album and spent countless hours imitating Rodgers' yodeling style. Unable to find work locally, he moved to San Antonio to work for the WPA; there he purchased his first guitar. In 1934, he talked his way into appearances on a local radio station. In 1935, he became friends with Carrie Rodgers, Jimmie's widow, who not only arranged a recording session for Tubb with RCA Records, but also lent him Jimmie's guitar. Tubb's recorded two tributes to Rodgers, "The Passing of Jimmie Rodgers" and "Jimmie Rodgers' Last Thoughts."

Tubb continued to struggle for five years. Then fate intervened. His tonsils were removed in 1939, and as a result, he could no longer yodel. Tubb was forced to develop his own singing style, which was a classic example of the hard-driving music that came to be known as "honky-tonk." In 1940, he was hired by the makers of

Gold Chain Flour to represent them as the Gold Chain Troubadour. The exposure led to his first film appearance, in the 1941 movie *Fightin' Buckaroos*. He reached true stardom in 1942 with the release of a song he wrote, "Walking the Floor Over You." Tubb auditioned for the Grand Ole Opry in December 1942 and was invited to join the Opry company in January 1943. He became one of the major stars of country music, releasing a string of hits through the late 1960s.

Tubb is also important in country music history as an innovator. In 1941, a nightclub owner complained that crowd noise drowned out records playing on the jukebox. Tubb then added an electric guitar to his band to increase the volume, the first major country music star to do so. Tubb was also the first major country star to insist on recording in Nashville, persuading Delta Records to open a branch there—the first step in making Nashville "Music City." In 1947, Tubb opened the Ernest Tubb Record Store, now a Nashville landmark. Finally, because there's never enough of a good thing, he started the "Midnight

Kitty Wells

Jamboree" radio show to follow "Grand Ole Opry" every Saturday.

GREATEST HITS
"Walking the Floor Over You"
"It's Been So Long, Darling"
"Slippin' Around"
"Blue Christmas"
"Goodnight Irene"
"I Love You Because"
"Half a Mind"
"Mr. And Mrs. Used-To-Be"
"Tomorrow Never Comes"
"Drivin' Nails in My Coffin"
"Let's Say Goodbye Like We Said Hello"
"Thanks a Lot"
"Walk Across Texas"

CAREER HIGHLIGHTS
- Tubb was elected to the Country Music Hall of Fame in 1965.
- He received the Academy of Country Music Pioneer Award in 1980.

COWLICKS
- Tubb was perhaps the hardest working star of his time, playing an average of 300 dates a year for decades.
- Tubb's eldest son, Justin, is a singer-guitarist who joined the Grand Ole Opry in 1955.
- Tubb broadcast his radio show from his own record shop.

KITTY WELLS

REAL NAME: Muriel Deason

NICKNAME: "Queen of Country Music"

INSTRUMENT: Guitar

BORN: August 30, 1919
Nashville, Tennessee

One of the few country stars actually born in Nashville, Muriel Deason had an average childhood as one of six children of a railroad brakeman. She learned to play the guitar at age 14, and at age 16 met a boy named Johnny Wright who shared her interest in music. Along with Johnny's cousin, Wright and Deason got a job singing on radio station WSIX in 1936. They began to tour and married in 1938. In 1939, Wright joined with singer Jack Anglin to form the duo "Johnny and Jack." They toured with their group, the Tennessee Mountain Boys, along with Muriel, who performed as a featured girl singer under the name Kitty Wells.

Johnny and Jack toured until 1942, when gasoline rationing made travel difficult. After the war, they were invited to join the Grand Ole Opry, but they left after a year to become stars on the new "Louisiana Hayride" show. Kitty Wells did some recording on her own, but the records didn't sell. When Johnny and Jack were invited back to the Grand Ole Opry in 1952, she decided to retire.

Then Johnny Wright ran into a Decca Records company executive who was looking for a female singer to record a female's "answer" to the current Hank Thompson hit, "The Wild Side of Life." Wright talked Wells into recording "It Wasn't God Who Made Honky Tonk Angels" on May 3, 1952. The song soared to number one on the charts, where it stayed for 16 weeks. In 1953, Wells, followed up with two more female answer songs that became number-one hits, and she became the first major female country music solo star. She was voted the number-one female country artist of the year for eleven consecutive years. As a virtual institution on the Grand Ole Opry, she was given the title "The Queen of Country Music." Her success paved the way for Patsy Cline, Loretta Lynn, and many other female stars of the 1960s, 1970s, and 1980s.

GREATEST HITS
"Honky Tonk Angels"
"I Heard the Jukebox Playing"
"A Wedding Ring Ago"
"I Don't Claim to Be an Angel"
"Cheatin's a Sin"
"Makin' Believe"
"Release Me"

"Searching"
"I Can't Stop Loving You"
"Amigo's Guitar"
"Heartbreak U.S.A."

CAREER HIGHLIGHTS
- Wells had 35 Top 10 hits between 1952 and 1965. She was the first woman to have a number-one country single.
- In 1954, Tennessee Governor Frank Clement created a Tennessee Womanhood Award for her.
- She was elected to the Country Music Hall of Fame in 1976.
- Wells received a Lifetime Achievement Award from the National Academy of Recording Arts and Sciences in 1991.

COWLICKS
- Johnny Wright named his wife Kitty Wells after an old folk song, "Sweet Kitty Wells."
- Kitty's son Bobby Wright played the role of Willie on the TV series "McHale's Navy."

HANK WILLIAMS, SR.

REAL NAME: Hiriam Williams

INSTRUMENT: Guitar

BORN: September 17, 1923
Mount Olive, Alabama

DIED: January 1, 1953
Oak Hill, West Virginia

Williams was born in rural Alabama but moved to Montgomery at age five, when his mother opened a boarding house. A domineering, strict woman, she made sure that he was thoroughly exposed to church and gospel music. On the streets, Williams spent countless days following a black street singer nicknamed "Tee-Tot," from whom he picked up blues chords and folk songs, including "My Bucket's Got A Hole In It." At age

14, Williams formed his own band, the Drifting Cowboys. They played in honky tonks, where Williams picked up some money—and, unfortunately, a tragic taste for alcohol. When World War II broke out, Williams was forced to disband his group and work in a shipyard to earn a living.

His big break came in 1946, when he and his wife, Audrey, traveled to Nashville and persuaded Fred Rose, of the famous Acuff-Rose Music Company, to purchase some of his songs. In April 1947, Williams recorded "Move It On Over," his first hit. He joined the "Louisiana Hayride" radio show in Shreveport, Louisiana in August 1948, and soon became the star. In February 1949, Williams released "Lovesick Blues," which stayed 16 weeks at the top of the country charts and sold more than three million copies.

The success of "Lonesome Blues" led to an invitation to perform at the Grand Ole Opry. Williams' debut performance, on June 11, 1949, has been called the single most dramatic moment in the long history of that institution. His rendition of "Lonesome Blues" so electrified the crowd and listening audience that overnight Williams became the most prominent star in country music. He immediately joined the Opry company while he wrote and recorded a dazzling series of hits.

His private life, however, was a disaster. Williams was an alcoholic who also became addicted to painkillers first prescribed for an aching back. His behavior became so erratic that he was finally fired from the Opry in August 1952. Just five months later, he died of a drug and alcohol overdose in the back seat of a car while being driven to a concert date in Oak Hill, West Virginia. Hank Williams was only 29 years old.

GREATEST HITS
"Move It On Over"
"Lonesome Blues"
"Mind Your Own Business"
"My Bucket's Got a Hole In It"
"Long Gone Lonesome Blues"
"Why Should We Try Anymore?"
"Cold, Cold Heart"
"Hey Good Lookin'"

"Crazy Love"
"I Can't Help It"
"Honky Tonk Blues"
"Jambalaya"
"I'll Never Get Out of This World Alive"
"Your Cheatin' Heart"
"Take These Chains From My Heart"

CAREER HIGHLIGHTS
- Williams was one of the first three electees to the Country Hall of Fame when it was started in 1961.
- Williams' music continues to serve as the essence of country music.
- In the early 1950s, Williams' income exceeded $200,000 per year, and his estate continues to receive millions in annual income today.

COWLICKS
- Despite his song-writing ability, Williams was nearly illiterate and could barely compose a short letter.
- Williams hated his given first name, Hiriam, which was a misspelling of the biblical King Hiram.
- Twenty thousand attended his funeral in Montgomery, Alabama.
- Hank Williams also recorded as Luke the Drifter.

BOB WILLS

REAL NAME: James Robert Wills

NICKNAME: "The King of Western Swing"

INSTRUMENT: Fiddle

BORN: March 6, 1905
Kosse, Texas

Wills, the oldest of ten children, picked up fiddling at an early age from his father, who often played at barn dances and house parties. In the 1920s, Wills roamed Texas, working odd jobs until he joined a medicine show. He settled in Fort Worth in 1929, forming a band with vocalist Milton Brown. When the band obtained a regular show sponsored by a local flour company, they became known as the Light Crust Doughboys. Fired for excessive drinking and personality conflicts, Wills eventually settled in Tulsa, Oklahoma, where he formed a new band known as Bob Wills and His Texas Playboys, featuring Tommy Duncan as vocalist and Wills' brother Johnnie Lee on banjo.

With the Playboys, Wills blended country music with the big band sound that was so popular across the country to create a style called "country swing." In 1935, Wills and the Playboys began recording, and by 1940 Wills was a major star and a leading influence on country music. In 1943, Wills moved to California, where he appeared in several films.

After the war, the popularity of the big bands declined, and Wills experimented with a new sound that combined the fiddle with electric steel guitars and other string instruments. The public responded positively, but Wills, a heavy drinker, began to have health problems. He had heart attacks in 1962 and 1964 and a stroke in 1969. In 1973, he had recovered enough to appear at a recording session featuring many of the original Texas Playboys and Merle Haggard. But he had another stroke after the first day and slipped into a coma that lasted until his death in 1975.

GREATEST HITS
"Spanish Two Step"
"Right or Wrong"
"San Antonio Rose"
"Stay a Little Longer"
"Faded Love"

NOTABLE MOVIES
Take Me Back to Oklahoma

CAREER HIGHLIGHTS
- Wills was elected to the Country Music Hall of Fame in 1968.
- He received the Academy of Country Music Pioneer Award in 1969.
- Wills was honored by the State of Texas on May 30, 1969.

COWLICKS

- In 1935, Wills hired the first drummer to play for a major country-music band.
- Johnny Lee Wills, Bob's brother, recorded the famous song "Peter Cottontail."

PAYING HOMAGE

These songs are dedicated to the legendary men of country music.

Razzy Bailey	"The Old Blue Yodeler" for Jimmie Rodgers
Ernest Tubb	"The Passing of Jimmie Rodgers," "Jimmie Rodgers' Last Thoughts"
Elton Britt	"The Jimmie Rodgers Blues"
Johnny Hardy	"In Memory of Johnny Horton"
Steven Lee Cook	"Please Play More Kenny Rogers"
R.W. Blackwood	"Dolly" for Dolly Parton"
David Allen Coe	"Willie, Waylon & Me" of Willie Nelson and Waylon Jennings
George Burns	"Willie, Won't You Sing a Song With Me"
Hank Cochran	"Willie" for Willie Nelson
Merle Haggard	"Leonard" about Tommy Collins
Don Bowman	"Chit Atkins, Make Me a Star" to Chet Atkins
Rosanne Cash	"Tennessee Flat Top Box" about her father Johnny Cash
Gordon Terry	"The Ballad of J.C." about Johnny Cash
Ray Stevens	"I Need Your Help, Barry Manilow"
Moe Bandy	"Where's the Dress?" about Boy George
Jerry Dycke	"Beethoven Was Before My Time"
Alabama	"Tar Top" (Randy Owens' nickname)
Sonny Curtis	"The Real Buddy Holly Story"
Becky Hobbs	"Jones on the Jukebox" about George Jones
Joe Stempley & Moe Bandy	"Hey Joe (Hey Moe)" to each other
Hank Williams, Jr.	"I Was With Red Foley (the Night He Passed Away"

COUNTRY MUSIC HALL OF FAME: THE MOVERS AND SHAKERS

The stars of country music are the household names in the Country Music Hall of Fame, but they didn't achieve stardom on their own. Over the last 75 years, country music has been blessed by non-performing geniuses with the imagination and talent to write songs, form record companies, arrange tours, and nurture shows that brought performers into living rooms across our land.

FRED ROSE
Songwriter and Music Publisher

Fred Rose was born in Evansville, Indiana, on August 24, 1897. After growing up in St. Louis, he moved to Chicago, where he pursued a moderately successful career as a piano player and songwriter. His first exposure to country music came in 1940, when he wrote 16 songs for Gene Autry. Soon afterward, he moved to Nashville to become the staff pianist for WSM radio. He became friends with Roy Acuff and began writing country songs. In 1942, Acuff and Rose established the first exclusively country music publishing firm, Acuff-Rose Publications, a business which became a huge success.

Rose left the running of the company to his son, Wesley, while he concentrated on writing songs for and with such stars as Hank Williams and Ray Whitley. His hits include "Be Honest with Me," "Blue Eyes Crying in the Rain," "Take These Chains from My Heart," "Tears on My Pillow," "Settin' the Woods on Fire," "No One Will Ever Know," and "Pins and Needles." Rose died in Nashville in 1954. In 1961, he became one of the first three people elected to the Country Music Hall of Fame.

WESLEY ROSE
Music Publisher and Record Company Founder

The son of Fred Rose, Wesley was born in Chicago in 1918. When his father formed Acuff-Rose Publications in 1942, Wesley moved to Nashville and became general manager of the company. He not only made that company the dominant force in the industry, he also moved into record production, forming his own label, Hickory Records. Rose died in 1990. In recognition of his many contributions to country music, he was elected to the Country Music Hall of Fame in 1986.

JAMES R. DENNY
Booking Agent for the Grand Ole Opry

Denny was born in Buffalo Valley, Tennessee, in 1911, and at age eleven he was sent to live with an aunt in Nashville. He earned money by selling newspapers and delivering telegrams for Western Union until, at age sixteen, he landed a job in the mailroom of the National Life and Accident Insurance Company, sponsors of the Grand Ole Opry. He slowly worked his way up, eventually becoming a department manager. At the same time, he spent every Saturday night selling tickets, running errands, and doing chores at the Grand Ole Opry. After a stint as concession manager for the Opry, he was named head of the Opry artists' service bureau, booking tours and concerts for the Opry performers. The Opry had under contract most of the big names in country music, who earned minimal salaries from the Opry, relying on touring Friday through Sunday of every week for most of their income. At one time, Denny was scheduling as many as 3,200 appearances around the world. For his skill in recognizing and nuturing talent, Denny was elected to the Country Music Hall of Fame in 1966.

GEORGE HAY
Creator and Builder of the Grand Ole Opry

George W. Hay was born on November 9, 1895 in Attica, Indiana. He became a newpaper reporter and columnist for a newspaper in Memphis, Tennessee. After World War I, Hay recognized the opportunities that a fledgling industry called radio might provide. He became an announcer on the station started by his Memphis paper, then moved to WLS in Chicago. In Chicago, he worked as announcer for the "WLS Barn Dance." He got into the habit of starting the show by blowing a steamboat whistle and referring to himself as the "Solemn Old Judge," which had been the title of his newspaper column. In 1925, he took a job as director of the newly established radio station WSM in Nashville. One of his first acts was to start a barn dance program resembling the "WSL Barn Dance." In 1929, he renamed this program the "Grand Ole Opry." Hay served as director of the program until 1951, shaping it into the premier showcase for country music. George Hay was elected to the Country Music Hall of Fame in 1966. He died on May 9, 1968.

J. L. FRANK
Agent and Promoter

Joe Frank, who was born in Rossai, Alabama, in 1900, moved into the big time in the early 1930s, when he took over managing the career of Gene Autry. In 1935, Frank moved to Louisville, where he placed Autry on radio station WHAS, along with a band that included Pee Wee King. When Autry went to Hollywood, Frank installed King as leader of a band called the Golden West Cowboys. Soon Frank arranged for the Cowboys to audition for the Grand Ole Opry, and, when they were hired, he moved to Nashville. Soon he became such a powerful agent and promoter that he was called the "Ziegfeld of Country Music." His clients were the superstars of the Grand Ole Opry, including Roy Acuff, Red Foley, Ernest Tubb, Pee Wee King, and Eddy Arnold. Joe Frank died in 1952. He was elected to the Country Music Hall of Fame in 1967.

STEVE SHOLES
R.C.A. Victor Record Company Executive

Born in Washington, D.C., in 1911, Sholes was head of RCA Victor's country division when he came to Nashville in 1946. Decca Records had been a successful recording studio in the hometown of the Grand Ole Opry, and Shole soon determined that RCA should establish a permanent office there. Among the artists he recruited for RCA were Jim Reeves, Hank Snow, Chet Atkins, and Elvis Presley. Sholes was elected to the Country Music Hall of Fame in 1967. He died in Nashville in 1968.

ARTHUR EDWARD SATHERLEY
Record Company Executive

Art Satherley was born in Bristol, England, and as a young man he came to the United States with a romanticized view of cowboys and brave mountain men. In the late 1920s, he became artists' manager for the American Record Company, which produced records for chain stores as well as Sears, Roebuck stores and catalog sales. In 1931, he signed Gene Autry, whose records, guitars, and songbooks became very popular through the Sears catalog. Satherley retained his job when ARC became Columbia Records in 1938. In the next 15 years, the man who came to be known as "Uncle Art" signed stars such as Lefty Frizzell, Marty Robbins, "Little" Jimmy Dickens, Bill Monroe and Carl Perkins. Satherley was elected to the Country Music Hall of Fame in 1971.

OWEN BRADLEY
Musician, Producer, Record Company Executive

Owen Bradley was born on October 10, 1915, in Westmoreland, Tennessee. He became an accomplished piano player and led one of the most popular dance bands in the Nashville area. In 1940, he was hired as director of WSM radio and, in 1947, became leader of the station's staff orchestra. About that time, he was asked by Paul Cohen of Decca Records to do some record producing for him. Bradley got more and more involved, until he and his brother built the first large Nashville studio, in 1952, on what would become Music Row. As a producer, Bradley played a significant role in creating the "Nashville sound," a melding of country with pop techniques to make it smoother and more palatable to casual listeners. As a producer for MCA, Bradley recorded Loretta Lynn, Conway Twitty, Brenda Lee, and many more. He later became an MCA executive, retiring as Vice-President in Charge of Nashville Operations. He was elected to the Country Music Hall of Fame in 1974.

PAUL COHEN
Record Company Executive

Paul Cohen, who was born in 1908, became a talent

scout for Decca Records in the 1930s. In the early 1940s, Cohen became the director of Decca's country division, which had signed such stars as Ernest Tubb, Bradley Kincaid, Jimmie Davis, Cliff Bruner, Johnie Lee Wills, Bill Carlisle and Red Foley. He had the vision to see that Nashville was a logical recording center, because of all the country stars that flocked to the Grand Ole Opry. In early 1945, he rented WSM's Studio B, an early home of the Opry, for a recording session with Red Foley, the first every major session in Nashville. Cohen also had shrewd musical judgements—it was his idea to have a female singer record an answer to Hank Thompson's "The Wild Side of Life." Kitty Wells' recording of "It Wasn't God Who Made Honky Tonk Angels" made her country music's first female solo star. Cohen was also active in industry affairs, and he was president of the Country Music Association when it opened the Hall of Fame and Museum in 1961. He was elected to the Country Music Hall of Fame in 1976, six years after his death.

HUBERT LONG
Talent Agent and Promoter
Hubert Long, who was born in 1923, began his career as selling records in a Texas department store. He became fascinated by the music business and he soon combined his love of music with his natural flair for promotion to found Nashville's first talent agencies. He and Jim Denny became the two most powerful agents in the business. Long was the first person to serve as both president and chairman of the Country Music Association. He died in 1972, seven years before he was elected to the Country Music Hall of Fame (1979).

CONNIE P. GAY
Country Music Entrepreneur
Connie P. Gay, a born salesman, was born in Lizard Lick, North Carolina. He migrated to Washington, D.C., during the Depression, supporting himself as a street huckster. In 1946, he went to an Arlington, Virginia radio station to ask for one hour of time to air a country music show called "Town and Country Time." His deal—no salary but a hefty cut of ad sales. The show

was a smash success. Gay went on to become one of the nation's leading country music entrepreneurs, running tours to Nashville, organizing cruises, promoting concerts, packaging tours, and producing radio shows. He was elected to the Country Music Hall of Fame in 1980.

GRANT TURNER
Opry Announcer

Grant Turner, born in Abilene, Texas, in 1912, had an early fascination with radio, even building his own set. He studied journalism in college and eventually worked his way up to the staff of a Dallas newspaper. Then radio beckoned, and he held a number of announcing jobs in Texas before being hired in 1942 at KBIR in Knoxville. In 1944, he was hired by WSM as a staff announcer, and he started work on D-Day, June 6, 1944. Shortly afterwards, George Hay assigned him as the announcer on a half hour segment of the "Grand Ole Opry." He went on to become the dean of Opry announcers. He was elected to the Country Music Hall of Fame in 1981.

CLIFFIE STONE
Songwriter, Manager, Publisher, Record Company Founder

Stone was born on March 1, 1917, in Burbank, California. His father was a well-known banjo player-comedian who called himself "Herman the Hermit." Cliffie learned to play the guitar and played in big bands as a teenager. He worked a series of country radio stations as a disc jockey, musician, comedian, and master of ceremonies. In 1946, he joined Capital Records as an executive, producing records as well as managing the careers of such stars as Tenessee Ernie Ford. He also performed and wrote several hit songs. In the 1960s, he started his own music publishing company. When he sold that, he started his own record label. He was elected to the Country Music Hall of Fame in 1989.

WHO'S WHO IN COUNTRY MUSIC

A POSSE OF COUNTRY GROUPS

ACE IN THE HOLE
George Strait's band.

ALABAMA
Country quartet formed in Fort Payne, Indiana, in 1969.
Top-selling country group of all time.

Alabama

ALLEY CATS
Western swing band based in Houston in the early 1930s,
founded by Shelly Lee Alley.

ARKANSAS COTTON PICKERS
This string band, led by Paul Howard, joined the Grand
Ole Opry in 1942.

ASLEEP AT THE WHEEL
An Austin, Texas-based band formed in 1975; it combines
western swing and rock-and-roll.

BAILLIE AND THE BOYS
A trio of East Coast songwriters and session vocalists
founded this band in l986. Kathy Baillie and her husband
Michael Bonagura became a duet after Alan LeBoeuf left
the group in early l989.

BAR-X COWBOYS
Traditional string band based in Houston in the
early 1930s.

BARN DANCE FIDDLERS
Formed by Tommy Dandurand, they performed on the
"National Barn Dance" for many years, beginning in 1925.

BARN DANCE SWEETHEARTS
Husband-and-wife team Martha and James Carson were
regulars on the WSB "Barn Dance" out of Atlanta.

BEAUSOLEIL
Cajun band that backed Mary-Chapin Carpenter on her
Grammy-winning song "Down at the Twist and Shout."

BEVERLY HILLBILLIES
An early California-based band formed in 1928.

BLUEGRASS ALLIANCE
Louisville-based bluegrass band of the 1980s.

BLUE GRASS BOYS
Bill Monroe's band, who created the sound that first
became identified as "Bluegrass."

BLUE GRASS CARDINALS
Group founded in 1975 by Kentucky banjo player
Don Parmley.

BLUE RIDGE ENTERTAINERS
Popular southeastern regional group in the 1930s.

BLUE GRASS KUN-TREE
Bluegrass band led by Joe Wilson in the 1960s and 1970s.

BLUE RIDGE MOUNTAIN FOLK
Band formed in Dallas by the Callahan Brothers in the
late 1930s.

BLUE RIDGE RAMBLERS
Although listed as a group, John Fogerty recorded solo
under this name.

THE BLUE SKY BOYS
Bill and Earl Bullick played together from 1935 to 1951.

BOONE CREEK
Bluegrass band formed by Ricky Scaggs in the 1970s.

BOYS FROM INDIANA
Bluegrass group led by Aubrey Hall.

BRAZOS VALLEY BOYS
Hank Thompson's band, voted top country group from 1953 to 1965.

Charlie Daniels

BRONCO BUSTERS
Led by Zeke Clements, this band played the Grand Ole Opry in the 1930s.

BROWN'S FERRY FOUR
All-star group that included the Delmore Brothers, Merle Travis, and Red Foley in the 1940s.

BUCKAROOS
Buck Owens's backup group, formed in 1952, which was very popular as a touring group.

CADILLAC COWBOYS
Mythical 1950s high school band created as a spoof by the Statler Brothers.

CAROLINA WILDCATS
Earl Scruggs played with this band in Gastonia, NC, in the early 1940s.

CHARLIE DANIELS BAND
Country-rock band formed by Charlie Daniels in 1970.

CHEROKEE COWBOYS
Ray Price's band, which at one time included Willie Nelson.

CHERRY BOMBS
Rodney Crowell's band, which once featured Vince Gill and Rosanne Cash.

CHUCK WAGON GANG
Texas-based gospel music group.

CLINCH MOUNTAIN BOYS
Bluegrass band led by the Stanley brothers in the 1950s.

CLINCH MOUNTAIN CLAN
Stoney Cooper and Wilma Lee's band, which helped keep old-time country music alive in the 1940s and 1950s.

CLODHOPPERS
Pioneer Grand Ole Opry band.

COLEMAN COUNTY COWBOYS
1970s western swing band formed in Texas by Red Steagall.

COMMANDER CODY AND HIS LOST PLANET AIRMEN
Wild western swing band formed in 1967 that continued to record into the 1980s.

COON CREEK GIRLS
All-girl band most popular in the 1930s.

COUNTRY GAZETTE
New wave bluegrass band formed in 1971.

COUNTRY GENTLEMEN
Progressive bluegrass band formed in 1957 that was active through the mid-1970s.

COWBOY RAMBLERS
Western swing band in 1930s led by Bill Boyd.

CRAZY HICKORY NUTS
Group sponsored by the Crazy Water Company on the "Crazy Barn Dance" on WBT in Charlotte, NC.

CRAZY MOUNTAINEERS
Group sponsored by the Crazy Water Company on the "Crazy Barn Dance" on WBT in Charlotte, NC.

CRAZY TENNESSEANS
Roy Acuff's second band, renamed in 1935.

THE CROOK BROTHERS
Early Opry band formed by Herman and Matthew Crook.

CUMBERLAND RIDGE RUNNERS
String band brought to the "National Barn Dance" in 1930.

DAVE & SUGAR
Trio consisting Dave Rowland, Vicki Hackman, and Jackie Frantz, which began as backup singers for Charlie Pride.

DESERT ROSE
Founded in 1986 by Chris Hillman, one of the original band members of The Byrds and founding member of the Flying Burrito Brothers, along with Herb Pederson and John Jorgenson. They have recorded several Number One hits since 1988.

DIAMOND RIO
Group named for a Harrisburg, Pennsylvania, trucking company. Formed in 1984. Their debut single was a Number One hit in 1991.

DIXIANA
Country-rock group with a debut album in 1992.

DIXIE EARLY BIRDS
First stage name of Johnny Wright and Jack Anglin, who later called themselves "Johnny and Jack."

DIXIE MOUNTAINEERS
Group that recorded as early as 1924, featuring Ernest "Pop" Stoneman.

DIXIELINERS
Early Grand Ole Opry band featuring Sam and Kirk McGee.

DOWN HOME FOLKS
Group formed in the 1960s by Buck White, featuring his wife and daughters.

DRIFTING COWBOYS
Hank Williams's famous band, that he formed as a teenager in the 1930s.

EARL SCRUGGS REVUE
Band formed by Earl Scruggs after his breakup with Lester Flatt in 1969.

EXILE
Top country group formed in 1963 that continues after 21 personnel changes.

EVANGELINE
All-girl Cajun band (except for the drummer) discovered by Jimmy Buffett.

FALLEN ANGELS BAND
Group formed by Gram Parsons in 1972, featuring Emmylou Harris.

FOGGY MOUNTAIN BOYS
Band formed by Lester Flatt and Earl Scruggs after leaving Bill Monroe's Blue Grass Boys in 1948.

THE FOUR GUYS
Nashville country-pop harmony group added to the Grand Ole Opry roster in 1967.

THE FRUIT JAR DRINKERS
Early band (1925), named because moonshine was consumed

from fruit jars. They were a fixture on the Grand
Ole Opry until the 1960s.

FLYING BURRITO BROTHERS
Country-rock group reformulated several times between
1968 and 1987.

The Highwaymen

GEORGIA WILDCATS
Progressive country band formed in 1931 by Clayton
McMichen.

GIRLS OF THE GOLDEN WEST
Dollie Good and Mollie Good.

GOLDEN WEST COWBOYS
Pee Wee King's band that he took over and renamed in the
1930s after Gene Autry went to Hollywood.

THE GRANDCHILDREN
Band formed by Grandpa Jones before he joined the Grand Ole Opry.

THE GREENBRIAR BOYS
A bluegrass group formed in New York City in 1958.

GULLY JUMPERS
Early Grand Ole Opry band that survived from its inception in 1928 until the 1960s.

THE HACKBERRY RAMBLERS
Early Cajun band.

HAPPY VALLEY BOYS
Tennessee band in the 1950s that for a time included the Louvin brothers.

HIGHWAY 101
Traditional quartet of singers founded in l986 which included Paulette Carlson. They have had several Number One hits.

THE HIGHWAYMEN
"Super group" of Waylon Jennings, Willie Nelson, Johnny Cash, and Kris Kristofferson that recorded a Number One album in 1985.

HILL BILLIES
A group of rural musicians, led by Al Hopkins, who traveled to New York in 1925. When asked to describe themselves, they said they were a bunch of hillbillies, which became their name and the new name for rural American music.

HILO FIVE HAWAIIAN ORCHESTRA
This string band that normally played only Hawaiian music was pressed into duty to play square dance music with a fiddler in the first country music broadcast on WBAP in Fort Worth on January 4, 1923.

HOMELAND HARMONY QUARTET
White gospel group that recorded the major hit "Gospel Boogie" in 1948.

HOOSIER HOT SHOTS
Band of comedians and musicians that starred on the WLS

"Barn Dance" beginning in 1935.

HOT BAND
Emmylou Harris's band, formed in the 1970s.

J. D. CROWE'S NEW SOUTH
Bluegrass band of the 1970s that at one time included Ricky Skaggs.

THE JORDANAIRES
Famous Nashville session group that backed up many Elvis Presley recordings as well as appearing on the Grand Ole Opry.

KENTUCKY HEADHUNTERS
Country-blues band formed in 1989 that became enormously popular.

KENTUCKY PARDNERS
Band formed in the late 1930s by Charlie Monroe, brother of Bill.

KENTUCKY RAMBLERS
Original name of the Prairie Ramblers.

LIGHT CRUST DOUGH BOYS
Early western swing band featuring Bob Wills and Milton Brown that evolved out of the Wills Fiddle Band in 1929.

LITTLE TEXAS
Country-rock group that debuted with a 1992 hit album, *First Time for Everything*.

LOG CABIN BOYS
Gene Autry's group in the early 1930s, of which Pee Wee King was a member.

MAINER'S MOUNTAINEERS
Very influential string band of the 1930s, led by J. E. Mainer.

MAVERICKS
1920s western band formed by Charlie Marshall.

THE MAVERICKS
Moe Bandy's first band which had their own TV show in the 1950s.

MCBRIDE & THE RIDE
Trio formed by Nashville session musicians Terry McBride (son of Dale McBride), Ray Herndon, and Billy Thomas.

MCGINTY COWBOYS
String band formed in the early 1920s that at first consisted of real cowboys

THE MELODY MASTERS
A 1930s Texas band that introduced the honky-tonk classic, "The Wild Side of Life."

THE MELODY RANCH GIRLS
All-girl band in the 1950s with Jean Shepard as bassist and singer.

THE MISSOURI MOUNTAINEERS
1930s Grand Ole Opry group of Jack Shook, Nap Bastien and Dee Simmons, all of whom were from Illinois.

MUNICH MOUNTAINEERS
Country music band formed from soldiers in Europe during World War II by Bradley Kincaid.

THE MUSICAL BROWNIES
Famous early western swing band, formed in 1934 by Milton Brown.

NASH RAMBLERS
Country band that recorded an album with Emmylou Harris in 1991.

NASHVILLE BRASS
Country brass band formed by trumpeter Danny Davis in the 1960s that so embodied the commercialization of country music that they were often parodied.

NASHVILLE GRASS
Band formed by Lester Flatt after his breakup with Earl Scruggs in 1969 as a gesture against commercial country music and a return to its roots.

NEW COON CREEK GIRLS
All-girl bluegrass band formed in the 1980s.

NEW GRASS REVIVAL
Bluegrass group formed in the 1980s.

NEW RIDERS OF THE PURPLE SAGE
Country rock group that was an offshoot of the acid-rock group the Grateful Dead.

NITTY GRITTY DIRT BAND
Country-rock group that in 1973 recorded *Will the Circle Be Unbroken*, a triple album featuring many great names in country music, such as Roy Acuff, Maybelle Carter, and Merle Travis. They changed their name to the Dirt Band in 1976, then returned to their original name in 1982.

NORTH CAROLINA RAMBLERS
Famous early country band formed in 1917 by Charlie Poole.

THE OAK RIDGE BOYS
The new name for the Oak Ridge Quartet, after they made the leap into country music in 1977. They remained one of the top groups in country music into the 1990s.

THE OAK RIDGE QUARTET
Gospel group originally led by Wally Fowler (1945) that were regulars on Roy Acuff's "Dinner Bell" show on WSM. The group went through numerous personnel changes into the 1960s.

OKLAHOMA COWBOYS
Led by Otto Gray, the band operated from 1924 to 1948.

OKLAHOMA PLAYBOYS
Western swing band founded by Jimmy Revard in 1936.

OKLAHOMA WRANGLERS
Vic, Skeeter and Guy Willis, who often played with Eddy Arnold in the late 1940s.

THE OUTLAWS
"Super group" of Waylon Jennings, Jessi Colter, Willie Nelson and Tompall Glaser that produced a hit album in 1976 and launched the "outlaw movement" in Nashville.

PEACOCK FIDDLE BAND
String band featured on WBAP square dances in 1923.

PICKARD FAMILY
A band from Waverly, Tennessee that played on the early

Grand Ole Opry.

THE PIONEER TRIO
Trio of Roy Rogers, Bob Nolan, and Tim Spencer.

THE PLAINSMEN
Formed by Andy Parker, this western harmony group appeared in eight western films and made recordings in the 1940s.

PLEASANT VALLEY BOYS
Austin, Texas-based group combining western swing and rock, formed in the 1980s.

PO' BOYS
Bill Anderson's band, named after his hit song, "Po' Folks."

THE POSSUM HUNTERS
Led by Dr. Humphrey Bates, the first group to play on the WSM "Barn Dance" (1925), which became the "Grand Ole Opry."

PRAIRIE RAMBLERS
Band that starred on the WLS "National Barn Dance" in the 1930s, with Patsy Montana as featured singer.

RADIO COWBOYS
Country-jazz band of the 1930s.

RIDERS IN THE SKY
Doug Green, Woody Paul and Too Slim, who brought the songs of the West back to the Grand Ole Opry in 1982.

RIDERS OF THE PURPLE SAGE
Country-western group that appeared with Monty Hale and Roy Rogers in many movies made by Republic pictures from 1942 to 1952.

THE ROADRUNNERS
Dave Dudley's group that formed in the 1960s to tour the Midwest.

SAWYER BROWN
Country-rock group formed in 1982 that got their big break when they won "Star Search" in 1984. Their name comes from a Nashville street.

SCHOOLHOUSE PLAYBOYS
Buck Owens played sax and trumpet for this group from 1951 to 1958.

SKILLET LICKERS
Early Grand Ole Opry band, led by Gid Tanner.

SMOKEY MOUNTAIN BOYS
Name of Roy Acuff's band after they joined the Grand Ole Opry in 1938.

SONS OF THE MOUNTAINEERS
Formed in 1937 by Wade Mainer, who left his brother's group, Mainer's Mountaineers.

THE SONS OF THE PIONEERS
Name changed from Pioneer Trio when Hugh and Karl Farr joined the group.

Roy Rogers and The Sons of the Pioneers

STAMPS QUARTET
Memphis-based country group in the 1950s that influenced Elvis Presley.

THE STATLER BROTHERS
Nine-time Country Music Association Vocal Group of the Year Award winners. Formed in 1963, they took their name from a box of Statler Tissue sitting on a dressing room table.

STONEY MOUNTAIN BOYS
A 1950s bluegrass group that played Carnegie Hall.

THE STORYTELLERS
Tom T. Hall's band, so-called for his ability to write songs that tell stories.

THE STRANGERS
Merle Haggard's band, formed in 1965.

SWEETHEARTS OF THE RODEO
This California band, named after a 1968 Byrds album, was formed by sisters Janis and Kristine Oliver. They won the Wrangler Country Showdown Talent Contest in 1985 and went on to record many hits.

SWIFT JEWEL COWBOYS
Band sponsored by Jewel Oil and Shortening that was formed in Houston in 1933, then moved to Memphis.

TENNESSEE CRACKERJACKS
Roy Acuff's first band, formed in 1933.

THE TENNESEE FIRECRACKERS
Curly Fox's band, formed in 1932.

THE TENNESSEE HILLBILLIES
Group formed in 1940 by Johnny Wright and Jack Anglin, with Kitty Wells as girl singer.

THE TENNESSEE MOUNTAIN BOYS
Later name of the Tennessee Hillbillies.

TENNESSEE RIVER BOYS
First name of Diamond Rio.

THE TENNESSEE TRAVELERS
Ralph Sloan's clog-dancing troop.

THE TENNESSEE TWO
Johnny Cash's first group, later the Tennessee Three, a trio with Luther Perkins on guitar and Marshall Grant on bass.

THE TENNEVA RAMBLERS
Popular band of the 1920s and 1930s that began as the Jimmie Rodgers Entertainers. They left Rodgers after an argument just before his first recording session in 1927.

THE TEXAS JEWBOYS
Band formed by Kinky Friedman in 1971, who moved to Los Angeles from Texas.

THE TEXAS PLAYBOYS
The most famous western swing band, formed by Bob Wills in 1934.

TEXAS TORNADOES
Eclectic band mixing country and rhythm and blues, formed in 1989.

TEXAS TROUBADOURS
Ernest Tubb's backup band, that gave him the nickname "The Texas Troubadour."

TEXAS WANDERERS
Well-known Texas band formed in 1937 by fiddler Cliff Bruner.

TEXAS WILDCATS
Jimmy Dean's band, formed 1952.

THREE LITTLE MAIDS
All-girl group in the early 1930s, one of whom married Red Foley.

THREE ROLLING STONES
First group to employ Roy Acuff in 1932.

TOMPALL AND THE GLASER BROTHERS
Family group from Spaulding, Nebraska, that joined the Opry in the early 1960s after being signed to Marty Robbins's own label in 1957.

TRINITY LANE
A trio comprised of Tom Grant, Allen Estes and Sharon Anderson based in Nashville.

VAGABONDS
A vocal trio from Chicago hired by the Grand Ole Opry in 1931.

VIRGINIA BOYS
Bluegrass group formed by Jim and Jesse McReynolds in the 1950s.

VIRGINIA BREAKDOWNERS
Group that recorded with Henry Whittier in 1945.

VIRGINIA REELERS
Group formed in the 1920s by Fiddlin' John Carson.

THE WAYLORS
Waylon Jennings's band, formed in 1960 in Phoenix.

WILD ROSE
All-female band formed by Wanda Vick.

NAME BEHIND THE NAME

Being born with a name like Julius Frank Kuczynski wasn't the most promising start for a country music star, which is why that young man changed his name to Pee Wee King. Following is a list of given names of other country stars:

GIVEN NAME	PROFESSIONAL NAME
David Akeman	Stringbean
Sylvia Kirby Allen	Sylvia
James Britt Baker	Elton Britt
Jack Barlow	Barefoot Jerry
Norma Jean Beaser	Norma Jean
Julie Marliene Bedra	Rosalie Allen
Molly Beechwood	Molly Bee
Ruby Blevins	Patsy Montana
Cyrus Whitfield Bond	Johnny Bond
Norma Jean Bowman	Jeanne Pruett
Bill Browder	T. G. Sheppard
Christina Ciminella	Wynonna Judd
Cecil Connor	Gram Parsons
Myrtle Eleanor Cooper	Lulu Belle
Paul Crosby	Jerry Jeff Walker

GIVEN NAME	PROFESSIONAL NAME
Jill Croston	Lucy J. Dalton
Muriel Deason	Kitty Wells
Ann Fowler	Patti Page
George Frayne	Commander Cody
William Fries	C. W. McCall
John Lee Harn	Johnny Lee
Jerry Reed Hubbard	Jerry Reed
Eleanor Johnson	Cristy Lane
Miriam Johnson	Jessi Colter
Harold Lloyd Jenkins	Conway Twitty
David Gordon Kilpatrick	Slim Dusty
Beecher Kirby	Bashful Brother Oswald
Julius Frank Kuczynski	Pee Wee King
Fred LaBour	Too Slim
Dickey Lipscomb	Dickey Lee
Jimmy Loden	Sonny James
Charles Loudermilk	Charlie Louvin
Ira Loudermilk	Ira Louvin
Don Eugene Lytle	Johnny Paycheck
Lecil Travis Martin	Boxcar Willie
Annie McGowan	Rattlesnake Annie
Warner McPherson	Warner Mack
James Morris	Jimmie Driftwood
George Nowlan	Danny Davis
Luther Ossenbrink	Arkie the Arkansas Woodchopper
Mary Francis Penick	Skeeter Davis
Marvin Karlton Percy	Marvin Rainwater
Albert Poindexter	Al Dexter
Virginia Wynette Pugh	Tammy Wynette
Martin David Robinson	Marty Robbins

GIVEN NAME	PROFESSIONAL NAME
Leonard Sipes	Tommy Collins
Marion Try Slaughter	Vernon Dalhart
Leonard Slye	Roy Rogers
Andrew J. Smik	Doc Williams
Francis Smith	Dale Evans
Jeanne Stephenson	Jeannie C. Riley
Roberta Streeter	Bobby Gentry
John Sullivan	Lonzo
Rollin Sullivan	Oscar
James Clell Summey	Cousin Jody
Brenda Mae Tarpley	Brenda Lee
Edward Thomas	Eddie Rabbitt
Randy Traywick	Randy Travis
Kathy Twitty	Jesseca James
Yvonne Vaughn	Donna Fargo
Mack Vickery	Atlanta James
Mary Ann Ward	Marion Worth
Howard Watts	Cedric Rainwater
Scott Wiseman	Skyland Scotty

TIGHT GENES

Entertainment has its dynasties, but in country music, kinship is serious business. A glance through the Who's Who of Country reveals a whole lotta talent in this gene pool. There's an old saw: "The son-in-law also rises." (See "Mergers & Acquisitions" for the marriages.)

Rosanne Cash	Daughter of Johnny Cash
Tommy Cash	Younger brother of Johnny Cash
Hoyt Axton	Son of Mae Axton
June Carter	Mother of Carlene Carter

Randy Newman	Nephew of Alfred, Emil and Lionel Newman
Barbara Mandrell	Older sister of Louise Mandrell
Peggy Sue	Younger sister of Loretta Lynn
Crystal Gayle	Youngest sister of Loretta Lynn
Loretta Lynn	Older sister of Jay Lee Webb & Ernest Ray
Billy Burnette	Son of Dorsey Burnette
Rex Allen, Jr.	Son of Rex Allen
Gabriel Ferrer	Son of Rosemary Clooney
Betty Foley	Daughter of Red Foley
Shelly West	Daughter of Dottie West
Allen Frizzell	Younger brother of David & Lefty Frizzell
Waylon Jennings	Older brother of Tommy Jennings
Johnny Horton	Cousin of Keith Stegall
Ann J. Morton	Sister of Jim Mundy and Bill White
Conway Twitty	Uncle of Larry Jenkins
Darrell Glenn	Son of Artie Glenn
Tompall Glaser	Eldest brother of Jim Glaser
La Costa	Older sister of Tanya Tucker
Pam Tillis	Daughter of Mel Tillis
Linda Gail Lewis	Youngest sister of Jerry Lee Lewis
Jerry Lee Lewis	Cousin of Mickey Gilley
Bobby Wright	Son of Kitty Wells and Johnny Wright
Ruby Wright	Daughter of Kitty Wells and Johnny Wright
Holly Dunn	Sister of composer Chris Waters
Johnny Duncan	Cousin of Jimmy Seals

Terry McBride	Son of Dale McBride
Jimmy Seals	Cousin of Troy Seals
Randy Parton	Younger brother of Dolly Parton
Stella Parton	Younger sister of Dolly Parton
Buddy Alan	Son of Buck Owens
Liz Anderson	Mother of Lynn Anderson
Debby Boone	Daughter of Pat Boone
Shirley Foley	Daughter of Red Foley
Billy Chinnock	Son-in-law of Dick Curless
Stonewall Jackson	Descended from General Stonewall Jackson
David Houston	Godson of Gene Austin and descended from Sam Houston and Robert E. Lee

MERGERS & ACQUISITIONS: FAMOUS MARRIAGES IN COUNTRY MUSIC

A comprehensive study of the marital ties that bind country singers would fill a book. Here's a page of famous mergers of talent.

Roy Rogers	Dale Evans
Kitty Wells	Johnny Wright
Rosanne Cash	Rodney Crowell
Johnny Cash	June Carter
June Carter	Carl Smith
Carl Smith	Goldie Hill
Pat Boone	Shirley Foley
Debby Boone	Gabriel Ferrer
Jack Blanchard	Misty Morgan

Shelly West	Allen Frizzell
Duane Eddy	Jessi Colter
Waylon Jennings	Jessi Colter
Vince Gill	Janis Oliver
Karen Taylor	Dennis Good

Waylon Jennings

Merle Haggard	Leona Williams
Leona Williams	Dave Kirby
Merle Haggard	Bonnie Owens
Lorrie Morgan	Keith Whitley
Jeannie Seely	Hank Cochran
R. C. Bannon	Louise Mandrell
Deborah Allen	Rafe Van Hoy
Amy Grant	Gary Chapman
Clint Black	Lisa Hartman
Reba McEntire	Charlie Battles
Reba McEntire	Narvel Blackstock
Randy Travis	Liz Hatcher
Goldie Hill	Carl Smith
Jerry Reed	Priscilla Mitchell

Margie Singleton	Leon Ashley
Peggy Sue	Sonny Wright
Tammy Wynette	George Jones
Tammy Wynette	George Richey
Virgil Doyle Wilburn	Margie Bowes
Sue Thompson	Hank Penny
Lynn Anderson	Glenn Sutton
Ricky Skaggs	Sharon White
Kris Kristofferson	Rita Coolidge

TODAY'S COUNTRY STARS

ALABAMA

FORMED: 1969, Fort Payne, Alabama

MEMBERS: Jeff Cook—lead guitar
Teddy Gentry—bass
Mark Herndon—drums
Randy Owen—guitar

The four musicians who make up Alabama were anything but an overnight success. The foundation of their success was laid in 1969, when three cousins—Jeff Cook, Randy Owen, and Jackie Owen—got together with Teddy Gentry to form a band they called Wild Country. They performed locally for four years, before moving to the resort community of Myrtle Beach, South Carolina. After honing their skills playing for tourists, they recorded for small regional labels and began to tour. But they had great difficulty making a living. In 1977, the group signed with GRT Records, changing their name to Alabama.

In 1978, a Dallas businessman named Larry McBride became their manager. He set up a record company and produced "I Wanna Come Over," which made the country charts. In 1979, Jackie Owen quit the group and was replaced by Mark Herndon. Their next song, "My

Home's in Alabama," was a smash hit. The group signed with RCA, and a stunning series of hit singles and albums has followed. Alabama has dominated the country charts and country awards like no other group in history. Their success encouraged the country music industry to stop concentrating on solo acts. In the late 1980s, dozens of fledgling groups have emerged.

GREATEST HITS
"I Wanna Come Over"
"My Home's in Alabama"
"Tennessee River"
"Why Lady Why"
"Feels So Right"
"Love in the First Degree"
"Mountain Music"
"The Closer You Get"

CAREER HIGHLIGHTS
- Alabama was given the Academy of Country Music's Artist of the Decade Award for the 1980s.
- Alabama has won two Grammy awards, has been the Country Music Association Entertainer of the Year three times, and has won the Vocal Group of the Year Award three times.
- The group had 21 consecutive Number One records from 1980 to 1987. They have had nine platinum albums, five of which were multi-platinum.

COWLICKS
- Alabama's first performances were at the Canyonland Amusement Park outside of Fort Payne, the community of 12,000 people in which all of the members were born.
- Alabama's use of rock-and-roll-type staging has made them one of the top-grossing tours of all time.

GARTH BROOKS

INSTRUMENT: Guitar

BORN: February 2, 1962
Tulsa, Oklahoma

Garth Brooks was born into a musical family. His

Garth Brooks

mother, Colleen, was a professional country musician with recording and radio credits. As a child, however, he was far more interested in sports. He played football, basketball, and track in high school and went on to Oklahoma State University on a track and field scholarship as a javelin thrower. He also learned to play the guitar while he was in high school and, while in college, he performed at parties and clubs. His early music was an eclectic mixture of folk, pop and country. After he graduated in 1984, he began to focus on country music, traveling to Nashville in 1985. He attracted no attention, so he went back home for two years and married Sandy Mahl. His second trip to Nashville in 1987 was quite different. Within a year, he had signed a contract with Capitol Records and hooked up with Allen Reynolds, an experienced producer. Brooks wrote all the songs except one for his first album, and Reynolds honed his style. The result, *Garth Brooks,* sold 500,000 copies in the first year. His second album, *No Fences,* sold 700,000 in just ten days. Both of his albums reached the one-million sales plateau in the same week in 1990 that he joined the Grand Ole Opry.

Brooks's popularity has soared higher more quickly than any other country artist. His third album, *Ropin' the Wind*, reached Number One on the pop charts in its first week—the first country album to reach the top that quickly and only the third country album to ever reach number 1 on the pop charts. Brooks's tours, videos, and TV specials were also smashing successes.

GREATEST HITS
"Much Too Young"
"If Tomorrow Never Comes"
"The Dance"
"Friends in Low Places"
"The Thunder Rolls"
"What's She Doing Now?"

CAREER HIGHLIGHTS
- Brooks was both the Country Music Association and the Academy of Country Music Entertainer of the of the Year in 1991 and 1992.
- He won the Country Music Association Album of the Year Award in both 1991 and 1992.
- His first three albums have sold close to 20 million copies in three years.

COWLICKS
- Brooks is very family-oriented. His half sister, Betsy, plays bass guitar in his band and his brother, Kelly, is the tour accountant.
- After nearly ruining his marriage through an admitted affair, Brooks shuns public attention and devotes himself to his wife and his young daughter.
- Brooks's favorite food is ice cream.

MARY CHAPIN CARPENTER

INSTRUMENT: Guitar

BORN: February 21, 1958
        Princeton, New Jersey

Carpenter's father was a *Life* magazine editor, and as a child she lived in Tokyo and Washington, DC. Like many others from upper-middle-class families, she went to an Ivy League college, Brown University, where she majored in American studies. She had begun to sing at amateur nights at local bars while in high school, and she continued to perform rock and folk songs while in college. After graduation, she moved to Washington, DC, where she made a living on the club circuit. At age 26, Carpenter realized that she had an alcohol addiction. After she conquered that problem, she met guitarist John Jennings, who became her mentor. She developed a distinctive style that she felt was rock-and-roll. In 1987, she cut a demo record in Jennings's basement. A CBS Records executive heard the tape and signed her as a country singer.

With just one song added to those on her demo tape, CBS released her debut album, *Hometown Girl*. Carpenter became a favorite on country radio stations. She reached stardom in 1991 with her third album, *Shooting Straight in the Dark.*

GREATEST HITS

"How Do"
"Never Had It So Good"
"Quittin' Time"
"Down at the Twist and Shout"
"Right Now"
"He Thinks He'll Keep Her"
"Walking Through Fire"

CAREER HIGHLIGHTS

- Carpenter was named American Country Music Best New Female Vocalist in 1990 and won the Country Music Association Horizon Award the same year.
- She won the Grammy Award for Best Country Female Vocalist in 1992.

COWLICKS

- Carpenter joined with such stars as Gloria Estefan, Carole King, Dionne Warwick, Emmylou Harris, and Rosanne Cash to record *Til Their Eyes Shine: The Lullaby Album*, a benefit for the Institute for Cultural Understanding.
- One of the artists she admires most is k.d. lang.

BILLY RAY CYRUS

INSTRUMENT: Guitar

BORN: Flatwoods, Kentucky

Cyrus, the grandson of a preacher, began to sing with his father's gospel group as a preschooler. During his school years, however, sports was his passion and he wanted to be a major-league catcher. At age twenty, he heard an "inner voice" tell him to get a guitar and start singing. He did, and formed a band the next day. He set a goal of playing in a bar in ten months, a deadline the band met. The band, Sly Dog, became popular locally until 1984, when a fire destroyed their equipment. Cyrus moved to Los Angeles, working during the day and trying to pursue a music career at night. Finally, he decided he needed to come back home. He took a job working five nights a week at a nightclub in Huntington, West Virginia. Forty-two times during his first year he made the six-hour drive to Nashville on his days off to try to get someone to listen to him. His persistance finally paid off when Del Reeves listened to him and cut one of his songs. Manager Jack McFadden signed Cyrus and booked him on tours with Reba McEntire and Highway 101. The tour led to a contract with Mercury Records. Cyrus wrote ten songs on his 1992 debut album *Some Gave All*. The song "Achy Breaky Heart" rocketed to the top of the charts and Cyrus was a national sensation.

GREATEST HITS
"Achy Breaky Heart"
"Wher'm I Gonna Live?"
"It Could Have Been Me"
"These Boots Are Made for Walkin'"

CAREER HIGHLIGHTS
• Cyrus's first album went platinum just two months after its release.

COWLICKS
• In California, Cyrus sold cars for a living, even though he

jokes, "I can't even change the oil in my car."
- Cyrus insisted on using his own band, rather than studio musicians, on his album.

VINCE GILL

INSTRUMENT: Guitar

BORN: April 12, 1957
       Norman, Oklahoma

Gill, the son of a judge who played guitar and banjo on the side, wanted to be a musician from an early age. After high school, he was fortunate to play with a series of well-known groups, including the Bluegrass Alliance, Boone Creek (where he played with Ricky Skaggs), Sundance, and the Pure Prairie Alliance. He then joined Rodney Crowell's band, the Cherry Bombs. In 1984, with the help of some other members of the band, he was signed to a recording contract. His first four singles made the country Top 40 charts. In 1985, both "If It Weren't for Him" and "Oklahoma Borderline" were in the Top 10.

His wife, Janis, was enjoying more success singing with her sister as Sweethearts of the Rodeo. Gill didn't break through to real stardom until he moved to MCA. In 1990, "When I Call Your Name," from the album of the same name, became a Number One hit. In 1991, Gill was invited to join the Grand Ole Opry, and he has continued to record smash hits.

GREATEST HITS
"If It Weren't for Him"
"Cinderella"
"When I Call Your Name"
"Never Knew Lonely"
"Never Alone"
"Pocket Full of Gold"
"Lisa Jane"
"Take Her Memory with You"

CAREER HIGHLIGHTS
- Gill won the Country Music Association Male Vocalist of

the Year in 1991 and 1992, as well as Grammy awards in both years.
- He had three consecutive platinum albums.

COWLICKS
- Gill has listed Emmylou Harris as one of his major influences.
- He has recorded hit duets with both Reba McEntire and Patty Loveless.
- His favorite pastime is golf.

MERLE HAGGARD

INSTRUMENT: Guitar

BORN: April 6, 1937
        Bakersfield, California

Merle Haggard

Haggard was born into a strict, religious family, but after his father died in 1946, he began to run wild. He was arrested a number of times and spent some time in a juvenile home. At age 20, he was convicted of armed robbery and sent to San Quentin prison. He became interested in music while in prison, an interest intensified by an appearance there by Johnny Cash. When he got out in 1960, he had two determinations: to go straight and to make a career in music. With some help from Bakersfield resident Buck Owens and his ex-wife Bonnie (whom Haggard later married), he started playing local clubs. In 1962, he cut a single with a tiny record company that sold 200 copies, but the next year, his "Sing a Sad Song" reached Number 19 on the country charts. Capitol Records took over the small label on which Haggard recorded and his career took off. In 1966, his "I'm a Lonesome Fugitive" hit Number One. His background fascinated fans and provided insight into some of his songs. His streak of Number One hits grew impressively. In 1970, he had his biggest success with "Okie from Muskogee" and "The Fightin' Side of Me." With his band, the Strangers, he played many different styles of music, producing hits through the 1980s.

GREATEST HITS
"Sing a Sad Song"
"All My Friends Are Gonna Be Strangers"
"I'm a Lonesome Fugitive"
"The Bottle Let Me Down"
"Workin' Man Blues"
"Today I Started Loving You Again"
"Okie from Muskogee"
"The Fightin' Side of Me"
"It's Not Love but It's Not Bad"
"If We Make It Through December"
"Big City"
"That's the Way Love Goes"

CAREER HIGHLIGHTS
- Merle Haggard has had 38 Number One singles, more than Hank Williams, Sr., and Johnny Cash combined.
- He has been nominated for more than 40 Country Music Association awards and was Entertainer of the Year in 1970.

COWLICKS
- Haggard's family, Okies who had migrated to California after the Dust Bowl in 1934, lived in a converted boxcar when he was born.
- He was not comfortable on television and once walked off the Ed Sullivan Show when he was instructed what to sing and how to sing it.
- Haggard recorded a tribute album to Elvis Presley, "My Fairwell to Elvis," in 1977.

EMMYLOU HARRIS

INSTRUMENT: Guitar

BORN: April 2, 1949
Birmingham, Alabama

Harris, the daughter of a career Marine Officer, was valedictorian of her high school class as well as a member of the cheerleading squad. She attended the University of North Carolina, but dropped out when she became interested in folk music. She moved to New York to play in folk clubs but abandoned the city at the end of an unhappy marriage. She began playing more country music in Washington, DC, when she met Gram Parsons, the most influential pioneer of country rock and founding member of the Flying Burrito Brothers. Parsons became more than a mentor, and she toured with him and the Fallen Angels Band. Parsons died of a drug-induced heart attack in 1973. Harris recovered by 1975 and recorded her first album, *Pieces of the Sky,* one track of which, "If I Could Only Win Your Love," was her first Number One hit. Emmylou formed the Hot Band, hiring some of the best musicians in the business. Hot Band alumni include Rodney Crowell and Ricky Skaggs. Her 1980 song "Roses on the Snow" established her as a country star, and she followed with country renditions of "Mister Sandman" and "How High the Moon." In 1986, she teamed with Dolly Parton and Linda Ronstadt on the Grammy Award-winning album *Trio.* In 1991, she recorded a hit album with the Nash Ramblers, and in 1992, she finally joined the Grand Ole Opry company.

Emmylou Harris

GREATEST HITS

"If I Could Only Win Your Love"

"Amarillo"

"Till I Gain Control Again"

"Roses on the Snow"

"Sweet Dreams"

"One of These Days"

"Mr. Sandman"

"How High the Moon"

"If I Needed You" (with Don Williams)

"Mystery Train"

CAREER HIGHLIGHTS

- Emmylou Harris has won five Grammies, three for her solo work and two as duets.

- She was the Country Music Association Female Vocalist of the Year in 1980.

COWLICKS
- While in high school, she won the "Miss Woodbridge" (Virginia) beauty pageant.
- Harris has recorded songs by writers as diverse as Bruce Springsteen, Paul McCartney and John Lennon, and she has sung duets with Bob Dylan, Johnny Cash and Bill Monroe.

WAYLON JENNINGS

INSTRUMENT: Guitar

BORN: June 15, 1937
Littlefield, Texas

Waylon Jennings was the son of a truck driver who played in a local band. At age 12, he got his first job as a d.j. on a local station. After he dropped out of high school, he moved to Lubbock, Texas, to take another radio job. There he met Buddy Holly, who hired him in 1958 to play bass guitar on his tour. Jennings was scheduled to be on Holly's plane on February 3, 1959, but he gave up his seat to J. P. "The Big Bopper" Richardson, an act of generosity that saved his life. Jennings spent the next six years working in Phoenix until Chet Atkins signed him for RCA in 1965. He recorded his first hit, "Stop the World," and made a guest appearance on the "Grand Ole Opry" TV show.

By this time, Jennings was developing his image as an "outlaw." He made hard-driving, rugged music in sharp contrast to the smooth, pop-like "Nashville sound." Professionally, he insisted on recording only with his own band, the Waylors, instead of Nashville session musicians. He played on the same bill as rock groups such as the Grateful Dead, and he cultivated a "rock star" image.

In 1969, he married Jessi Colter; in 1976, they combined to produce the Country Music Association Song of the Year in "Suspicious Minds." With Colter, Willie Nelson, and Tompall Glaser, he was involved in *Wanted: The Outlaws*, the Album of the Year in 1976. He con-

Waylon Jennings

tinued to pile up hits on his own, but frequently teamed up with Willie Nelson for other hit singles, such as "Mammas, Don't Let Your Babies Grow Up to Be Cowboys." In 1985, he joined with Willie Nelson, Johnny Cash and Kris Kristofferson for the best-selling album *The Highwaymen*. He continues to be a legendary performer in the 1990s.

GREATEST HITS

"Stop the World"
"Only Daddy That'll Walk the Line"
"Delta Dawn"
"Suspicious Mind" (with Jessi Colter)
"Good Hearted Woman" (with Willie Nelson)
"Are You Ready for the Country?"
"Luckenback, Texas" (with Willie Nelson)
"I've Always Been Crazy"
"Mammas, Don't Let Your Babies Grow Up to Be
  Cowboys" (with Willie Nelson)
"Good Ol' Boys" (Theme to the "Dukes of Hazzard")

CAREER HIGHLIGHTS

• *Wanted: The Outlaws* was the first Nashville album to go platinum, selling over 1 million copies.

- Jennings has won two Grammys and was Country Music Association Male Vocalist of the Year in 1974.
- He has had nine gold, two platinum, two double-platinum, and one quadruple-platinum albums.

COWLICKS
- Jessi Colter, Jennings' fourth wife, was formerly married to guitar great Duane Eddy.
- When he recorded his album *Turn the Page* in 1985, Jennings admitted it was the first recording he'd done without using drugs in 20 years.
- Jennings' admiration for the greats of country music was evident in two 1974 hit singles "Bob Wills Is Still the King" and "Are You Sure Hank Done It This Way?"

WYNONNA JUDD

REAL NAME: Christina Ciminella

BORN: May 30, 1964
  Ashland, Kentucky

INSTRUMENT: Guitar

Wynonna Judd was born in a small Kentucky town, the daughter of Naomi Judd. When she was four, her ambitious 20-year-old mother took her to Hollywood, California. Naomi, who divorced Wynonna's father in 1972, worked as a secretary and professional model until she moved the family back to the tiny community of Morrill, Kentucky in 1975. Because there was no television in the house, Wynonna took up the guitar and passed the time singing duets with her mother. A year later, Naomi returned to California, got her nursing degree, and tried to get into show business.

It soon became apparent that singing as a mother-daughter duo was their most likely route to fame. The Judds headed for Nashville in 1979 and spent three years passing out demo tapes made on a $30 K-Mart recorder. Wynonna won a high school talent contest while in 10th grade. Her evenings were spent singing in clubs with her mom. Their big break came when Naomi gave a tape of their duets to a producer whose daughter she was nursing. Wynonna and Naomi sang the 1936 bluegrass bal-

The Judds

lad "The Sweetest Gift" at their RCA Records audition. RCA immediately signed them as The Judds.

The Judds were in immediate sensation. Their first single, "Had a Dream," hit the Top 20 and their follow-up, "Mama He's Crazy," hit Number One. They went on to win the Country Music Association's Horizon Award, given to the most promising new act of the year. An astonishing string of Number One hits followed, as did more than a dozen major awards. Suddenly, their story-book career came to a sudden conclusion. Naomi announced her retirement on October 15, 1990, because she suffered from incurable chronic hepatitis. The Judds' final performance was a pay-per-view cable broadcast on December 4, 1991, that ranked as one of the top-grossing pay-per-view telecasts of all time.

Wynonna was reluctant to continue on her own, but with her mother's encouragement, she went back to the studio. Her first single, "She Is His Only Need," debuted at Number 30 on the "Radio & Records" country singles charts, the first single by a female in 20 years to accomplish that feat. Two other singles, "My Strongest Weakness" and "I Saw the Light," also made the country charts in her first year. Her 1992 solo tour was one of top five grossing country tours of the year.

JUDDS' GREATEST HITS
"Had a Dream"
"Mama He's Crazy"
"Why Not Me?"
"Love is Alive"
"Girls' Night Out"
"Grandpa (Tell Me About the Good Old Days)"
"Rockin' with the Rhythm of the Rain"
"Don't Be Cruel"
"Born to Be Blue"
"Love Can Build a Bridge"

CAREER HIGHLIGHTS
- The Judds won Grammy Awards for Best Country Performance by a Duo or Group in 1984, 1985, 1986, 1988, and 1991.
- The Country Music Association voted the Judds the Vocal Group of the Year in 1985, 1986, and 1987 and Vocal Duo of the Year in 1988, 1989, 1990, and 1991.
- The Judds had 16 Number One singles as well as four gold, two platinum, and two double-platinum albums.

COWLICKS
- Wynonna appeared as an extra in the film *American Graffiti* when producers spotted her mom's used 1957 Chevy on a Hollywood street.
- Bonnie Raitt is her favorite singer and biggest influence.
- Her favorite recreation is riding her Harley-Davidson motorcycle, and her favorite nail polish is hot red.
- She's engaged to Tony King of the trio Mathews, Wright and King.

ALAN JACKSON

INSTRUMENT: Guitar

BORN: October 17, 1958
             Newnan, Georgia

Born in the same Georgia town as Doug Stone, Jackson followed the path of many of his friends by marrying young and taking a variety of jobs that included driving a forklift. But his heart was in music, and he devoted his spare time to writing songs. At his wife's urging, Jackson decided to move to Nashville. Then fate intervened. His wife, Denise, a flight attendant, ran into Glen Campbell at the Atlanta Airport. She asked Campbell for advice, and he gave her the name of his music publishing company. Jackson's first job in Music City in 1985 was in the mail-

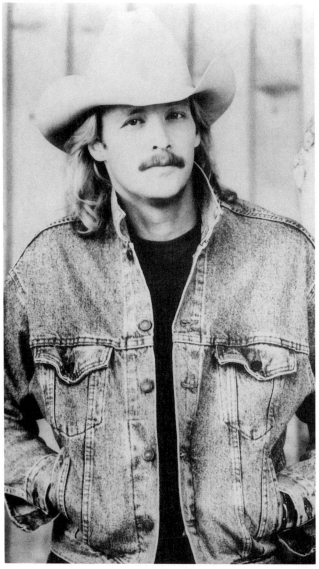

Alan Jackson

room of the Nashville Network, but he soon landed a job as a songwriter at Campbell's publishing company. Later, the same company booked him on a grueling tour schedule, where he gained a modest reputation. His recording breakthrough came when Arista released his first album in 1989. In April 1990, a single from that album, "Here in the Real World," reached Number One. The album of the same title went gold, then platinum. Jackson has since reached stardom as both a singer and songwriter.

GREATEST HITS
"Here in the Real World"
"Chasin' That Neon Rainbow"
"Someday"
"Don't Rock the Jukebox"
"Walkin' the Floor Over Me"
"Midnight in Montgomery"
"Dallas"

CAREER HIGHLIGHTS
- Jackson won the Academy of Country Music Award for Best Single and Best Album in 1992.
- His first three albums were certified platinum.

COWLICKS
- George Jones was Jackson's biggest influence, and the two men have become close friends. Jackson's pickup truck has a bumper sticker that readers, "I Love George Jones," and Jones' pickup, an identical model, has a bumper sticker that reads, "I Love Alan Jackson
- Jackson is a dedicated family man whose hobbies are restoring old cars, boating and fishing. His favorite TV viewing is "Andy Griffith Show" reruns.

REBA McENTIRE

INSTRUMENT: Guitar

BORN: March 28, 1954
       Chockie, Oklahoma

Reba McEntire was born into a different arena of show business—rodeo. As a child, she and her siblings

Reba McEntire

traveled the rodeo circuit while her father, Clark, competed as a steer roper. While in high school, McEntire competed as a barrel racer at rodeos and played clubs at night with her sister and brother as the Singing McEntires. She went on to college, planning to be an elementary school teacher. Then she was invited to sing the national anthem at the National Rodeo Finals. Red Steagall was impressed with her and arranged for her to cut a demo tape. She soon signed with Mercury Records but was not an overnight success. She struggled for four years before she first made the Top 20 in 1979 with "Sweet Dreams" and the Top 10 in 1980 with "You Lift Me up to Heaven."

Her first Number One hit came with "Can't Even Get the Blues" in 1983. She switched to MCA Records, and began recording an impressive series of hits in 1984. A cascade of awards followed, and she continued a career that has led her to be called the "crown jewel of country music."

GREATEST HITS

"Sweet Dreams"
"You Lift Me up to Heaven"
"You're the First Time I've Thought About Leaving"
"Just a Little Love"
"How Blue"
"Somebody Should Leave"
"Whoever's in New England"
"I Know How He Feels"
"Cathy's Clown"
"Rumor Has It"

CAREER HIGHLIGHTS

- McEntire won the top female vocalist honors four years in a row (1984-87) from both the Academy of Country Music and the Country Music Association.
- She was named the Country Music Association Entertainer of the Year in 1986, and she won a Grammy the same year.
- She has three platinum and seven gold albums.

COWLICKS

- Her first husband, Charley Battles, was a rodeo champion. They were divorced in 1987. McEntire married her manager, Narvel Blackstock, in 1989.
- In 1991, her road manager and seven members of her band were killed in a plane crash en route to a concert. McEntire didn't make the trip because she was ill. Her next album, *For My Broken Heart*, was devoted to her feelings about the tragedy.
- McEntire appeared in the TV mini-series, "Luck of the Draw: The Gambler IV."

WILLIE NELSON

INSTRUMENT: Guitar

BORN: April 30, 1933
          Abbott, Texas

Raised by his grandparents, Nelson spent a lot of time listening to late-night radio. His influences were not only country musicians, but also sources ranging from New Orleans jazz to Frank Sinatra. As a teenager, he played with local bands before joining the Air Force. Discharged for a back problem, he moved to Waco, Texas, where he held a variety of jobs until he talked his way into a job as a disc jockey. He worked in California, Texas, Canada, then back to Texas again, all the while performing in honky tonks and writing songs. In 1960, he made his way to Nashville, intending to become a songwriter. Shortly after, he was hired to play bass guitar in Ray Price's band, the Cherokee Cowboys. At the same time, he began writing a series of hits that included "Crazy" (recorded by Patsy Cline) and "Hello Walls" (recorded by Faron Young). Nelson himself became a regular on the Grand Ole Opry in 1964, but began to be increasingly alienated by the smooth Nashville sound. In 1970, he fled Nashville, returning to Texas.

Nelson reached stardom in the mid-1970s with his smash hit album *Red-Headed Stranger*. He went on to participate, with his friend Waylon Jennings, Jessi Colter, and Tompall Glaser, on the platinum album *Wanted: The Outlaws*. His early eclectic tastes were reflected in his recording albums of pop standards, gospel music, and jazz. In the 1980s, he recorded duet albums with Waylon Jennings, Merle Haggard, Roger Miller, Ray Price, Faron Young, and Webb Pierce. He also became a movie star, winning critical praise for his role in *Honeysuckle Rose*. In 1990, Nelson made the headlines when the Internal Revenue Service seized all his property to pay off a whopping $16.7 million tax lien. Even as a maverick, Nelson continues to be one of the dominant figures in American entertainment.

GREATEST HITS
"The Party's Over"
"Touch Me"
"Blue Eyes Crying in the Rain"
"If You've Got the Money, I've Got the Time"
"Good Hearted Woman" (with Waylon Jennings)
"My Heros Have Always Been Cowboys"
"On the Road Again"
"Mamas, Don't Let Your Babies Grow Up to Be Cowboys" (with Waylon Jennings)

"Always on My Mind"
"Without a Song"
"If Loving You Were Easy"

CAREER HIGHLIGHTS
- Willie Nelson has won three Grammys and eight Country Music Association Awards.
- He was honored with the National Academy of Popular Music's Lifetime Achievement Award in 1983 and the Academy of Country Music's Pioneer Achievement Award in 1992.
- Nelson has had seven gold, nine platinum, and two triple-platinum albums.

COWLICKS
- Nelson's first professional job was with the Bohemian Polka Band.
- More than 70 artists have recorded his song "Night Life."
- Nelson endured the tragedy of having his only son, Billy, commit suicide on December 25, 1991, at age 34.

THE OAK RIDGE BOYS

FORMED: 1945, in Oak Ridge, Tennessee

MEMBERS: Duane Allen—lead
Joe Bonsall—tenor
William Lee Golden—baritone
Richard Sterban—bass

The group originated in 1945, when a group known as the Country Cut-ups changed their name to the Oak Ridge Quartet because they played at the nuclear power facility in Oak Ridge, Tennessee. After World War II they disbanded, but reformed again in 1957 as a gospel group and became full-time professionals in 1961. They were very successful but very controversial because their hair was longer and their music livelier than many other country groups. They did, however, garner four Grammy awards in the 1970s for Gospel Performance, and one for Country Performance for Duo or Group in 1981.

In 1975, while playing Las Vegas, the Oak Ridge Boys

began to move toward country music. In 1977, their "Y'All Come Back Saloon" was a smash hit. They followed with a series of hit albums that made them one of the most popular touring groups.

In 1987, their longtime member Bill Golden, renowned for his baritone voice, left the group to pursue a solo career. The Oak Ridge Boys have recorded with Johnny Cash and Barbara Mandrell.

GREATEST HITS
"Y'All Come Back Saloon"
"I'll Be True to You"
"Sail Away"
"Trying to Love Two Women"
"Elvira"
"Bobbie Sue"
"American Made"
"Come on In"

CAREER HIGHLIGHTS
- The Oak Ridge Boys have had 11 gold and platinum albums.
- They won the Country Music Association Group of the Year Award in 1978 and Single of the Year Award in 1981 for "Elvira".

COWLICKS
- William Lee Golden joined the group in 1964, followed by Duane Allen in 1966, Richard Sterban in 1972, and Joe Bonsall in 1972.
- Sterban played with the Stamps Quartet, which backed Elvis Presley, before joining the Oaks.
- The Oak Ridge Boys were a favorite of President Bush and once spent the night at the White House.

BUCK OWENS

INSTRUMENT: Guitar, saxophone, trumpet

BORN: August 12, 1929
       Sherman, Texas

Owens was the son of a sharecropper who moved his family to Arizona during the Depression to escape the Dust Bowl. Times were still hard, and Owens dropped out of

Buck Owens

school to help support the family. Married at 17 and a father at 18, he seemed to be stuck in a pattern that would perpetuate poverty. But music was his salvation. He had learned to play several instruments and performed on Arizona stations. In 1951, he moved to Bakersfield, California, to play sax and trumpet with the Schoolhouse Playboys. After working as a session man for other stars and playing lead guitar in Tommy Collins's band, he signed his own record contract in 1957. In 1959, "Second Fiddle" established him as a budding star. In 1962, he formed his own group, the Buckaroos, and launched a string of hits. Beginning in 1969, Owens co-hosted "Hee Haw," where he provided both comedy and music. Owens never relocated to Nashville, preferring the independence he got from staying in Bakersfield. The rhythm of his hard-driving sound, with its emphasis on drums, inspired many other performers, luring them to the city that has been called "Nashville West." His recordings became infrequent in the 1980s, but his duet with Dwight Yoakam, "Streets of Bakersfield," was a Number One hit in 1988.

GREATEST HITS
"Second Fiddle"
"Under Your Spell Again"
"Above and Beyond"
"Excuse Me"

"Under the Influence of Love"
"Act Naturally"
"My Heart Skips a Beat"
"I've Got a Tiger by the Tail"
"The Kansas City Song"
"Streets of Bakersfield"

CAREER HIGHLIGHTS
- Owens had 32 consecutive Top 10 hits between 1963 and 1972, and has had 12 Number One albums.
- Owens was named *Billboard* top Country Male Singles and Album Artist of the Decade in 1969.

COWLICKS
- Owens is a shrewd businessman whose broadcasting and publishing interests have made him wealthy.
- Owens recorded a series of duet hits with Rose Maddox, Susan Raye, and his son Buddy Allan.
- Buck Owens's marriage to Jana Grief lasted just two days.

DOLLY PARTON

INSTRUMENT: Guitar, banjo

BORN: January 19, 1946
       Locust Ridge, Tennessee

Dolly Parton was born in the most unlikely place to produce one of America's best known entertainers—a dirt-poor mountain community in Sevier County, Tennessee. Parton was the fourth of 12 children born to a man who could neither read nor write. Her uncle gave her a guitar when she was eight, and by age ten she was performing regularly on radio and TV. She made her first appearance at the Grand Ole Opry at age 13, and after her graduation from high school in 1964, she moved to Nashville permanently. On her first day in Nashville, she met an asphalt paving contractor named Carl Dean, whom she married in 1966. She struggled at writing songs with her uncle, Bill Owen, but a Top 10 hit she wrote for Bill Phillips, "Put It off Until Tomorrow," led to a recording contract with Monument Records in 1966. In 1967, "Dumb Blonde" and

Dolly Parton

"Something Fishy" were her first two hits.

That same year, Porter Wagoner hired her to replace Norma Jean as the "girl singer" on his TV show and touring company. The two combined for a series of hit records, beginning with "Last Thing on My Mind." After six years, Parton was anxious to strike out on her own. She branched out musically, recording rock and pop songs as well as country songs. In 1980, her performance in *9 to 5* proved her acting ability and popular appeal. While her physical appearance has always attracted attention, it's Parton's talent that has propelled her to major stardom. She continues to be a multi-faceted entertainer into the 1990s.

GREATEST HITS
"Dumb Blonde"

"Something Fishy"
"Last Thing on My Mind" (with Porter Wagoner)
"Mule Skinner Blues"
"Coat of Many Colors"
"Jolene"
"Is Forever Longer than Always?" (with Porter
  Wagoner)
"Here You Come Again"
"9 to 5"
"Applejack"
"Islands in the Stream" (with Kenny Rogers)
"Real Love"

CAREER HIGHLIGHTS
- Parton has won three Grammys and seven Country Music Association Awards, including Entertainer of the Year in 1978.
- She won an Academy Award for Best Song for the film *9 to 5*.

COWLICKS
- Parton's other movies include *The Best Little Whorehouse in Texas*, *Rhinestone* and *Straight Talk*.
- She developed and owns a theme amusement park called Dollywood, near Pigeon Forge, Tennessee, which funds an educational foundation.
- In 1989, Parton bought the radio station where she first performed.

CHARLIE PRIDE

INSTRUMENT: Guitar

BORN: March 18, 1938
        Sledge, Mississippi

Along with the other members of his large family, Pride spent time in his boyhood picking cotton on a Mississippi Delta farm. He eventually earned ten dollars to purchase a Sears guitar, and he taught himself to play. But his real love was baseball. He played two seasons for the Memphis Red Sox of the old Negro Leagues before a stint in the service. After his discharge, he played semi-

Charlie Pride

pro ball, but he eventually failed to obtain a contract after tryouts with the California Angels and New York Mets. Pride held a variety of jobs before he sang on a show headlined by touring stars Red Sovine and Red Foley. Encouragement sent him to Nashville, where he eventually signed with RCA records in 1965. His first single, "Snakes Crawl at Night," was given significant airplay by d.j.'s who had no idea that the smooth-voiced singer was black. Subsequently, he received enormous attention when his next record, "Just Between You and Me," was nominated for a Grammy. Pride went on to become not only the most successful black musician in country music history, but also one of the most successful musicians in the business. He became a Grand Ole Opry member in 1967, and he produced Top Ten hits for two decades. When he moved to Dallas, Texas, he became one of the city's biggest sports fans.

GREATEST HITS
  "Snakes Crawl at Night"

"Just Between You and Me"
"I'm So Afraid of Losing You"
"Is Anybody Going to San Antonio"
"I'm Just Me"
"Kiss An angel Good Morning"
"You're My Jamaica"
"Honky Tonk Blues"

CAREER HIGHLIGHTS

- Charley Pride has won three Grammy Awards and was the Country Music Association Entertainer of the Year in 1971.
- Pride had five consecutive Number One hits from 1969 to 1971 and has had a total of 28 Number One hits in his career. He has six gold records.

COWLICKS

- Pride's idol was Hank Williams, and in 1980, he recorded an entire album of Williams's hits, *There's a Little Bit of Hank in Me.* The album reached Number One on the country charts.
- Pride was RCA's best-selling country artist since Elvis Presley, who, ironically, was strongly influenced by black musicians.

KENNY ROGERS

INSTRUMENT: Guitar

BORN: August 21, 1938
 Houston, Texas

Rogers was the son of a man who worked on the docks during the day and played the fiddle at night. He tasted success at a very early age when his high school band, The Scholars, had a pop hit with "Crazy Feeling" in 1958. After attending the University of Houston for a while, he played with numerous bands, including the well-known folk group The New Christy Minstrels. With some other ex-Minstrels, Rogers formed The First Edition, a folk-pop-country group who had their first hit, "Just Dropped In," in 1968. They went on to produce several other hits, including the Mel Tillis song "Ruby, Don't Take Your Love to Town."

Kenny Rogers

In the mid-1970s, Rogers went solo. In 1977, his version of "Lucille" was a Number One country hit and a Top 10 pop chart song. He followed it with "The Gambler" and other hits. His 1981 recording of the Lionel Richie song "Lady" was Number One on the pop charts for six weeks. Rogers sold an estimated 35 million records in five years for UA/Liberty, before moving to RCA. His duet with Dolly Parton, "Islands in the Stream," was one of the biggest hits of the 1980s. In addition to recording, Rogers has starred in "The Gambler" and other TV movies and has hosted several network television specials.

GREATEST HITS
"Just Dropped In" (with the First Edition)

"Ruben James" (with the First Edition)
"Ruby, Don't Take Your Love to Town" (with the First Edition)
"Lucille"
"The Gambler"
"She Believes in Me"
"Coward of the County"
"Lady"
"Islands in the Stream" (with Dolly Parton)
"Real Love"
"Morning Desire"

CAREER HIGHLIGHTS
- Kenny Rogers has had 11 platinum albums, more than any other country artist. He has also had seven gold albums.
- In 1977, Rogers won the Country Music Association's Best Country Vocal Performance, Single of the Year, and Song of the Year award for "Lucille."

COWLICKS
- He signed a $20 million contract with RCA in 1983, the largest deal of any recording artist at that time. In 1984 alone, he sold an estimated $250 million in records.
- Rogers designed his own Bel Air, California mansion, an Italian-style palace with 13 bathrooms.
- Rogers described himself as "a country singer who's capable of doing other things."

MEL TILLIS

INSTRUMENT: Guitar

BORN: August 8, 1932
       Pahokee, Florida

Mel Tillis, a Florida native, developed a life-long stutter after contracting malaria at age three. He learned to play the guitar at an early age and was a drummer in his high school band, but his main interest was football. He dropped out of the University of Florida, enlisted in the Air Force, and later took a railroad job. During the entire period, he worked on songwriting and singing. In 1957, he headed to Nashville with his songs, including "I'm Tired," which soon became a Number One hit for Webb Pierce. Tillis had firmly established himself as a songwriter. He went on to write such huge hits as "Ruby, Don't Take Your Love to Town" (for Kenny Rogers and the First Edition) and "Detroit City" (for Bobby Bare).

In 1958, he had his first hit as a performer, "The Violet and the Rose." His first Top 10 song was "Wine" in 1965, followed by a series of successful records. In 1976, he had his first Number One hit, "Good Woman Blues," and he visited that position with five more songs in the next five years.

Tillis's stutter did not inhibit him. He sought out public appearances and was a popular talk show guest. He made fun of himself in his album title, *M...M...Mel Live.* In 1986, he wrote an autobiography entitled *Stutterin' Boy.*

GREATEST HITS
"The Violet and the Rose"
"Wine"
"Who's Julie?"
"These Lonely Hands of Mine"
"Good Woman Blues"
"I Believe in You"
"Coca-Cola Cowboy"
"Southern Rains"
"In the Middle of the Night"

CAREER HIGHLIGHTS:
- Tillis was named Entertainer of the Year in 1976 by the Country Music Association.
- He has published more than 500 songs in his career as a songwriter.

COWLICKS
- Tillis produced the 1985 film *Uphill All the Way,* which starred Roy Clark and featured Tillis in a supporting role.
- His daughter, Pam Tillis, is one of the top female stars of country music today.

GEORGE STRAIT

INSTRUMENT: Guitar

BORN: May 18, 1952
Pearsall, Texas

Strait was born on a ranch in South Texas, where his father taught junior high school and raised cattle. A few months after his high school graduation, he eloped to Mexico with his high school sweetheart, Norma, then joined the Army. While in the service, Strait began singing with a country band that frequently performed on military bases. After his discharge, he returned to work on the family ranch and began singing at night with a local group called Aces in the Hole. Strait's rendition of traditional country favorites by legends such as Bill Wills and Merle Haggard brought him a considerable local reputation. Despite having recorded for a Houston company, Strait couldn't make any headway in Nashville. He almost gave up music in 1979, but a San Marcos, Texas, nightclub owner finally arranged for Strait to record in Nashville for MCA. His first single, "Unwound," was a Top 10 hit.

Strait went on to record ten Number One hits over the next five years. His traditional country ballads and western attire influenced an entire generation of country singers. He continued to pour out hit singles and gold and platinum albums into the 1990s, yet he stayed with his family on his South Texas ranch, far away from the glitter of Nashville.

GREATEST HITS
"Unwound"
"Fool Hearted Memory"
"Amarillo by Morning"
"You Look So Good in Love"
"Right or Wrong"
"Does Fort Worth Ever Cross Your Mind"
"The Chair"
"Ocean Front Property"
"All My Ex's Live in Texas"

"Love Without End, Amen"
"Chill of an Early Fall"

CAREER HIGHLIGHTS
- Strait has had nine platinum and eight gold albums.
- He was named Academy of Country Music Top Male Vocalist in 1984, 1985, and 1988, as well as Country Music Association Male Vocalist in 1986 and Entertainer of the Year in 1989 and 1990.
- His "Ocean Front Property" was the first single in country music history to debut at Number One.

COWLICKS
- Strait graduated from Southwest Texas State University with a degree in agriculture.
- A personal tragedy occurred in 1986, when his 13-year-old daughter, Jennifer, was killed in an automobile accident.

Randy Travis

RANDY TRAVIS

REAL NAME: Randy Traywick

INSTRUMENT: Guitar

BORN: May 4, 1959
Marshville, North Carolina

Born in a town with a population of 2,000 people, Travis grew up with the songs of Hank Williams, Lefty Frizzell and Ernest Tubb playing in his house. He learned to play the guitar at eight years old, and by the time he was a teenager, he and his brother were playing in local clubs as the Traywick Brothers. About the same time, he stopped going to school and started drinking, doing drugs, and getting in trouble with the law. He ran away to Charlotte, North Carolina at age 16. At 17, just before he was to stand trial for breaking and entering, he entered a talent contest at a night club called Country Music City USA. He so impressed the club's co-owner, Liz Hatcher, that she persuaded the court to place Travis on probation in her custody. In 1980, the two moved to Nashville, where Hatcher got a job managing the Nashville Palace. Travis cooked and swept up in the club between sets as a vocalist. For four years, Hatcher worked tirelessly to obtain a record contract for Travis, to no avail. Finally, in 1985, she persuaded a Warner Bros. executive to hear Travis, and the young singer finally got a contract.

Travis's second single, "1982," was a Top 10 hit, and he became a major star virtually overnight. His first album, *Storms of Life*, became the first debut country album to sell one million copies in its first year. He was immediately invited to join the Grand Ole Opry. His second album spent ten months at the top of the charts. His string of smash hits has continued into the 1990s.

GREATEST HITS
"1982"
"On the Other Hand"
"Always and Forever"
"I Won't Need You Anymore"

"For Ever and Ever, Amen"
"Too Gone Too Long"
"Deeper than the Holler"
"Heroes and Friends"
"Better Class of Losers"

CAREER HIGHLIGHTS

- Travis was the Academy of Country Music's Top Male Vocalist in 1986 and 1987 and he won the Country Music Association awards for Male Vocalist of the Year, Album of the Year, and Single of the Year in 1987.
- He had six platinum albums and three gold albums between 1986 and 1992.
- Twice Travis won the Grammy Award for Best Country Vocal Performance, Male in 1988 and 1989.

COWLICKS

- Travis completely abandoned his wild youthful ways. He no longer drinks, and he exercises regularly.
- Randy Travis and Liz Hatcher were married in May, 1991.

CONWAY TWITTY

REAL NAME: Harold Jenkins

INSTRUMENT: Guitar

BORN: September 1, 1933
Friars Point, Mississippi

At age five, Harold Jenkins would sing and play the guitar while riding the Mississippi River on a ferryboat piloted by his father. A talented athlete, he was contacted by the Philadelphia Phillies, but he was drafted by the Army before he could sign. After two years in the service, he went to Memphis to look for work as a rock-and-roll singer. Sun Studios owner Sam Phillips suggested Jenkins could use a more distinctive name, so from a map he picked out two towns—Conway, Arkansas and Twitty, Texas. As Conway Twitty, he had two hit rock records, "I Need Your Lovin'" and "It's Only Make Believe." His first country music venture was writing a song that became a Ray Price hit. After gaining regional fame as the host of a syndicated TV show, "The Conway Twitty Show," he moved to Nashville.

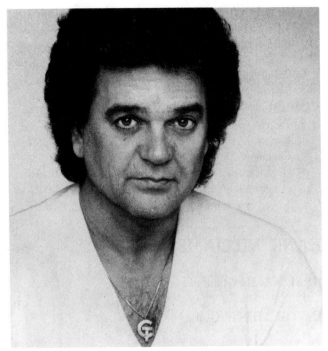
Conway Twitty

In 1968, he began an impressive series of hits that began with "Next in Line." In 1971, he teamed with Loretta Lynn for a second series of hits that included "After the Fire Is Gone." His recording success gave him the income to develop Twitty City, a Nashville theme park. His additional investments included a music promotion company, real estate, and the Nashville Sounds, a minor league baseball team. He continued to record hit solos throughout the 1980s.

GREATEST HITS
"I Need Your Lovin'"
"It's Only Make Believe"
"Next in Line"
"How Much More Can We Stand"
"I Can't Stop Loving You"
"To See My Angel Cry"
"Hello, Darlin'"
"After the Fire Is Gone" (with Loretta Lynn)
"Louisiana Woman, Mississippi Man" (with Loretta Lynn)
"She Needs Someone to Hold Her"
"The Rose"
"Ain't She Somethin' Else"

CAREER HIGHLIGHTS
- Twitty had 30 consecutive Number One country hits from 1968 to 1977.
- He and Loretta Lynn won the Country Music Association Vocal Duo of the Year for four straight years.

COWLICKS
- Twitty appeared in three teen movies in the 1950s: *Sex Kittens Go to College, Platinum High School,* and *College Confidential.*
- He was made an honorary chief of the Chocktaw nation and given the Indian name "Hatako-Chtokchito-A-Yakni-Toloa," which means "Great Man of Country Music."

HANK WILLIAMS, JR.

REAL NAME: Randall Hank Williams

INSTRUMENT: Guitar

BORN: May 26, 1949
Shreveport, Louisiana

Williams was just three years old when his famous father died of a drug and alcohol overdose. Hank Williams's departed spirit seemed to leave a heavy burden on his young son. He was touring with his mother's "Caravan of Stars" show at the age of eight, and by the time he was 16 he had already recorded two hits. He changed his name from Randall to Hank, Jr., and at the urging of his mother, performed his father's old songs in his father's style. The title of his 1966 hit, "Standing in the Shadows (of a Very Famous Man)," vividly demonstrated his feelings. The more uncomfortable he felt, the more he seemed to lapse into a trait inherited from his father—a weakness for drugs and alcohol.

Finally, in 1974, Hank rebelled, moving from Nashville to Cullman, Alabama. He celebrated his liberation by cutting a country-rock album with the assistance of musicians like Charlie Daniels and Chuck Leavell of the Allman Brothers. When the album was completed, Williams rewarded himself with a hunting trip to Montana. But he slipped while mountain climbing, tumbling 500 feet down a rocky slope and suffering

Hank Williams, Jr.

massive head injuries that nearly cost him his life. The success of *Hank Williams, Jr., and Friends* helped him endure two long years of rehabilitation and several operations. He came roaring back in 1978 with "I Fought the Law," a hit single, and two gold albums. Despite his success, he was shunned by the Nashville country music establishment and ignored by awards programs. Although he sold more than 20 million records, he received no recognition until 1985, when he won the Country Music Association Award for best video. This opened the door once more, and Hank Williams, Jr., for the first time was universally accepted as a major star on his own terms.

GREATEST HITS
"Long Gone Lonesome Blues"
"Standing in the Shadows"
"I Fought the Law"
"Whiskey Bent and Hell Bound"
"Family Tradition"
"The Conversation" (with Waylon Jennings)

"All My Rowdy Friends"
"Women I've Never Had"
"Old Habits"
"Born to Boogie"
"There's a Tear in My Beer" (with Hank Williams)
"Hotel Whiskey" (with Clint Black)

CAREER HIGHLIGHTS
- The Country Music Association named Williams Entertainer of the Year in 1987 and 1988, as did the Academy of Country Music in 1986, 1987, and 1988.
- At one point he had eight albums on the country charts at one time.
- Williams has had 14 gold and three platinum albums.

COWLICKS
- In 1990, Williams won a Grammy for a video in which he was superimposed in an old piece of film with his late father to sing "There's a Tear in My Beer."
- Williams titled his autobiography, *Living Proof*, after his song in which a drunkard taunts him, saying he'll never be the man his father was.

TAMMY WYNETTE

REAL NAME: Tammy Wynette Pugh

NICKNAME: "The First Lady of Country Music"

INSTRUMENT: Guitar

BORN: May 5, 1942
Tupelo, Mississippi

Tammy Wynette was born in a shack on her grandfather's farm. She was raised by her grandparents after her father died and her mother moved to Birmingham, Alabama to obtain work during World War II. She learned to play several instruments and took singing lessons as a child, but she married at 17 and had three children in three years. Just before her third child was born, the marriage broke up, and Wynette began to appear first on radio shows, then on Porter Wagoner's syndicated TV show. She made numerous trips to

Tammy Wynette

Nashville and eventually signed a contract with Epic Records in 1966. Her first song, "Apartment No. 9," was a modest hit and her second recording, "Your Good Girl's Gonna Go Bad," hit Number Three.

She went on to record a string of hits into which she seemed to pour all the emotions stored up from her turbulent early years. In 1968, she recorded "Stand by Your Man," which became the all-time best-selling country single by a female singer. At the same time, her personal life was also making headlines. Her relationship with George Jones produced so much gossip that the two announced they were married six months before they actually had the ceremony performed. Although they recorded many hits together, their marriage was stormy and they were divorced six years later. Wynette has had a hit recording as recently as 1992, and her autobiography, *Stand by Your Man*, was made into a movie in 1982.

GREATEST HITS
"Apartment No. 9"
"Your Good Girl's Gonna Go Bad"
"I Don't Wanna Play House"
"My Elusive Dreams"
"Take Me to Your World"
"D-I-V-O-R-C-E"
"Stand by Your Man"
"Starting Over"
"We Loved It Away" (with George Jones)
"Sometimes when We Touch" (with Mark Gray)
"You and Me"

CAREER HIGHLIGHTS
- Wynette was the Country Music Association's Female Vocalist of the Year from 1968 through 1970.
- She received Grammy Awards in 1967 and 1969.

COWLICKS
- Wynette has been married five times, in addition to relationships that included Burt Reynolds and Rudy Gatlin of the Gatlin Brothers.
- Her *Greatest Hits* album was certified platinum in 1989, and the total number of her albums has passed 50.

COUNTRY MUSIC TRAGEDIES

1953   Hank Williams died of a drug and alcohol overdose while being driven to a concert date in Canton, Ohio.

Betty Jack Davis was killed in a car accident that seriously injured her singing partner, Skeeter Davis.

1954   R.W. Blackwood, a member of gospel's most famous quartet, the Blackwood Brothers, died in a plane crash in 1954.

1956   In March, Carl Perkins was seriously injured in an automobile accident that killed his musician brother Jay.

1960   On November 5, Johnny Horton died in a car accident while driving to Nashville.

1961   Spade Cooley, in a drunken rage, beat and stomped his wife to death. He was convicted of manslaughter and died two months before he was to be paroled while performing at the Oakland Sheriff's Show.

1963   On March 5, Patsy Cline, Hawkshaw Hawkins, Randy Hughes and Cowboy Copas were killed in a plane crash.

Jack Anglin was killed in a car crash on his way to Patsy Cline's funeral.

Texas Ruby, wife of Curly Fox and sister of Tex Owen, was killed in a fire that destroyed her house trailer on March 29.

1964   On July 31, Jim Reeves was killed in the crash of a rented aircraft while returning to Nashville for an Opry appearance.

1965   Ira Louvin, the elder of the Louvin Brothers, was killed in an auto accident.

1968   Jan Howard's son Jim was killed in Vietnam two weeks after her tribute to him, "My Son" was released.

1973   Stringbean, beloved banjo player and comedian on the Grand Ole Opry and TV's "Hee Haw," was murdered with his wife outside their Nashville home.

Gram Parsons died of a heart attack after a night of drugs and drinking.

1975   Hank Williams, Jr., suffered severe disfigurement after barely surviving a 490-foot fall in a mountain-climbing accident.

1980   Red Sovine was killed in an automobile accident in Nashville at age 61.

1984   Loretta Lynn's son Jack drowned while trying to cross a river on horseback at age 34.

1985	On October 23, Merle Watson was killed when the tractor he was driving rolled over on him.
	On December 31, Rick Nelson was killed in a plane crash.
1986	George Strait's 13-year-old daughter Jennifer was killed in an automobile accident.
1989	On May 9, Keith Whitley died of alcohol poisoning.
1991	Reba McEntire's road manager and seven members of her band were killed in a plane crash.
	Billy Nelson, Willie Nelson's only son, committed suicide on Christmas Day at age 33.

SONGS ABOUT HANK WILLIAMS

Hank Williams was by far the most influential country artist for the recent generation of artists. Some have honored him the best way they know how—through song. Following are some tributes:

"Hank Williams, You Wrote My Life"
Moe Bandy

"Rollin' and Ramblin' (The Death of Hank Williams)"
Emmylou Harris

"Hank, It Will Never Be the Same Without You"
Ernest Tubb

"Are You Sure Hank Done It This Way?"
Waylon Jennings

"Hank Williams Will Live Forever"
Johnny and Jack

"Tribute to Hank Williams"
Tim Hardin

"Death of Hank Williams"
Jack Cardwell

"Singing Teacher in Heaven"
Jimmie Skinner

"Hank"
Hank Williams, Jr.

"The Long Gone Lonesome Blues"
Hank Williams, Jr.

"Hank and Lefty Raised My Country Soul"
Stoney Edwards

"Hank Drank"
Bobby Lee Springfield

"Hank Williams's Guitar"
Freddie Hart

"Midnight in Montgomery"
Alan Jackson

"The Ride"
David Allan Coe

NORTH OF THE BORDER

A surprising number of country singers come from that hotbed of country music, Canada. Some are still there; some commute. Nashville loves Canadians, because country is big, and somebody's got to fill it.

k.d. lang
Michelle Wright
Hank Snow
The Family Brown (Tracey & Barry Brown)
Mary Bailey
Burton Cummings
Alibi
Ray Griff
Carroll Baker (Top Female Country Singer, 1975)
Audie Henry
Gary Buck
Tommy Hunter
Wilf "Montana Slim" Carter
Iris Larratt
Debbie Lori Kaye
Billy Thunderkloud and the Chieftones (yes, "kloud")
Gale Garnett

ELVIS CITINGS

What would this book be if we didn't include Elvis's country connections—even if he's not been sighted lately on the stage of the Grand Ole Opry?

- Bill Black's Combo provided backup for Elvis.

- Mac Davis wrote "In the Ghetto" and "Don't Cry, Daddy" for Elvis.

- Wayne Carson wrote "Always on My Mind" for Elvis.

- Mae Axton, mother of Hoyt, wrote "Heartbreak Hotel" for Elvis.

- Larry Gatlin wrote numerous songs for Elvis.

- "From Graceland to the Promised Land" was recorded by Merle Haggard and the Jordanaires in 1977 after the death of Elvis.

- Wanda Jackson toured with Elvis in 1955 and 1956. Touring with Elvis was also part of the careers of Floyd Cramer, Skeeter Davis, Ace Cannon, June Carter, and Janie Frickie.

- Red Foley's song "Old Shep" was what Elvis sang to win his first talent contest at the age of ten.

- At 19, Elvis performed on both "Louisiana Hayride" and "The Grand Ole Opry," where the talent co-ordinator advised him to return to truck driving until he learned to sing.

- "Unknown" was an Elvis impersonator who, in 1988, recorded "Spelling on the Stone" about the name on Elvis's gravestone.

- "Orion" is the moniker of a masked Elvis Presley impersonator, born Jimmy Ellis from Alabama, who signed with Sun records until he put on the mask in 1979 for five years during which he managed to get ten songs on the charts.

COUNTRY MUSIC FAN CLUBS

Alabama Fan Club
P.O. Box 529
East Payne, AL 35967

Hoyt Axton Fan Club
P.O. Box 1077
Hendersonville, TN 37077

Baillie & the Boys
International Fan Club
P.O. Box 121185
Arlington, TX 76012

Clint Black Fan Club
P.O. Box 299386
Houston, TX 77299

Suzy Bogguss Fan Club
P.O. Box 7535
Marietta, GA 30065

Garth Brooks
The Believer Magazine
27 Music Square East, #172
Nashville, TN 37203

Jann Browne Fan Club
c/o Tracy Gersham
P.O. Box 158400
Nashville, TN 37215

Paulette Carlson
International Fan Club
c/o Ned & Julie Sheils
P.O. Box 1144
Arvada, CO 80001

Carlene Carter International
Fan Club
P.O. Box 120845
Nashville, TN 37212

Lionel Cartwright
International Fan Club
27 Music Square East,
Suite 182
Nashville, TN 37203

Rosanne Cash
c/o Side One Management
1775 Broadway, 7th Floor
New York, NY 10019

Mark Chesnutt International
Fan Club
P.O. Box 12803
Nashville, TN 37212

Linda Davis International
Fan Club
P.O. Box 121027
Nashville, TN 37212

Billy Dean Fan Club
P.O. Box 23362
Nashville, TN 37202

Diamond Rio International
Fan Club
P.O. Box 128031
Nashville, TN 37215

Desert Rose Band Fan Club
P.O. Box 1053
Arvada, CO 80001

Friends of Holly Dunn
P.O. Box 120964
Nashville, TN 37212

Evangeline Fan Club
Lafayette Square Station
P.O. Box 2700
New Orleans, LA 71076

Cleve Francis Productions
P.O. Box 15258
Alexandria, VA 22309

Vince Gill Fan Club
27 Music Square East,
Suite 107
Nashville, TN 37203

John Wesley Harding
c/o UpLate Management
P.O. Box 1429
London W6 0QI England

Emmylou Harris Fan Club
P.O. Box 99497
Louisville, KY 40299

Alan Jackson Fan Club
P.O. Box 121945
Nashville, TN 37212

The Judds International
Fan Club

P.O. Box 17325
Nashville, TN 36217

The Kentucky HeadHunters
International Fan Club
Ridgecrest Drive
Goodlettsville, TN 37072

Sammy Kershaw Fan Club
P.O. Box 23362
Nashville, TN 37202

Hal Ketchum Fan Club
P.O. Box 120205
Nashville, TN 37212

Little Texas Fan Club
P.O. Box 121950
Nashville, TN 37212

Patti Loveless Fan Club
P.O. Box 363
Groveport, OH 43125

Shelby Lynne Fan Club
P.O. Box 190
Monroeville, AL 36461

Barbara Mandrell
International
Fan Club
P.O. Box 620
Hendersonville, TN 37077

Kathy Mattea Fan Club
P.O. Box 158482
Nashville, TN 37215

Martina McBride Fan Club
P.O. Box 291627
Nashville, TN 37229

McBride & the Ride
Fan Club
P.O. Box 17617
Nashville, TN 37217

Charlie McClain Fan Club
c/o Marilyn J. Davis
P.O. Box 2014
Brentwood, TN 37027

Reba McEntire International
Fan Club
P.O. Box 121996
Nashville, TN 37212

Molly & the Haymakers
Fan Club
P.O. Box 1160
Hayward, WI 54843

Lorrie Morgan International
Fan Club
P.O. Box 2204
Brentwood, TN 37027

Garry Morris Fan Club
607 West Church Drive
Sugarland, TX 77478

Willie Nelson Fan Club
118 16th Avenue South
Nashville, TN 37203

Juice Newton Fan Club
c/o Maxine Young
P.O. Box 293323
Louisville, TX 75029

Nitty Gritty Dirt Band
Fan Club
c/o Lori M. Zmudka
P.O. Box 121742
Nashville, TN 37212

Oak Ridge Boys Fan Club
329 Rockland Road
Hendersonvile, TN 37075

Pirates of the Mississippi
Fan Club
P.O. Box 17617
Nashville, TN 37217

Eddie Rabbitt Fan Club
P.O. Box 125
Lewisboro, OH 43333

Ronna Reeves Fan Club
c/o Rene Laughlin
P.O. Box 80424
Midland, TX 79709

Dennis Robbins Fan Club
P.O. Box 120964
Nashville, TN 37212

Doug Stone Fan Club
P.O. Box 40465
Nashville, TN 37204

George Strait Fan Club
P.O. Box 2119
Hendersonville, TN 37077

Mary Stuart Fan Club

P.O. Box 67
St. Croix Falls, WI 54024

Sweethearts of the Rodeo
Fan Club
P.O. Box 160077
Nashville, TN 37216

Pam Tillis International
Fan Club
P.O. Box 25304
Nashville, TN 37202

Aaron Tippin Fan Club
P.O. Box 121709
Nashville, TN 37212

Karen Tobin Fan Club
P.O. Box 3822
Palos Verdes Peninsula, CA
90274

Randy Travis Fan Club
P.O. Box 38
Ashland City, TN 37015

Travis Tritt Country Club
P.O. Box 440099

Kennesaw, GA 30144

Tanya Tucker Fan Club
P.O. Box 2449
Brentwood, TN 37027

Ricky Van Shelton Fan Club
P.O. Box 20548
Nashville, TN 37212

Steve Wariner Fan Club
P.O. Box 1209
Nolensville, TN 37135

Wild Rose Fan Club
P.O. Box 121705
Nashville, TN 37212

Hank Williams, Jr., Fan Club
P.O. Box 1350
Paris, TN 38242

Michelle Wright Fan Club
P.O. Box 52
Morpeth, Ontario
Canada N0P 1X0

Trisha Yearwood Fan Club
P.O. Box 64
Monticello, GA 31064

Dwight Yoakam Fan Club
15840 Ventura Blvd., #465
Encino, CA 91436

Loretta Lynn

STEEL MAGNOLIAS
WITH STEEL GUITARS

Feminism in country music startled everyone when Loretta Lynn scored a hit single in 1972 with "The Pill." Following in her footsteps, the women belting out country songs nowadays are less concerned about standing by their men than about standing up for themselves and their families. Rosanne Cash is perhaps the most outspoken on subjects such as physical abuse ("Pack Your Bags, Rosie") and female intelligence ("Hold On"). Still, it doesn't keep her or any of the women listed here from the traditional lyrics about cheapskates, cheaters, and regretting a morning after the night before. Here's a list of freedom fightin' songs.

Loretta Lynn	"The Pill," "Who's Gonna Take the Garbage Out"
Patti Loveless	"The Night's Too Long," "On Down the Line"
k.d. lang	"Shadowland"
K. T. Oslin	"Clean Your Own Tables"
Sammi Smith	"You Just Hurt My Last Feeling"
Janie Frickie	"I'm Down to My Last Broken Heart"
Jeannie Seely	"Alright I'll Sign the Papers"
Barbara Mandrell	"Fast Lanes & Country Roads"
Norma Jean	"Don't Let that Doorknob Hit You"
Jennifer Warnes	"Don't Make Me Over"
Bonnie Owens	"Don't Take Advantage of Me"
Margo Smith	"Either You're Married or You're Single"
Lynn Anderson	"Even Cowgirls Get the Blues"
Dolly Parton	"9 to 5"
Lacy J. Dalton	"Can't Make a Rock from a Rolling Stone"
Jeannie C. Riley	"Another Football Year," "Harper Valley P.T.A.

Libby Hurley	"Don't Get Me Started"
Audrey Henry	"You'll Never Find a Good Man (Playin' in a Country Band)"
Jan Howard	"Marriage Has Ruined More Good Love Affairs"
Cindy Hurt	"Don't Come Knockin'"
Terri Lane	"Daisy May (and Daisy May Not)"
Charly McClain	"Lay Something on My Bed Besides a Blanket"
Debbie Rich	"I Ain't Gonna Take This Layin' Down"
Judy Rodman	"Girls Ride Horses Too"
Connie Cato	"You Better Hurry Home (Somethin's Burnin')"
Helen Cornelius	"I Don't Want to Have to Marry You"
Gail Davis	"Unwed Fathers"
Reba McEntire	"Why Do We Want (What We Know We Can't Have)"
Kathy Mattea	"She Came From Fort Worth," "Untold Stories"
Emmylou Harris	"Tougher than the Rest"
Tanya Tucker	"Bidding America Goodbye (the Auction)"
Suzie Boggus	"Fear of Flying"
Mary Chapin Carpenter	"He Thinks He'll Keep Her"

COUNTRY
SONGS

GOLD & PLATINUM ALBUMS

The following is a list of every gold and platinum release by a country artist since 1958 (with the year of release).

ALABAMA
Gold
Just Us (1988)
Alabama Live (1988)
Southern Star (1989)
Pass It On Down (1990)
Greatest Hits Vol II (1991)
American Pride (1992)

Platinum
My Home's in Alabama (1981)
Feels So Right (1981)
Mountain Music (1982
The Closer You Get (1983)
40 Hour Week (1985)
Alabama Christmas (1985)
Greatest Hits (1986)
The Touch (1987)
Roll On (1984)

Alabama

JOHN ANDERSON
Gold
Wild & Blue (1984)

Platinum
Seminole Wind (1992)

LYNN ANDERSON
Platinum
Rose Garden (1971)

EDDY ARNOLD
Gold
My World (1966)
The Best of Eddy Arnold (1968)

GENE AUTRY
Gold
Rudolph the Red-Nosed Reindeer (1969)

CLINT BLACK
Platinum
Killin' Time (1989)
Put Yourself in My Shoes (1990)
The Hard Way (1992)

SUZY BOGGUSS
Gold
Aces (1991)

BROOKS & DUNN
Platinum
Brand New Man (1991)

GARTH BROOKS
Platinum
Garth Brooks (1990)
No Fences (1990)
Ropin' the Wind (1991)
Beyond the Season (1992)
The Chase (1992)

JIMMY BUFFETT
Gold
Feeding Frenzy (1990)

Platinum
Songs You Know By Heart (1985)
Boats, Beaches, Bars & Ballads (1992)

Clint Black

Garth Brooks

GLEN CAMPBELL
Gold
Hey, Little One (1968)
That Christmas Feeling (1968)
Live (1969)
Try a Little Kindness (1970)
Rhinestone Cowboy (1975)
Southern Nights (1977)

Platinum
Gentle On My Mind (1967)
By the Time I Get to Phoenix (1967)
Wichita Lineman (1968)
Galveston (1969)
Glen Campbell's Greatest Hits (1971)

MARY CHAPIN CARPENTER
Gold
Shooting Straight in the Dark (1990)
Come On, Come On (1992)

JOHNNY CASH
Gold
Ring of Fire (1963)
I Walk the Line (1964)
Hello, I'm Johnny Cash (1970)
The World of Johnny Cash (1970)
The Johnny Cash Collection (1971)

Platinum
Johnny Cash's Greatest Hits, Vol. 1 (1967)
Johnny Cash at Folsom Prison (1968)
Johnny Cash at San Quentin (1969)

ROSANNE CASH
Gold
Seven Year Ache (1981)

MARK CHESNUTT
Gold
Too Cold At Home (1990)
Longnecks and Short Stories (1992)

PATSY CLINE
Gold
Sweet Dreams (1985)
Platinum
Greatest Hits (1967)

JERRY CLOWER
Gold
Greatest Hits (1979)

DAVID ALLAN COE
Gold
Greatest Hits (1978)

JOHN CONLEE
Gold
John Conlee's Greatest Hits (1983)

Johnny Cash

EARL THOMAS CONLEY
Gold
Greatest Hits (1985)

RITA COOLIDGE
Gold
Love Me Again (1978)

Platinum
Anytime...Anywhere (1977)

RODNEY CROWELL
Gold
Diamonds & Dirt (1988)

Billy Ray Cyrus

BILLY RAY CYRUS
Platinum
Some Gave All (1992)

THE CHARLIE DANIELS BAND
Gold
Saddle Tramp (1976)
Windows (1982)
Simple Man (1989)

Platinum
Fire on the Mountain
(1974)
Million Mile Reflections (1979)
Full Moon (1980)
A Decade of Hits (1983)

MAC DAVIS
Gold
Baby Don't Get Hooked on Me (1972)
Stop and Smell the Roses (1974)
All the Love in the World (1978)
Greatest Hits (1979)
It's Hard to Be Humble (1980)

BILLY DEAN
Gold
Billy Dean

JOHN DENVER
Gold
Poems, Prayers & Promises (1971)
Aerie (1971)
Rocky Mountain High (1972)
Farewell Andromeda (1973)
John Denver's Greatest Hits (1973)
Back Home Again (1974)
An Evening With John Denver (1975)
Windsong (1975)
Rocky Mountain Christmas (1975)
John Denver (1979)
Some Days Are Diamonds (1981)
Seasons of the Heart (1982)

Platinum
Spirit (1976)
John Denver's Greatest Hits, Vol. 2 (1977)
I Want to Live (1977)
A Christmas Together (1979)

Billy Dean

DIAMOND RIO
Gold
Diamond Rio (1991)

TENNESSEE ERNIE FORD
Gold
Spirituals (1957)
Nearer the Cross (1959)

Platinum
Hymns (1956)
The Star Carol (1958)

LARRY GATLIN
Gold
Larry Gatlin's Greatest Hits Vol. 1 (1978)
Straight Ahead (1979)

CRYSTAL GAYLE
Gold
Miss the Mississipi (1979)
Classic Crystal (1979)

John Denver

Platinum
We Must Believe in Magic (1977)
When I Dream (1978)

BOBBIE GENTRY
Gold
Ode to Billy Joe (1967)

BOBBIE GENTRY AND GLEN CAMPBELL
Gold
Bobbie Gentry and Glen Campbell

Crystal Gayle

VINCE GILL
Platinum
When I Call Your Name (1989)
Pocket Full of Gold (1991)
I Still Believe in You (1992)

MICKEY GILLEY
Gold
Encore (1980)

LEE GREENWOOD
Gold
Inside Out (1982)
Somebody's Gonna Love You (1983)
You've Got a Great Love Comin' (1984)

Platinum
Greatest Hits (1985)

Vince Gill

MERLE HAGGARD
Gold
The Best of Merle Haggard (1968)
The Fightin' Side of Me (1970)
Big City (1981)
His Epic Hits: The First 11 (1984)

Platinum
Okie From Muskogee (1970)
The Best of the Best of Merle Haggard (1972)

MERLE HAGGARD & WILLIE NELSON
Platinum
Poncho & Lefty (1983)

EMMYLOU HARRIS
Gold
Pieces of the Sky (1975)
Elite Hotel (1976)
Luxury Liner (1977)
Quarter Moon in a Ten Cent Town (1978)
Profile/Best of Emmylou Harris (1978)
Blue Kentucky Girl (1979)
Roses in the Snow (1980)
Evangeline (1981)

EMMYLOU HARRIS, DOLLY PARTON & LINDA RONSTADT
Platinum
Trio (1987)

THE HIGHWAYMEN
Gold
Highwaymen (1985)

JOHNNY HORTON
Platinum
Johnny Horton's Greatest Hits (1961)

Emmylou Harris

ALAN JACKSON
Platinum
Here in the Real World (1990)
Don't Rock the Jukebox (1991)
A Lot About Livin' (And a Little 'Bout Love) (1992)

WAYLON JENNINGS
Gold
Dreaming my Dreams (1975)
Are You Ready For The Country (1976)
Waylon Live (1976)
I've Always Been Crazy (1978)
What Goes Around Comes Around (1979)
Music Man (1980)

Platinum
Ol' Waylon (1977)
Greatest Hits (1988)

WAYLON JENNINGS
& JESSI COLTER
Gold
Leather And Lace (1981)

WAYLON JENNINGS
& WILLIE NELSON
Gold
WWII (1982)

Platinum
Waylon & Willie (1978)

Waylon Jennings

WAYLON JENNINGS, WILLIE NELSON,
JESSI COLTER,
& TOMPALL GLASER
Platinum
Wanted! The Outlaws (1976)

GEORGE JONES
Gold
Still the Same Old Me (1980)
Super Hits (1987)
Platinum
I Am What I Am (1980)

WYNONNA JUDD
Platinum
Wynonna (1992)

THE JUDDS
Gold
Rivers of Time (1989)
Love Can Build a Bridge (1990)
Greatest Hits Vol. II (1991)

Platinum
Why Not Me (1984)
Rockin' With The Rhythm (1985)
Heartland (1987)
Greatest Hits (1988)

THE KENDALLS
Gold
Heaven's Just A Sin Away (1977)

The Judds

THE KENTUCKY HEADHUNTERS
Gold
Electric Banyard (1991)

Platinum
Pickin' On Nashville (1989)

SAMMY KERSHAW
Gold
Don't Go Near the Water (1991)

HAL KETCHUM
Gold
Past the Point of Rescue (1991)

Kris Kristofferson

KRIS KRISTOFFERSON
Gold
The Silver Tongued Devil and I (1971)
Me And Bobby McGee (1971)
Jesus Was A Capricorn (1972)
Songs of Kristofferson (1977)

k.d. lang
Gold
Shadowland (1989)
Absolute Torch & Twang (1989)
Ingenue (1992)

TRACY LAWRENCE
Gold
Sticks and Stones (1991)

JOHNNY LEE
Gold
Lookin' For Love (1980)

PATTY LOVELESS
Gold
Honky Tonk Angel (1988)

Loretta Lynn

LYLE LOVETT
Gold
Lyle Lovett and His Large Band (1989)

LORETTA LYNN
Gold
Don't Come Home A Drinkin' (1967)
Loretta Lynn's Greatest Hits (1968)
Coal Miner's Daughter (1971)
Greatest Hits Vol. II (1974)

LORETTA LYNN AND CONWAY TWITTY
Gold
We Only Make Believe (1971)
Lead Me On (1972)
The Very Best of Conway Twitty & Loretta Lynn (1979)

BARBARA MANDRELL
Gold
The Best of Barbara Mandrell (1979)
Barbara Mandrell Live (1981)

KATHY MATTEA
Gold
Willow in the Wind (1989)
A Collection of Hits (1990)

C. W. McCALL
Gold
Black Bear Road (1975)

REBA McENTIRE
Gold
My Kind of Country (1984)
Whoever's In New England (1986)
What Am I Gonna Do About You (1986)
The Last One To Know (1987)
Reba (1988)
Sweet Sixteen (1989)
Reba McEntire Live (1989)

Platinum
Reba McEntire's Greatest Hits (1987)
Rumor Has It (1990)
For My Broken Heart (1991)

ROGER MILLER
Gold
Dang Me (1964)

Reba McEntire

The Return of Roger Miller (1965)
Golden Hits (1965)

RONNIE MILSAP
Gold
Live (1976)
It Was Almost Like a Song (1977)
Only One Love in My Life (1979)
There's No Gettin' Over Me (1981)
Lost in the Fifties (1986)
Platinum
Greatest Hits (1980)
Greatest Hits Vol. II (1985)

LORRIE MORGAN
Gold
Leave the Light On (1989)
Platinum
Something in Red (1991)

GARY MORRIS
Gold
Why Lady Why (1983)

ANNE MURRAY
Platinum
Greatest Hits (1980)
Christmas Wishes (1981)

Willie Nelson

WILLIE NELSON
Gold
The Sound in Your Mind (1976)
The Troublemaker (1976)
Willie Nelson Sings Kristofferson (1979)
Pretty Paper (1979)
The Electric Horseman (1979)
Without a Song (1983)
City of New Orleans (1984)
Half Nelson (1985)
Platinum
Stardust (1978)
Willie & Family Live (1978)
Willie Nelson Sings Kristofferson (1979)
Honeysuckle Rose (1980)
Somewhere Over the Rainbow (1981)

Willie Nelson's Greatest Hits (1981)
Always on My Mind (1982)

WILLIE NELSON & RAY PRICE
Gold
San Antonio Rose (1980)

WILLIE NELSON & LEON RUSSELL
Gold
One for the Road (1979)

NEW RIDERS OF THE PURPLE SAGE
Gold
The Adventures of Panama Red (1973)

JUICE NEWTON
Gold
Greatest Hits (1986)

NITTY GRITTY DIRT BAND
Gold
Will the Circle Be Unbroken (1972)

THE OAK RIDGE BOYS
Gold
Y'All Come Back Saloon (1977)
Room Service (1978)
The Oak Ridge Boys Have Arrived (1979)
Together (1980)
Greatest Hits (1980)
Bobbie Sue (1982)
Christmas (1982)
American Made (1983)
Deliver (1983)
Greatest Hits 2 (1984)
Platinum
Fancy Free (1981)

The Oak Ridge Boys

K. T. OSLIN
Gold
Love in a Small Town (1990)

BUCK OWENS
Gold
The Best of Buck Owens (1964)

OZARK MOUNTAIN DAREDEVILS
Gold
Ozark Mountain Daredevils (1973)

DOLLY PARTON
Gold
The Best of Dolly Parton (1975)
Heartbreaker (1978)
Great Balls of Fire (1979)
9 to 5 and Odd Jobs (1980)
White Limousine (1989)

Platinum
Here You Come Again (1977)
Greatest Hits (1982)
Eagle when She Flies (1991)

Dolly Parton

DOLLY PARTON & KENNY ROGERS
Platinum
Once upon a Christmas (1989)

RAY PRICE
Gold
For the Good Times (1970)
Ray Price's All-Time Greatest Hits (1982)

CHARLEY PRIDE
Gold
Country (1966)
The Country Way (1967)
In Person (1969)
The Sensational Charley Pride (1969)
The Best of Charley Pride (1969)
Just Plain Charley (1970)
Charley Pride's 10th Album (1970)
From Me to You (1971)
Did You Think to Pray (1971)
Charley Pride Sings Heart Songs (1971)
The Best of Charlie Pride, Vol. 2 (1972)

PURE PRAIRIE LEAGUE
Gold
Bustin' Out (1972)

EDDIE RABBITT
Gold
The Best of Eddie Rabbitt (1979)
Step by Step (1981)

Platinum
Horizon (1980)

COLLIN RAYE
Gold
All I Can Be (1991)

JIM REEVES
Gold
The Best of Jim Reeves (1964)
Distant Drums (1966)

RESTLESS HEART
Gold
Big Dreams in a Small Town (1988)
Fast Movin' Train (1990)

DOLLY PARTON, EMMYLOU HARRIS & LINDA RONSTADT
Platinum
Trio (1987)

CHARLIE RICH
Gold
There Won't Be Anymore (1974)
Very Special Love Songs (1974)

Platinum
Behind Closed Doors (1973)

JEANNIE C. RILEY
Gold
Harper Valley P.T.A. (1968)

MARTY ROBBINS
Gold
Marty Robbins's All-Time Greatest Hits (1972)
Platinum
Gunfighter Ballads and Trail Songs (1959)

KENNY ROGERS
Gold
Greatest Hits (1971)
Kenny Rogers (1976)
Daytime Friends (1977)
Love or Something Like It (1978)
Love Will Turn You Around (1982)
We've Got Tonight (1983)
Heart of the Matter (1985)
Something Inside So Strong (1989)

Platinum
Ten Years of Gold (1978)
The Gambler (1978)
Kenny (1979)
Gideon (1980)
Kenny Rogers' Greatest Hits (1980)
Share Your Love (1983)
Christmas (1981)
Eyes that See in the Dark (1983)
Twenty Greatest Hits (1983)
What About Me? (1984)

Kenny Rogers

KENNY ROGERS & DOTTIE WEST
Gold
Classics (1979)

RICKY VAN SHELTON
Gold
Wild-Eyed Dream (1987)
Loving Proof (1988)
The Road Not Taken (1989)
Greatest Hits Plus (1992)

Platinum
RSV III (1990)
Backroads (1991)

Ricky Skaggs

RICKY SKAGGS
Gold
Waitin' for the Sun to Shine (1982)
Don't Cheat in Our Hometown (1983)

Platinum
Highways & Heartaches (1982)

THE STATLER BROTHERS
Gold
Entertainers...On and Off the Record (1978)
The Statler Brothers Christmas Carol (1978)
The Originals (1979)
The Best of the Statler Bros. Rides Again, Vol. II (1979)

Platinum
The Best of the Statler Bros. (1975)

RAY STEVENS
Gold
He Thinks He's Ray Stevens (1984)
I Have Returned (1985)
Greatest Hits (1987)

DOUG STONE
Gold
Doug Stone (1990)
I Thought It Was You (1991)

GEORGE STRAIT
Gold
Strait Country (1981)
Strait From The Heart (1982)
Right or Wrong (1983)
Something Special (1985)
#7 (1986)
Merry Christmas to You (1986)
Ten Strait Hits (1991)
Holding My Own (1992)

George Strait

Platinum
Does Fort Worth Ever Cross Your Mind (1984)
Greatest Hits (1985)
Ocean Front Property (1987)
Greatest Hits, Vol. Two (1987)
If You Ain't Lovin' (1988)
Beyond the Blue Neon (1989)
Livin' It Up (1990)
Chill of an Early Fall (1991)
Pure Country (1992)

SYLVIA
Gold
Just Sylvia (1982)

B.J. THOMAS
Gold
*Raindrops Keep Fallin' On
My Head* (1969)

PAM TILLIS
Gold
Put Yourself in My Place (1991)

AARON TIPPIN
Gold
Read Between the Lines (1992)

RANDY TRAVIS
Gold
An Old Time Christmas (1989)
High Lonesome (1991)
Greatest Hits Vol. I (1992)

Platinum
Storms of Life (1986)
Always & Forever (1987)
Old 8 X 10 (1988)
No Holdin' Back (1989)
Heroes and Friends (1990)
Storms of Life (1992)

TRAVIS TRITT
Gold
T-R-O-U-B-L-E (1992)

Platinum
Country Club (1990)
It's All About to Change (1991)

TANYA TUCKER
Gold
Greatest Hits (1975)
TNT (1978)
Can't Run from Yourself (1992)

Platinum
What Do I Do with Me (1991)

CONWAY TWITTY
Gold
Hello Darlin' (1970)
Greatest Hits Volume 1 (1972)

Tanya Tucker

Randy Travis

Travis Tritt

You've Never Been This Far Gone Before (1973)
Conway Twitty's Greatest Hits, Vol. II (1976)
Number Ones (1982)
Platinum
The Very Best of Conway Twitty (1978)

CONWAY TWITTY & LORETTA LYNN
Gold
We Only Make Believe (1971)
Lead Me On (1972)
The Very Best of Conway Twitty & Loretta Lynn (1979)

DOTTIE WEST
Gold
Classics (1979; with Kenny Rogers)

JERRY JEFF WALKER
Gold
Viva Terlingua! (1973)

DON WILLIAMS
Gold
The Best of Don Williams, Vol. III (1984)
Platinum
I Believe in You (1980)

HANK WILLIAMS
Gold
Greatest Hits (1963)
24 Greatest Hits (1971)

HANK WILLIAMS, JR.
Gold
Your Cheatin' Heart (1964)
Family Tradition (1979)
Whiskey Bent & Hell Bound (1979)
Rowdy (1981)
High Noon (1982)
Strong Stuff (1983)
Man of Steel (1983)
Major Moves (1984)
Five-O (1985)
Montana Cafe (1986)
Hank "Live" (1987)
Wild Streak (1988)

Hank Williams, Jr.

Greatest Hits III (1989)
Lone Wolf (1990)

Platinum
The Pressure Is On (1981)
Hank Williams, Jr.'s Greatest Hits (1982)
Greatest Hits, Vol. 2 (1985)
Born to Boogie (1987)

TAMMY WYNETTE
Platinum
Tammy's Greatest Hits (1969)

TRISHA YEARWOOD
Gold
Hearts in Armor (1992)

Platinum
Trisha Yearwood (1991)

Dwight Yoakam

DWIGHT YOAKAM
Gold
Hillbilly DeLuxe (1987)
Buenas Noches from a Lonely Room (1988)
Just Lookin' for a Hit (1989)
If There Was a Way (1990)

Platinum
Guitars, Cadillacs, Etc. Etc. (1986)

THE SILLIEST SONG TITLES

Every country singer has a repertoire of deliberately funny songs, many of which have the silliest song titles.

"How Come Your Dog Don't Bite Nobody but Me?"
"Whatcha Gonna Do with a Dog Like That?"
"How Much is that Hound Dog in the Window?"
"Your Squaw Is on the Warpath"
"My Uncle Used to Love Me But She Died"
"You Can't Rollerskate in a Buffalo Herd"
"A Good Old Fashioned Saturday Night Honky Tonk Barroom Brawl"
"Don't Worry Bout the Mule, Just Load the Wagon"
"May the Bird of Paradise Fly up Your Nose"
"Take an Old Cold 'Tater (and Wait)"
"My Bucket's Got a Hole in It"

"Slap 'er Down Again, Paw"
"Hello Mexico, and Adios Baby to You"
"Rebels Without a Clue"
"The Lawrence Welk-Hee Haw Counter-Revolution Polka"
"Divers Do It Deeper"
"The Letter that Johnny Walker Read"
"Changes in Latitudes, Changes in Attitudes"
"Cheaper Crude or No More Food"
"I Owe, I Owe (It's Off to Work I Go)"
"Old Betsy Goes Boing, Boing, Boing"
"Grandma Got Run Over by a Reindeer"
"Bull Smith Can't Dance the Cotton-Eyed Joe"
"Don't Get Above Your Raisin'"
"If You Can't Bite, Don't Growl"
"I Come Home A-Drinkin' (to a Worn Out Wife Like You)"
"Nag, Nag, Nag"
"No Tell Motel"
"I Wish a Buck Was Still Silver"
"Money Greases the Wheels"
"Even Cowgirls Get the Blues"
"Who's Gonna Mow Your Lawn"
"I'm Not Leavin', I'm Just Gettin' Out of Your Way"
"I May Be Used (But Baby I Ain't Used Up)"
"When You're Ugly Like Us (You Just Naturally Got
    to Be Cool)"
"Rocket 'Til the Cows Come Home"
"Don't Telephone, Don't Telegraph, Tell a Woman"
"Life Gets Tee-jus, Don't It"

DOIN' TIME

Sometimes jail seems like an occupational hazard for country musicians, as in the case of Charlie Bandy, whose career ended when he was arrested for selling cocaine. Or Cajun fiddler Harry Choates, who died in an Austin jail at the age of 25. Singer Spade Cooley went to Vacaville State Prison for life for murdering his wife. The most famous case is Johnny Cash, who spent only one night in jail but can thank the tank for some big hits. Others are just poetic cons.

Johnny Cash   "Folsom Prison Blues"
                         "Orleans Parish Prison"

Elton Britt   "I'm a Convict With Old
                         Glory in My Heart"

Jimmie Rodgers	"In the Jailhouse Now"
Johnny Paycheck	"Me and the I.R.S." "The Outlaw's Prayer"
Roy Clark	"Chain Gang of Love" (purely poetic)
Tommy Collins	"I Made the Prison Band"
John Conlee	"Busted"
Sonny Curtis	"I Fought the Law"
Jimmy Dean	"Ninety Days"
Dick Curless	"Drag 'em Off the Interstate, Sock it to 'em, J.P. Blues"
Tex Ritter	"Fort Worth Jail"
Tom T. Hall	"A Week in a Country Jail"
Lynn & Molly Davis	"Poor Ellen Smith"
Sonny James	"The Prisoner's Song"
Waylon Jennings	"Don't You Think This Outlaw Bit's Done Got out of Hand"
Waylon Jennings & Johnny Cash	
	"There Ain't No Good Chain Gang"
George Jones	"Life to Go"
Don King	"Maximum Security to Minimum Wage"
Charlie Lomin	"Will You Visit Me on Sundays"
Webb Pierce	"Tupelo County Jail"
Kenny Price	"The Sheriff of Boone County"
Garth Brooks	"Mama's in the Graveyard Papa's in the Pen (Papa Loved Mama, and Mama Loved Men)"

HOW LONG CAN
THIS SONG GO ON?

Listed below are the country artists with recordings that have gone to Number One on the Billboard charts for at least one week—and how long the recordings have remained in the Top 100.

BAND/SONG	YEAR	WEEKS ON CHART
ALABAMA		
"Tennessee River"	1980	17
"Why Lady Why"	1980	19
"Old Flame"	1981	14
"Feels So Right"	1981	13
"Love in the First Degree"	1981	16
"Mountain Music"	1982	18
"Take Me Down"	1982	17
"Close Enough to Perfect"	1982	17
"Dixieland Delight"	1983	16
"The Closer You Get"	l983	17
"Lady Down on Love"	1983	20
"Roll On (Eighteen Wheeler)"	l984	17
"When We Make Love"	1984	19
"If You're Gonna Play in Texas (You Gotta Have a Fiddle in the Band)"	1984	19
"(There's a) Fire in the Night"	1984	19
"There's No Way"	1985	21
"Forty Hour Week (For a Livin')"	1985	19
"Can't Keep a Good Man Down"	1985	22
"She and I"	1986	21
"Touch Me When We're Dancing"	1986	20
"You've Got the Touch"	1987	22
"Face to Face"	1987	22
"Fallin' Again"	1988	17
"Song of the South"	1988	19
BILL ANDERSON		
"Mama Sang a Song"	1962	27
"Still"	1963	27
"I Get the Fever"	1966	20
"My Life (Throw It Away if I Want To)"	1969	19
"World of Make Believe"	1973	14
"For Loving You" (with		

Jan Howard)	1967	20
"Sometimes" (with Mary Lou Turner)	1975	16

JOHN ANDERSON

"Wild and Blue"	1982	20
"Swingin'"	1983	22
"Black Sheep"	1983	21

LYNN ANDERSON

"Rose Garden"	1970	20
"You're My Man"	1971	15
"How Can I Unlove You"	1971	16
"Keep Me in Mind"	1973	16
"What a Man, My Man Is"	1974	13

EDDY ARNOLD

"What Is Life Without Love?"	1947	22
"It's a Sin"	1947	38
"I'll Hold You in My Heart (Till I Can Hold You in My Arms)"	1947	46
"Anytime"	1948	39
"Bouquet of Roses"	1948	54
"Texarkana Baby"	1948	26
"Just a Little Lovin'"	1948	32
"A Heart Full of Love (for a Handful of Kisses)"	1948	21
"Don't Rob Another Man's Castle"	1949	31
"One Kiss Too Many"	1949	22
"I'm Throwing Rice at the Girl I Love"	1949	22
"Take Me in Your Arms and Hold Me"	1949	17
"There's Been a Change in Me"	1951	23
"Kentucky Waltz"	1951	17
"I Wanna Play House with You"	1951	24
"Easy on the Eyes"	1952	14
"A Full Time Job"	1952	18
"Eddy's Song"	1953	13
"I Really Don't Want to Know"	1954	37
"The Cattle Call"	1955	26
"That Do Make it Nice"	1955	15
"What's He Doing in My World"	1965	25
"Make the World Go Away"	1965	25
"I Want to Go With You"	1966	19

"Somebody Like Me"	1966	19
"Lonely Again"	1967	16
"Turn the World Around"	1967	16
"Then You Can Tell Me Goodbye"	1968	14

LEON ASHLEY
| "Laura (What's He Got that I Ain't Got)" | 1967 | 18 |

ERNEST ASHWORTH
| "Talk Back Trembling Lips" | 1963 | 36 |

GENE AUTRY
| "At Mail Call Today" | 1945 | 22 |
| "Rudolph the Red-Nosed Reindeer" | 1949 | 5 |

RAZZY BAILEY
"Lovin' Up a Storm"	1980	15
"I Keep Coming Back"	1980	17
"Friends"	1981	16
"Midnight Hauler"	1981	18
"She Left Love All Over Me"	1981	20

MOE BANDY
| "I Cheated Me Right out of You" | 1979 | 14 |
| "Just Good Ol' Boys" (with Joe Stampley) | 1979 | 16 |

BOBBY BARE
| "Marie Laveau" | 1974 | 18 |

THE BELLAMY BROTHERS
"If I Said You Have a Beautiful Body Would You Hold It Against Me?"	1979	15
"Sugar Daddy"	1980	14
"Dancin' Cowboys"	1980	17
"Do You Love as Good as You Look"	1981	13
"For All the Wrong Reasons"	1982	18
"Redneck Girl"	1982	18
"When I'm Away from You"	1983	18
"I Need More of You"	1985	20
"Too Much Is Not Enough"	1986	20

"Kids of the Baby Boom"
  (with the Forester Sisters) 1987 22

JACK BLANCHARD & MISTY MORGAN
"Tennessee Bird Walk" 1970 19

DEBBY BOONE
"Are You on the Road to
  Lovin' Me Again?" 1980 15

LANE BRODY
"The Yellow Rose"
  (with Karen Johnny Lee) 1984 22

BROOKS
"Faking Love" (with T.G. Sheppard) 1982 20

JIM ED BROWN
"I Don't Want to Have to Marry
  You" (with Helen Cornelius) 1976 16

T. GRAHAM BROWN
"Hell and High Water" 1986 23
"Don't Go to Strangers" 1987 21
"Darlene" 1988 21

THE BROWNS
"The Three Bells" 1959 19

ED BRUCE
"You're the Best Break This
  Old Heart Ever Had" 1981 21

BUCK OWENS & THE BUCKAROOS
"Buckaroo" 1965 17

CARL BUTLER & PEARL
"Don't Let Me Cross Over" 1962 24

GLEN CAMPBELL
"I Wanna Live" 1968 16
"Wichita Lineman" 1968 19
"Galveston" 1969 14

"Rhinestone Cowboy"	1975	21
"Southern Nights"	1977	17

HENSON CARGILL
"Skip a Rope"	1967	19

THE CARLISLES
"No Help Wanted"	1953	24

JOHNNY CASH
"I Walk the Line"	1956	43
"There You Go"	1956	28
"Ballad of a Teenage Queen"	1958	23
"Guess Things Happen That Way"	1958	24
"Don't Take Your Guns to Town"	1959	20
"Ring of Fire"	1963	26
"Understand Your Man"	1964	22
"Folsom Prison Blues"	1968	18
"Daddy Sang Bass"	1968	20
"A Boy Named Sue"	1969	14
"Sunday Morning Coming Down"	1970	15
"Flesh and Blood"	1970	13
"One Piece at a Time"	1976	15
"Highwayman" (With Waylon Jennings, Kris Kristofferson, Willie Nelson)	1985	20

ROSANNE CASH
"Seven Year Ache"	1981	19
"My Baby Thinks He's a Train"	1981	16
"Blue Moon With Heartache"	1981	18
"I Don't Know Why You Don't Want Me"	1985	24
"Never Be You"	1985	24
"The Way We Make a Broken Heart"	1987	23
"Tennessee Flat Top Box"	1987	22
"It's Such a Small World" (with Rodney Crowell)	1988	23
"If You Change Your Mind"	1988	22
"Runaway Train"	1988	23

RAY CHARLES
"Seven Spanish Angels"	1984	27

ROY CLARK
"Come Live With Me"	1973	16

PATSY CLINE
"I Fall to Pieces"	1961	39
"She's Got You"	1962	19

THE KING COLE TRIO
"Straighten up and Fly Right"	1944	15

JESSI COLTER
"I'm Not Lisa"	1975	18

JOHN CONLEE
"Lady Lay Down"	1978	16
"Backside of Thirty"	1979	15
"Common Man"	1983	19
"I'm Only in It for the Love"	1983	20
"In My Eyes"	1983	23
"As Long As I'm Rockin' With You"	1984	19
"Got My Heart Set on You"	1986	22

EARL THOMAS CONLEY
"Fire & Smoke"	1981	19
"Somewhere Between Right and Wrong"	1982	18
"Your Love's On the Line"	1983	19
"Holding Her and Loving You"	1983	25
"Don't Make it Easy for Me"	1984	18
"Angel in Disguise"	1984	21
"Chance of Lovin' You"	1984	22
"Honor Bound"	1985	22
"Love Don't Care (Whose Heart It Breaks)"	1985	19
"Nobody Falls Like a Fool"	1985	21
"Once in a Blue Moon"	1986	22
"I Can't Win for Losin' You"	1986	23
"That Was a Close One"	1987	21
"Right from the Start"	1987	23
"What She Is (Is a Woman in Love)"	1988	23
"We Believe in Happy Endings" (with Emmylou Harris)	1988	21
"What'd I Say"	1988	24

SPADE COOLEY

"Shame on You"	1945	31

COWBOY COPAS

"Alabam"	1960	34

HELEN CORNELIUS

"I Don't Want to Have to Marry You" (with Jim Ed Brown)	1976	16

BILLY "CRASH" CRADDOCK

"Rub It In"	1974	16
"Ruby, Baby"	1974	14
"Broken Down in Tiny Pieces"	1976	16

BING CROSBY

"Pistol Packin' Mama"	1944	11

RODNEY CROWELL

"It's Such a Small World" (with Rosanne Cash)	1988	23
"I Couldn't Leave You if I Tried"	1988	21
"She's Crazy for Leavin'"	1988	19

DAVE & SUGAR

"The Door Is Always Open"	1976	19
"Tear Time"	1976	16
"Golden Tears"	1979	14

THE DAVIS SISTERS

"I Forgot More Than You'll Ever Know"	1953	26

JIMMIE DAVIS

"There's a New Moon Over My Shoulder"	1945	18

PAUL DAVIS

"You're Still New to Me" (with Marie Osmond)	1986	21
"I Won't Take Less than Your Love" (with Tanya Tucker, Paul Overstreet)	1987	24

JIMMY DEAN

"Big Bad John"	1961	22
"The First Thing Ev'ry Morning		
(and the Last Thing Ev'ry Night)"	1965	17

DELMORE BROTHERS

"Blues Stay Away from Me"	1949	23

JOHN DENVER

"Back Home Again"	1974	14
"Thank God I'm a Country Boy"	1975	14
"I'm Sorry"	1975	18

THE DESERT ROSE BAND

"He's Back and I'm Blue"	1988	19
"I Still Believe in You"	1988	20

AL DEXTER

"Pistol Packin' Mama"	1944	10
"Rosalita"	1944	25
"So Long, Pal"	1944	30
"Too Late to Worry,		
Too Blue to Cry"	1944	30
"I'm Losing My Mind Over You"	1945	21
"Guitar Polka"	1946	29
"Wine, Woman and Song"	1946	13

"LITTLE" JIMMY DICKENS

"May the Bird of Paradise Fly		
up Your Nose"	1965	19

ROY DRUSKY

"Yes, Mr. Peters"		
(with Priscilla Mitchell)	1965	23

DAVE DUDLEY

"The Pool Shark"	1970	16

JOHNNY DUNCAN

"Thinkin' of a Rendezvous"	1976	17
"It Couldn't Have Been Any Better"	1977	15
"She Can Put Her Shoes Under		
My Bed Anytime"	1978	17

SHEENA EASTON
"We've Got Tonight"
   (with Kenny Rogers)   1983   17

THE EVERLY BROTHERS
"Bye Bye Love"   1957   26
"Wake up Little Susie"   1957   22
"All I Have to Do Is Dream"   1958   13
"Bird Dog"   1958   13

EXILE
"Woke Up in Love"   1983   22
"I Don't Want to Be a Memory" 1984   24
"Give Me One More Chance"   1984   26
"Crazy for Your Love"   1984   23
"She's a Miracle"   1985   22
"Hang on to Your Heart"   1985   24
"I Could Get Used to You"   1985   22
"It'll Be Me"   1986   22
"She's Too Good to Be True"   1987   23
"I Can't Get Close Enough"   1988   22

BARBARA FAIRCHILD
"Teddy Bear Song"   1972   19

DONNA FARGO
"The Happiest Girl in the
   Whole U.S.A."   1972   23
"Funny Face"   1972   16
"Superman"   1973   14
"You Were Always There"   1973   14
"You Can't Be a Beacon
   (If Your Light Don't Shine)" 1974   15
"That Was Yesterday"   1977   14

FREDDY FENDER
"Before the Next Teardrop Falls" 1975   17
"Wasted Days and Wasted Nights" l975   16
"Secret Love"   1975   16
"You'll Lose a Good Thing"   1976   15

FLATT & SCRUGGS
"The Ballad of Jed Clampett"   1962   20

RED FOLEY

"Smoke on the Water"	1944	27
"New Jole Band"	1947	16
"Tennessee Saturday Night"	1948	40
"Chattanoogie Shoe Shine Boy"	1950	20
"Birmingham Bounce"	1950	9
"M-I-S-S-I-S-S-I-P-P-I"	1950	14
"Midnight"	1952	11
"Goodnight, Irene"	1950	15
"Shame on You"		
(with Lawrence Welk)	1945	14
"One by One"	1954	41

TENNESSEE ERNIE FORD

"Mule Train"	1949	10
"The Shot Gun Boogie"	1950	25
"Sixteen Tons"	1955	21

THE FORESTER SISTERS

"I Fell in Love Again Last Night"	1985	22
"Just in Case"	1986	20
"Mama's Never Seen Those Eyes"	1986	22
"Too Much Is Not Enough"		
(with the Bellamy Brothers)	1986	20
"You Again"	1987	24

JANIE FRICKIE

"On My Knees" (with Charlie Rich)	1978	14
"Don't Worry Bout Me Baby"	1982	18
"It Ain't Easy Bein' Easy"	1982	19
"He's a Heartache		
(Looking for a Place to Happen)"	1983	20
"Tell Me a Lie"	1983	20
"Let's Stop Talkin' About It"	1984	18
"Your Heart's Not in It"	1984	23
"A Place to Fall Apart"		
(with Merle Haggard)	1985	22
"Always Have Always Will"	1986	1

DAVID FRIZZELL

"I'm Gonna Hire a Wino to		
Decorate Our Home"	1982	23
"You're the Reason God Made		
Oklahoma" (with Shelly West)	1981	17

LEFTY FRIZZELL

"If You've Got the Money I've Got the Time"	1950	22
"I Love You a Thousand Ways"	1951	32
"I Want to Be with You Always"	1951	27
"Always Late (with Your Kisses)"	1951	28
"Give Me More, More, More"	1952	21
"Saginaw, Michigan"	1964	26

LARRY GATLIN & THE GATLIN BROTHERS

"I Just Wish You Were Someone I Love"	1978	16
"All the Gold in California"	1979	15
"Houston (Means I'm One Day Closer)"	1983	22

CRYSTAL GAYLE

"I'll Get Over You"	1976	18
"You Never Miss a Real Good Thing"	1977	16
"Don't It Make My Brown Eyes Blue"	1977	18
"Ready for the Times to Get Better"	1978	14
"Talking in Your Sleep"	1978	16
"Why Have You Left the One You Left Me For"	1979	14
"It's Like We Never Said Goodbye"	1980	14
"If You Ever Change Your Mind"	1980	18
"Too Many Lovers"	1981	17
"You and I" (with Eddie Rabbitt)	1982	19
"Til I Gain Control Again"	1982	22
"Our Love Is on the Faultline"	1983	16
"Baby, What About You"	1983	19
"The Sound of Goodbye"	1984	21
"Turning Away"	1984	20
"Cry"	1986	19
"Straight to the Heart"	1987	22
"Makin' Up for Lost Time" (with Gary Morris)	1986	19

DON GIBSON

"Oh Lonesome Me"	1958	34
"Blue Blue Day"	1958	24
"Woman (Sensuous Woman)"	1972	18

MICKEY GILLEY

"Room Full of Roses"	1974	16
"I Overlooked an Orchid"	1974	18
"City Lights"	1975	12
"Window Up Above"	1975	15
"Don't the Girls All Get Prettier at Closing Time"	1976	16
"Bring It on Home to Me"	1976	14
"She's Pulling Me Back Again"	1977	17
"True Love Ways"	1980	16
"Stand By Me"	1980	17
"That's All that Matters"	1980	16
"A Headache Tomorrow (or a Heartache Tonight)"	1981	15
"You Don't Know Me"	1981	16
"Lonely Nights"	1982	18
"Put Your Dreams Away"	1982	16
"Talk to Me"	1983	18
"Fool for Your Love"	1983	18
"Paradise Tonight" (with Charly McClain)	1983	22

JIM GLASER

"You're Gettin' to Me Again"	1984	24

BOBBY GOLDSBORO

"Honey"	1968	15

VERN GOSDIN

"I Can Tell By the Way You Dance (You're Gonna Love Me Tonight)"	1984	25
"Set 'em Up Joe"	1988	22

JACK GREENE

"There Goes My Everything"	1966	23
"All the Time"	1967	20
"You Are My Treasure"	1968	15
"Until My Dreams Come True"	1968	17
"Statue of a Fool"	1969	18

LEE GREENWOOD

"Somebody's Gonna Love You"	1983	22
"Going, Going, Gone"	1983	19
"Dixie Road"	1985	20
"I Don't Mind the Thorns		

(If You're the Rose)"	1985	23
"Don't Underestimate		
My Love For You"	1985	20
"Hearts Aren't Made to Break		
(They're Made to Love)"	1986	22
"Mornin' Ride"	1987	24

JACK GUTHRIE

"Oklahoma Hills"	1945	19

MERLE HAGGARD

"The Fugitive"	1966	18
"Branded Man"	1967	16
"Sing Me Back Home"	1968	20
"The Legend of Bonnie and Clyde"	1968	15
"Mama Tried"	1968	15
"Hungry Eyes"	1969	17
"Workin' Man Blues"	1969	15
"Okie from Muskogee"	1969	16
"The Fightin' Side of Me"	1970	14
"Daddy Frank (The Guitar Man)"	1971	14
"Carolyn"	1971	16
"Grandma Harp"	1972	15
"It's Not Love (but It's Not Bad)"	1972	14
"I Wonder if They Ever		
Think of Me"	1972	14
"Everybody's Had the Blues"	1973	16
"If We Make It Through December"	1973	17
"Things Aren't Funny Anymore"	1974	15
"Old Man from the Mountain"	1974	14
"Kentucky Gambler"	1975	15
"Always Wanting You"	1975	14
"Movin' On"	1975	15
"It's All in the Movies"	1975	15
"The Roots of My Raising"	1976	14
"Cherokee Maiden"	1976	13
"I Think I'll Just Stay		
Here and Drink"	1981	17
"Pancho and Lefty"		
(with Willie Nelson)	1983	21

TOM T. HALL

"A Week in a Country Jail"	1969	15
"The Year that Clayton		
Delaney Died"	1971	20

"Old Dogs, Children, and Watermelon Wine"	1972	15
"I Love"	1974	18
"Country Is"	1974	16
"I Care"	1975	15
"Faster Horses (the Cowboy and the Poet)"	1976	16

GEORGE HAMILTON IV

"Abilene"	1963	24

EMMYLOU HARRIS

"Together Again"	1976	14
"Sweet Dreams"	1976	14
"Two More Bottles of Wine"	1978	14
"Beneath Still Waters"	1980	14
"(Lost His Love) on Our Last Date"	1983	20
"We Believe in Happy Endings" (with Earl Thomas Conley)	1988	21
"To Know Him Is to Love Him" (with Linda Ronstadt, Dolly Parton)	1987	19

FREDDIE HART

"Easy Loving"	1971	24
"My Hang-Up Is You"	1972	19
"Bless Your Heart"	1972	14
"Got the All Overs for You (All Over Me)"	1972	17
"Super Kind of Woman"	1973	14
"Trip to Heaven"	1973	16

HAWKSHAW HAWKINS

"Lonesome 7-7203"	1963	25

BOBBY HELMS

"Fraulein"	1957	52
"My Special Angel"	1957	26

GOLDIE HILL

"I Let the Stars Get in My Eyes"	1953	9

JOHNNY HORTON

"When It's Springtime in Alaska (It's Forty Below)"	1959	23

| "The Battle of New Orleans" | 1959 | 21 |
| "North to Alaska" | 1961 | 22 |

DAVID HOUSTON

"Almost Persuaded"	1966	25
"With One Exception"	1967	18
"My Elusive Dreams"		
(with Tammy Wynette)	1967	18
"You Mean the World to Me"	1967	17
"Have a Little Faith"	1968	14
"Already It's Heaven"	1968	16
"Baby, Baby, I Know You're a Lady"	1979	17

JAN HOWARD

| "For Loving You" | | |
| (with Bill Anderson) | 1967 | 20 |

FERLIN HUSKY

"A Dear John Letter"		
(with Jean Shepard)	1953	23
"Gone"	1957	27
"Wings of a Dove"	1960	36

STONEWALL JACKSON

| "Waterloo" | 1959 | 19 |
| "B.J. the D.J." | 1963 | 22 |

SONNY JAMES

"Young Love"	1956	24
"You're the Only World I Know"	1965	25
"Behind the Tear"	1965	22
"Take Good Care of Her"	1966	20
"Need You"	1967	18
"I'll Never Find Another You"	1967	17
"It's the Little Things"	1967	18
"A World of Her Own"	1968	17
"Heaven Says Hello"	1968	17
"Born to Be with You"	1968	16
"Only the Lonely"	1969	16
"Running Bear"	1969	15
"Since I Met You Baby"	1969	15
"It's Just a Matter of Time"	1970	14
"My Love"	1970	15
"Don't Keep Me Hangin' On"	1970	15
"Endlessly"	1970	16

"Empty Arms"	1971	16
"Bright Lights, Big City"	1971	13
"Here Comes Honey Again"	1971	15
"That's Why I Love You Like I Do"	1972	11
"When the Snow Is on the Roses"	1972	15
"Is It Wrong (for Loving You)"	1974	15

WAYLON JENNINGS

"This Time"	1974	13
"I'm a Ramblin' Man"	1974	13
"Are You Sure Hank Done It This Way"	1975	16
"Luckenbach, Texas (Back to the Basics of Love)"	1977	18
"The Wurlitzer Prize (I Don't Want to Get Over You)"	1977	16
"I've Always Been Crazy"	1978	13
"Amanda"	1979	14
"Come with Me"	1979	13
"I Ain't Livin' Long Like This"	1980	15
"Theme from the Dukes of Hazzard"	1980	17
"Lucille (You Won't Do Your Daddy's Will)"	1983	16
"Rose in Paradise"	1987	19
"Good Hearted Woman" (with Willie Nelson)	1976	17
"Mammas, Don't Let Your Babies Grow up to Be Cowboys" (with Willie Nelson)	1978	16
"Just to Satisfy You" (with Willie Nelson)	1982	18
"Highwayman" (with Willie Nelson, Kris Kristofferson, Johnny Cash)	1985	20

JOHNNY & JACK

"Oh Baby Mine (I Get So Lonely)"	1954	18

MICHAEL JOHNSON

"Give Me Wings"	1986	23
"The Moon Is Still Over Her Shoulder"	1987	26

GEORGE JONES

"White Lightning"	1959	22
"Tender Years"	1961	32
"She Thinks I Still Care"	1962	23

"Walk Through This World with Me"	1967	22
"The Grand Tour"	1974	17
"The Door"	1975	13
"He Stopped Loving Her Today"	1980	18
"Still Doin' Time"	1981	17
"I Always Get Lucky with You"	1983	18
"Yesterday's Wine" (with Merle Haggard)	1982	15
"We're Gonna Hold On" (with Tammy Wynette)	1973	17
"Golden Ring" (with Tammy Wynette)	1976	15
"Near You" (with Tammy Wynette)	1977	16

TOM JONES

"Say You'll Stay Until Tomorrow"	1977	17

LOUIS JORDAN

"Ration Blues"	1944	13
"Is You Is or Is You Ain't (Ma' Baby)"	1944	9

THE JUDDS

"Mama He's Crazy"	1984	23
"Why Not Me"	1984	22
"Girls Night Out"	1985	22
"Love Is Alive"	1985	21
"Have Mercy"	1985	22
"Grandpa (Tell Me 'Bout the Good Old Days)"	1986	20
"Rockin' with the Rhythm of the Rain"	1986	18
"Cry Myself to Sleep"	1987	20
"I Know Where I'm Going"	1987	19
"Maybe Your Baby's Got the Blues"	1987	22
"Turn It Loose"	1988	17
"Change of Heart"	1989	20

THE KENDALLS

"Heaven's Just a Sin Away"	1977	20
"Sweet Desire"	1978	15
"Thank God for the Radio"	1984	23

CLAUDE KING
"Wolverton Mountain"   1962   26

PEE WEE KING
"Slow Poke"   1951   31

KRIS KRISTOFFERSON
"Why Me"   1973   20
"Highwayman"
   (with Waylon Jennings,
   Willie Nelson, Johnny Cash)   1985   20

CHRISTY LANE
"One Day at a Time"   1980   18

DICKEY LEE
"Rocky"   1975   18

JOHNNY LEE
"Lookin' for Love"   1980   14
"One in a Million"   1980   16
"Bet Your Heart on Me"   1981   15
"The Yellow Rose"
   (with Lane Brody)   1984   22
"You Could've Heard a Heart Break"   1984   24

JERRY LEE LEWIS
"Whole Lot of Shakin' Going On"   1957   23
"Great Balls of Fire"   1958   19
"To Make Love Sweeter for You"   1968   15
"There Must Be More to
   Love than This"   1970   15
"Would You Take Another
   Chance on Me"   1971   17
"Chantilly Lace"   1972   15

HANK LOCKLIN
"Let Me Be the One"   1953   32
"Please Help Me, I'm Falling"   1960   36

THE LOUVIN BROTHERS
"I Don't Believe You've
   Met My Baby"   1956   24

LORETTA LYNN

"Don't Come Home A'Drinkin'		
with Lovin' on Your Mind"	1966	19
"Fist City"	1968	17
"Woman of the World		
(Leave My World Alone)"	1969	16
"Coal Miner's Daughter"	1970	15
"One's on the Way"	1971	16
"Rated X"	1972	16
"Love Is the Foundation"	1973	15
"Trouble in Paradise"	1974	17
"Somebody Somewhere		
(Don't Know What He's		
Missin' Tonight)"	1976	17
"She's Got You"	1977	17
"Out of My Head and		
Back in My Bed"	1978	15
"After the Fire is Gone"		
(with Conway Twitty)	1971	14
"Lead Me On"	1971	17
"Louisiana Woman, Mississippi Man"	1973	14
"As Soon as I Hang up the Phone"	1974	15
"Feelin's"	1975	16

WARNER MACK

"The Bridge Washed Out"	1965	23

CLEDUS MAGGARD & THE CITIZEN'S BAND

"The White Knight"	1976	14

BARBARA MANDRELL

"Sleeping Single in a Double Bed"	1978	15
"(If Loving You Is Wrong) I Don't		
Want to Be Right"	1979	14
"Years"	1979	15
"I Was Country when Country		
Wasn't Cool"	1981	13
"'Till You're Gone"	1982	19
"One of a Kind Pair of Fools"	1983	21

KATHY MATTEA

"Goin' Home"	1987	24
"Eighteen Wheels and a		
Dozen Roses"	1988	20

C.W. McCALL
"Convoy"	1975	15

CHARLY McCLAIN
"Who's Cheatin' Who"	1981	17
"Radio Heart"	1985	23
"Paradise Tonight"	1983	22

MEL DANIEL
"Baby's Got Her Blue Jeans On"	1984	28

SKEETS McDONALD
"Don't Let the Stars Get in Your Eyes"	1952	18

RONNIE McDOWELL
"Older Women"	1981	16
"You're Gonna Ruin My Bad Reputation"	1983	22

REBA McENTIRE
"Can't Even Get the Blues"	1983	22
"You're the First Time I've Thought About Leaving"	1983	21
"How Blue"	1984	23
"Somebody Should Leave"	1985	22
"Whoever's in New England"	1986	23
"Little Rock"	1986	19
"What Am I Gonna Do About You"	1987	22
"One Promise Too Late"	1987	21
"The Last One to Know"	1987	22
"Love Will Find Its Way to You"	1988	20
"I Know How He Feels"	1988	22
"New Fool at an Old Game"	1989	21

ROGER MILLER
"Dang Me"	1964	25
"King of the Road"	1965	20

RONNIE MILSAP
"Pure Love"	1974	15
"Please Don't Tell Me How the Story Ends"	1974	14
"(I'd Be a) Legend in My Time"	1975	13

"Daydreams About Night Things"	1975	16
"What Goes on When the Sun Goes Down"	1976	14
"(I'm a) Stand By My Woman Man"	1976	14
"Let My Love Be Your Pillow"	1977	15
"It Was Almost Like a Song"	1977	18
"What a Difference You've Made in My Life"	1978	16
"Only One Love in My Life"	1978	13
"Let's Take the Long Way Round the World"	1978	12
"Nobody Likes Sad Songs"	1979	15
"Why Don't You Spend the Night"	1980	15
"My Heart"	1980	15
"Cowboys and Clowns"	1980	16
"Smoky Mountain Rain"	1980	14
"Am I Losing You"	1981	14
"There's No Gettin' Over Me"	1981	15
"I Wouldn't Have Missed It for the World"	1981	16
"Any Day Now"	1982	17
"He Got You"	1982	18
"Inside"	1982	19
"Don't You Know How Much I Love You"	1983	19
"Show Her"	1984	19
"Still Losing You"	1984	19
"She Keeps the Home Fires Burning"	1985	20
"Lost in the Fifties Tonight (in the Still of the Night)"	1985	23
"Happy, Happy Birthday Baby"	1986	20
"In Love"	1986	20
"How Do I Turn You On"	1987	21
"Snap Your Fingers"	1987	19
"Make No Mistake, She's Mine" (with Kenny Rogers)	1987	17
"Where Do the Nights Go"	1988	20
"Don't You Ever Get Tired of Hurting Me" (with Mike Reid)	1988	20

PRISCILLA MITCHELL
"Yes, Mr. Peters" (with Roy Drusky)	1965	23

MELBA MONTGOMERY
"No Charge"	1974	16

GEORGE MORGAN
"Candy Kisses"   1949   23

GARY MORRIS
"Baby, Bye Bye"   1985   20
"I'll Never Stop Loving You"   1985   23
"100% Chance of Rain"   1986   20
"Leave Me Lonely"   l987   21
"Makin' up for Lost Time
    (Dallas Theme)"   1986   19

MOON MULLICAN
"I'll Sail My Ship Alone"   1950   35

MICHAEL MARTIN MURPHY
"What's Forever For"   1982   24
"A Long Line of Love"   l987   23

ANNE MURRAY
"He Thinks I Still Care"   l974   17
"I Just Fall in Love Again"   l979   15
"Shadows in the Moonlight"   1979   15
"Broken Hearted Me"   1979   14
"Could I Have This Dance"   1980   16
"Blessed Are the Believers"   1981   14
"A Little Good News"   1983   20
"Just Another Woman in Love"   1984   20
"Nobody Loves Me Like You Do"   1984   22
"Now and Forever (You and Me)"   1986   19

WILLIE NELSON
"Blue Eyes Crying in the Rain"   1975   18
"If You've Got the Money
    I've Got the Time"   1976   15
"Georgia on My Mind"   1978   16
"Blue Skies"   1978   13
"My Heroes Have Always
    Been Cowboys"   1980   14
"On the Road Again"   1980   16
"Angel Flying Too
    Close to the Ground"   1981   14
"Always on My Mind"   1982   21
"City of New Orleans"   1884   25
"Forgiving You Was Easy"   1985   22
"Living in the Promised Land"   1986   20

"Seven Spanish Angels" (with Ray Charles)	1985	27
"Pancho and Lefty" (with Merle Haggard)	1983	21
"To All the Girls I've Loved Before" (with Julio Iglesias)	1984	20
"Good Hearted Woman" (with Waylon Jennings)	1976	17
"Mammas, Don't Let Your Babies Grow Up to Be Cowboys" (with Waylon Jennings)	1978	16
"Just to Satisfy You" (with Waylon Jennings)	1982	18
"Highwayman" (with Waylon Jennings, Kris Kristofferson, Johnny Cash)	1985	20
"Heartbreak Hotel" (with Leon Russell)	1980	13

JUICE NEWTON

"The Sweetest Thing"	1982	19
"You Make Me Want to Make You Mine"	1985	22
"Hurt"	1986	24
"Both to Each Other" (with Eddie Rabbitt)	1986	20

NITTY GRITTY DIRT BAND

"Modern Day Romance"	1985	21
"Fishin' in the Dark"	1987	23
"Long Hard Road"		

THE OAK RIDGE BOYS

"I'll Be True to You"	1978	15
"Leaving Louisiana in the Broad Daylight"	1979	15
"Trying to Love Two Women"	1980	16
"Elvira"	1981	14
"Fancy Free"	1981	15
"Bobbie Sue"	1982	15
"American Made"	1983	16
"Love Song"	1983	18
"I Guess It Never Hurts to Hurt Sometimes"	1984	22
"Everyday"	1984	21

"Make My Life with You"	1985	21
"Little Things"	1985	20
"Touch a Hand, Make a Friend"	1985	21
"It Takes a Little Rain to Make Love Grow"	1987	24
"This Crazy Love"	1987	23
"Gonna Take a Lot of River"	1988	21

THE O'KANES

"Can't Stop My Heart from Loving You"	1987	22

K. T. OSLIN

"Do Ya'"	1987	25
"I'll Always Come Back"	1988	21
"Hold Me"	1989	20

MARIE OSMOND

"Paper Roses"	1973	16
"Meet Me in Montana" (with Dan Seals)	1985	23
"There's No Stopping Your Heart"	1986	21
"You're Still New to Me" (with Paul Davis)	1986	21

PAUL OVERSTREET

"I Won't Take Less than Your Love" (with Tanya Tucker, Paul Davis)	1987	24

BUCK OWENS

"Act Naturally"	1963	28
"Love's Gonna Live Here"	1963	30
"My Heart Skips a Beat"	1964	26
"Together Again"	1964	27
"I Don't Care"	1964	27
"I've Got a Tiger by the Tail"	1965	20
"Before You Go"	1965	20
"Only You (Can Break My Heart)"	1965	19
"Buckaroo"	1965	17
"Waitin' in Your Welfare Line"	1966	19
"Think of Me"	1966	21
"Open Up Your Heart"	1966	20
"Where Does the Good Times Go"	1967	16
"Sam's Place"	1967	16
"Your Tender Loving Care"	1967	16

"How Long Will My Baby Be Gone"	1968	15
"Who's Gonna Mow Your Grass"	1969	15
"Johnny B. Goode"	1969	15
"Tall Dark Stranger"	1969	15
"Made in Japan"	1972	15
"Streets of Bakersfield" (with Dwight Yoakam)	1988	18

DOLLY PARTON

"Joshua"	1971	15
"Jolene"	1974	19
"I Will Always Love You"	1974	15
"Love Is Like a Butterfly"	1974	17
"The Bargain Store"	1975	13
"Here You Come Again"	1977	19
"It's All Wrong, But It's All Right"	1978	14
"Heartbreaker"	1978	13
"I Really Got the Feeling"	1978	14
"You're the Only One"	1979	14
"Starting Over Again"	1980	14
"Old Flames Can't Hold a Candle to You"	1980	16
"9 to 5"	1980	14
"But You Know I Love You"	1981	17
"I Will Always Love You"	1982	19
"Tennessee Homesick Blues"	1984	20
"Think About Love"	1986	22
"Islands in the Stream" (with Kenny Rogers)	1983	23
"Real Love"	1983	29
"To Know Him Is to Love Him" (with Linda Ronstadt, Emmylou Harris)	1987	19
"Please Don't Stop Loving Me"	1974	17

JOHNNY PAYCHECK

"Take This Job and Shove It"	1978	18

LEON PAYNE

"I Love You Because"	1949	32

CARL PERKINS

"Blue Suede Shoes"	1956	24

WEBB PIERCE

"Wondering"	1952	27
"That Heart Belongs to Me"	1952	20
"Back Street Affair"	1952	23
"It's Been So Long"	1953	22
"There Stands the Glass"	1953	27
"Slowly"	1954	36
"Even Tho"	1954	31
"More and More"	1954	18
"In the Jailhouse Now"	1955	37
"I Don't Care"	1955	32
"Love, Love, Love"	1955	32
"Honky Tonk Song"	1957	22
"Why Baby Why" (with Red Sovine)	1956	25

ELVIS PRESLEY

"I Forgot to Remember to Forget"	1955	39
"Heartbreak Hotel"	1956	27
"I Want You, I Need You, I Love You"	1956	20
"Don't Be Cruel"	1956	27
"Hound Dog"	1956	20
"All Shook Up"	1957	16
"(Let me Be Your) Teddy Bear"	1957	16
"Jailhouse Rock"	1957	24
"Moody Blue"	1976	16
"Way Down"	1977	17

RAY PRICE

"Crazy Arms"	1956	45
"My Shoes Keep Walking Back to You"	1957	37
"City Lights"	1958	34
"The Same Old Me"	1959	30
"For the Good Times"	1970	26
"I Won't Mention It Again"	1971	19
"She's Got to Be a Saint"	1972	16
"You're the Best Thing that Ever Happened to Me"	1973	16

CHARLEY PRIDE

"All I Have to Offer You (Is Me)"	1969	17
"(I'm So) Afraid of Losing You Again"	1969	16

"Is Anybody Goin' to San Antone"	1970	17
"Wonder Could I Live There Anymore"	1970	17
"I Can't Believe that You've Stopped Loving Me"	1970	16
"I'd Rather Love You"	1971	14
"I'm Just Me"	1971	16
"Kiss an Angel Good Mornin'"	1971	19
"It's Gonna Take a Little Bit Longer"	1972	16
"She's Too Good to Be True"	1972	16
"A Shoulder to Cry On"	1973	14
"Don't Fight the Feelings of Love"	1973	15
"Amazing Love"	l973	16
"Then Who Am I"	1975	12
"Hope You're Feelin' Me Like I'm Feelin' You"	1975	14
"My Eyes Can Only See as Far as You"	1976	14
"She's Just an Old Love Turned Memory"	1977	14
"I'll Be Leaving Alone"	1977	14
"More to Me"	1977	14
"Someone Loves You Honey"	1978	15
"Where Do I Put Her Memory"	1979	15
"You're My Jamaica"	1979	15
"Honky Tonk Blues"	1980	13
"To Win Again"	1980	15
"Never Been So Loved in All My Life"	1981	15
"Mountain of Love"	1982	18
"You're So Good when You're Bad"	1982	17
"Why Baby Why"	1982	19
"Night Games"	1983	21

JEANNE PRUETT

"Satin Sheets"	1973	18

EDDIE RABBITT

"Drinkin' My Baby off My Mind"	1976	16
"You Don't Love Me Anymore"	1978	14
"I Just Want to Love You"	1978	14
"Every Which Way But Loose"	1978	15
"Suspicions"	1979	14
"Gone Too Far"	1980	14
"Drivin' My Life Away"	1980	15
"I Love a Rainy Night"	1980	17

"Step By Step"	1981	16
"Someone Could Lose a Heart Tonight"	1981	17
"You and I" (with Crystal Gayle)	1982	19
"You Can't Run from Love"	1983	17
"The Best Year of My Life"	1985	23
"Both to Each Other" (with Juice Newton)	1986	20
"I Wanna Dance With You"	1988	20
"The Wanderer"	1988	18

WAYNE RANEY

"Why Don't You Haul Off and Love Me"	1949	22

EDDY RAVEN

"I Got Mexico"	1984	22
"Shine, Shine, Shine"	1987	24
"I'm Gonna Get You"	1988	21
"Joe Knows How to Live"	1988	21

JERRY REED

"When You're Hot, You're Hot"	1971	15
"Lord, Mr. Ford"	1973	15
"She Got the Goldmine"		

DEL REEVES

"Girl on the Billboard"	1965	20

JIM REEVES

"Mexican Joe"	1953	26
"Bimbo"	1954	21
"Four Walls"	1957	26
"Billy Bayou"	1958	25
"He'll Have to Go"	1960	34
"I Guess I'm Crazy"	1964	26
"This Is It"	1965	23
"Is It Really Over?"	1965	21
"Distant Drums"	1966	21
"Blue Side of Lonesome"	1966	19
"I Won't Come in While He's There"	1967	16

RESTLESS HEART

"That Rock Won't Roll"	1986	23
"I'll Still Be Loving You"	1987	25

"Why Does It Have to Be"
"Wheels"	1987	23
"Bluest Eyes in Texas"	1988	21
"A Tender Lie"	1988	23

CHARLIE RICH

"Behind Closed Doors"	1973	20
"The Most Beautiful Girl"	1973	18
"There Won't Be Anymore"	1974	17
"A Very Special Love Song"	1974	14
"I Don't See Me in Your Eyes Anymore"	1974	13
"I Love My Friend"	1974	15
"She Called Me Baby"	1974	15
"Rollin' with the Flow"	1977	19
"On My Knees" (with Janie Frickie)	1978	14

JEANNIE C. RILEY

| "Harper Valley P.T.A." | 1968 | 14 |

TEX RITTER

"I'm Wastin' My Tears on You"	1944	20
"You Two-Timed Me One Time Too Often"	1945	20
"You Will Have to Pay"	1946	7

MARTY ROBBINS

"I'll Go Alone"	1953	18
"Singing the Blues"	1956	30
"A White Sport Coat (and a Pink Carnation)"	1957	22
"The Story of My Life"	1957	23
"Just Married"	1958	25
"El Paso"	1959	26
"Don't Worry"	1961	19
"Devil Woman"	1962	21
"Ruby Ann"	1962	14
"Begging to You"	1964	23
"Ribbon of Darkness"	1965	21
"Tonight Carmen"	1967	16
"I Walk Alone"	1968	15
"My Woman, My Woman, My Wife"	1970	17

"El Paso City"	1976	16
"Among My Souvenirs"	1976	14

JUDY RODMAN
"Until I Met You"	1986	25

JOHNNY RODRIGUEZ
"You Always Come Back to Hurting Me"	1973	16
"Ridin' My Thumb to Mexico"	1973	17
"That's the Way Love Goes"	1974	14
"I Just Can't Get Her out of My Mind"	1975	12
"Just Get up and Close the Door"	1975	18
"Love Put a Song in My Heart"	1975	15

KENNY ROGERS
"Lucille"	1977	20
"Daytime Friends"	1977	14
"Love or Something Like It"	1978	14
"The Gambler"	1978	16
"She Believes in Me"	1979	16
"You Decorated My Life"	1979	12
"Coward of the County"	1979	15
"Lady"	1980	14
"I Don't Need You"	1981	15
"Love Will Turn You Around"	1982	16
"Crazy"	1985	21
"Morning Desire"	1985	22
"Thumb of the Unknown Love"	1986	20
"We've Got Tonight" (with Sheena Easton)	1983	17
"Make No Mistake, She's Mine" (with Ronnie Milsap)	1987	17
"Islands in the Stream" (with Dolly Parton)	1983	23
"Real Love"	1985	20
"Every Time Two Fools Collide"	1978	17
"All I Ever Need Is You"	1979	15
"What Are We Doin' in Love"	1981	15

LINDA RONSTADT
"When Will I Be Loved"	1975	15
"To Know Him Is to Love Him" (with Dolly Parton, Emmylou Harris)	1987	19

LEON RUSSELL
"Heartbreak Hotel"
   (with Willie Nelson)   1979   13

SAWYER BROWN
"Step that Step"   1985   21

JOHN SCHNEIDER
"I've Been Around Enough to Know"   1984   28
"Country Girls"   1985   23
"What's a Memory Like You"
   (Doing in a Love Like This)   1986   24
"You're the Last Thing
   I Needed Tonight"   1986   20

SCHUYLER, KNOBLOCH & OVERSTREET
"Baby's Got a New Baby"   1986   22

DAN SEALS
"Meet Me in Montana"
   (with Marie Osmond)   1985   23
"Bop"   1986   27
"Everything that Glitters
   (Is Not Gold)"   1986   23
"You Still Move Me"   1986   22
"I Will Be There"   1987   19
"Three Time Loser"   1987   21
"One Friend"   1988   26
"Addicted"   1988   22
"Big Wheels in the Moonlight"   1988   21

JEAN SHEPARD
"A Dear John Letter"   1953   23

T. G. SHEPARD
"Devil in the Bottle"   1974   19
"Tryin' to Beat the Mornin' Home"   1975   15
"Last Cheater's Waltz"   1979   14
"I'll Be Coming Back for More"   1979   15
"Do You Wanna Go to Heaven"   1980   15
"I Feel Like Loving You Again"   1980   13
"I Loved 'em Every One"   1981   15
"Party Time"   1981   16
"Only One You"   1982   19

"Finally"	1981	16
"War Is Hell (on the Homefront Too)"	1982	19
"Faking Love" (with Karen Brooks)	1982	20
"Slow Burn"	1983	21
"Strong Heart"	1986	23

RICKY SKAGGS

"Crying My Heart out Over You"	1982	23
"I Don't Care"	1982	18
"Heartbroke"	1982	17
"I Wouldn't Change You if I Could"	1982	20
"Highway 40 Blues"	1983	19
"Don't Cheat in Our Hometown"	1983	20
"Honey (Open that Door)"	1984	18
"Uncle Pen"	1984	19
"Country Boy"	1985	19
"Cajun Moon"	1986	20

CAL SMITH

"The Lord Knows I'm Drinking"	1972	17
"Country Bumpkin"	1974	15
"It's Time to Pay the Fiddler"	1974	16

CARL SMITH

"Let Old Mother Nature Have Her Way"	1952	33
"(When You Feel Like You're in Love) Don't Just Stand There"	1952	24
"Are You Teasing Me"	1952	19
"Hey, Joe"	1953	26
"Loose Talk"	1955	32

CONNIE SMITH

"Once a Day"	1964	28

MARGO SMITH

"Don't Break the Heart That Loves You"	1977	18
"It Only Hurts for a Little While"	1978	15

SAMMI SMITH

"Help Me Make It Through the Night"	1971	20

HANK SNOW

"I'm Moving On"	1950	44
"The Golden Rocket"	1950	23
"Rhumba Boogie"	1951	27
"I Don't Hurt Anymore"	1954	41
"Let Me Go, Lover"	1954	16
"I've Been Everywhere"	1962	22
"Hello Love"	1974	15

RED SOVINE

"Giddyup Go"	1965	22
"Teddy Bear"	1976	13
"Why Baby Why"		
(with Webb Pierce)	1955	25

BILLY JO SPEARS

"Blanket on the Ground"	1975	17

JOE STAMPLEY

"Soul Song"	1973	15
"Roll on Big Mama"	1975	14
"All These Things"	1976	16
"Just Good Ol' Boys"		
(with Moe Bandy)	1979	16
"Elizabeth"	1983	23
"My Only Love"	1984	20
"Too Much on My Heart"	1985	25

GARY STEWART

"She's Actin' Single		
(I'm Drinkin' Doubles)"	1975	13

WYNN STEWART

"It's Such a Pretty World Today"	1967	22

GEORGE STRAIT

"Fool Hearted Memory"	1982	18
"A Fire I Can't Put Out"	1983	23
"You Look So Good in Love"	1984	23
"Right or Wrong"	1984	23
"Let's Fall to Pieces Together"	1984	21
"Does Fort Worth Ever		
Cross Your Mind"	1984	23
"The Chair"	1985	22

"Nobody in His Right Mind Would've Left Her"	1986	22
"It Ain't Cool to Be Crazy About You"	1986	22
"Ocean Front Property"	1987	21
"All My Ex's Live in Texas"	1987	16
"Am I Blue"	1987	18
"Famous Last Words of a Fool"	1988	19
"Baby Blue"	1988	19
"If You Ain't Lovin' (You Ain't Livin')"	1988	20

BILLY SWAN

"I Can Help"	1974	14

SYLVIA

"Drifter"	1981	14
"Nobody"	1982	24

B. J. THOMAS

"(Hey Won't You Play) Another Somebody Done Somebody Wrong Song"	1975	16
"Whatever Happened to Old Fashioned Love"	1983	21
"New Looks from an Old Lover"	1983	21

HANK THOMPSON

"The Wild Side of Life"	1952	30
"Rub-a-Dub-Dub"	1953	20
"Wake Up, Irene"	1953	19

MEL TILLIS

"I Ain't Never"	1972	15
"Good Woman Blues"	1976	16
"Heart Healer"	1977	14
"I Believe in You"	1978	14
"Coca Cola Cowboy"	1979	15
"Southern Rains"	1981	16

FLOYD TILLMAN

"They Took the Stars out of Heaven"	1944	13

MITCHELL TOROK
"Caribbean"	1953	24

MERLE TRAVIS
"Divorce Me C.O.D."	1946	23
"So Round, So Firm, So Fully Packed"	1947	22

RANDY TRAVIS
"On the Other Hand"	1986	23
"Diggin' Up Bones"	1986	21
"Forever and Ever, Amen"	1987	22
"I Won't Need You Anymore"	1987	22
"Too Gone Too Long"	1988	19
"I Told You So"	1988	18
"Honky Tonk Moon"	1988	17
"Deeper than the Holler"	1988	18

ERNEST TUBB
"Soldier's Last Letter"	1944	29
"It's Been So Long, Darling"	1945	13
"Rainbow at Midnight"	1946	20
"Slippin' Around"	1949	20
"Blue Christmas"	1950	6
"Good Night, Irene" (with Red Foley)	1950	15

TANYA TUCKER
"What's Your Mama's Name"	1973	17
"Blood Red and Goin' Down"	1973	16
"Would You Lay with Me in a Field of Stone"	1974	17
"Lizzie and the Rainman"	1975	15
"San Antonio Stroll"	1975	15
"Here's Some Love"	1976	15
"Just Another Love"	1986	24
"I Won't Take Less than Your Love" (with Paul Davis & Paul Overstreet)	1987	24
"If It Don't Come Easy"	1988	20
"Strong Enough to Bend"	1988	23

MARY LOU TURNER
"Sometimes" (with Bill Anderson)	1975	16

WESLEY TUTTLE

"With Tears in My Eyes"	1945	14

CONWAY TWITTY

"Next in Line"	1968	17
"I Love You More Today"	1969	17
"To See My Angel Cry"	1969	14
"Hello Darlin'"	1970	20
"Fifteen Years Ago"	1970	18
"How Much More Can She Stand"	1971	17
"(Lost Her Love) On Our Last Date"	1972	15
"I Can't Stop Loving You"	1972	15
"She Needs Someone to Hold Her (When She Cries)"	1973	15
"You've Never Been This Far Gone Before"	1973	19
"There's a Honky Tonk Angel (Who'll Take Me Back In)"	1974	15
"I See the Want to in Your Eyes"	1974	17
"Linda on My Mind"	1975	13
"Touch the Hand"	1975	13
"This Time I've Hurt Her More than She Loves Me"	1975	14
"After All the Good is Gone"	1976	13
"The Games that Daddies Play"	1976	13
"I Can't Believe She Gives it All to Me"	1976	14
"Play, Guitar, Play"	1977	16
"I've Already Loved You in My Mind"	1977	15
"Don't Take It Away"	1979	14
"I May Never Get to Heaven"	1979	15
"Happy Birthday Darlin'"	1979	14
"I'd Love to Lay You Down"	1980	13
"Rest Your Love on Me"	1981	16
"Red Neckin' Love Makin' Night"	1981	18
"The Clown"	1982	17
"Slow Hand"	1982	16
"The Rose"	1982	19
"Somebody's Needin' Somebody"	1984	19
"I Don't Know a Thing About Love (the Moon Song)"	1984	19
"Ain't She Somethin' Else"	1985	21
"Don't Call Him a Cowboy"	1985	20
"Desperado Love"	1986	21
"After the Fire is Gone" (with Loretta Lynn)	1971	14
"Lead Me On" (with Loretta Lynn)	1971	17
"Louisiana Woman, Mississippi Man"		

(with Loretta Lynn)	1973	14
"As Soon as I Hang up the Phone"		
(with Loretta Lynn)	1974	15
"Feelin's" (with Loretta Lynn)	1975	16

LEROY VAN DYKE

"Walk on By"	1961	37

PORTER WAGONER

"A Satisfied Mind"	1955	33
"Misery Loves Company"	1962	29
"Please Don't Stop Loving Me"		
(with Dolly Parton)	1974	17

JIMMY WAKELY

"One Has My Name		
(the Other Has My Heart)"	1948	32
"I Love You So Much It Hurts"	1948	28
"Slipping Around"		
(with Margaret Whiting)	1948	28

BILLY WALKER

"Charlie's Shoes"	1962	23

JERRY WALLACE

"If You Leave Me Tonight I'll Cry"	1972	17

STEVE WARINER

"All Roads Lead to You"	1981	18
"Some Fools Never Learn"	1985	22
"You Can Dream of Me"	1985	22
"Life's Highway"	1986	24
"Small Town Girl"	1986	24
"The Weekend"	1987	23
"Lynda"	1987	23

GENE WATSON

"Fourteen Carat Mind"	1981	19

KITTY WELLS

"It Wasn't God Who Made		
Honky Tonk Angels"	1952	18
"Heartbreak, U.S.A."	1961	23
"One by One" (with Red Foley)	1954	41

DOTTIE WEST

"A Lesson in Leavin'"	1980	15
"Are You Happy Baby?"	1980	16
"Every Time Two Fools Collide"		
(with Kenny Rogers)	1978	17
"All I Ever Need Is You"	1979	15
"What Are We Doin' in Love"	1981	15

SHELLY WEST

"Jose Cuervo"	1983	23
"You're the Reason God Made		
Oklahoma" (with David Frizzell)	1981	17

SLIM WILLET

"Don't Let the Stars Get in Your Eyes"	1952	23

DON WILLIAMS

"I Wouldn't Want to Live If		
You Didn't Love Me"	1974	17
"You're My Best Friend"	1975	17
"(Turn Out the Light and)		
Love Me Tonight"	1975	16
"Til the Rivers All Run Dry"	1976	16
"Say It Again"	1976	16
"Some Broken Hearts Never Mend"	1977	16
"I'm Just a Country Boy"	1977	15
"Tulsa Time"	1978	16
"It Must Be Love"	1979	14
"Love Me Over Again"	1980	16
"I Believe in You"	1980	16

HANK WILLIAMS

"Lovesick Blues"	1949	42
"Long Gone Lonesome Blues"	1950	21
"Why Don't You Love Me"	1950	25
"Moanin' the Blues"	1950	15
"Cold, Cold Heart"	1951	46
"Hey, Good Lookin'"	1951	25
"Jambalaya (on the Bayou)"	1952	29
"I'll Never Get Out of		
This World Alive"	1953	13
"KawLiga"	1953	19
"Your Cheatin' Heart"	1953	23
"Take These Chains from My Heart"	1953	13

HANK WILLIAMS, JR.

"All for the Love of Sunshine"	1970	15
"Eleven Roses"	1972	16
"Texas Women"	1981	13
"Dixie on My Mind"	1981	14
"All My Rowdy Friends (Have Settled Down)"	1981	19
"Honky Tonkin'"	1982	15
"I'm for Love"	1985	23
"Ain't Misbehavin'"	1986	18
"Mind Your Own Business" (with Willie Nelson, Reba McEntire, Reverend Ike)	1986	18
"Born to Boogie"	1987	20

TEX WILLIAMS

"Smoke! Smoke! Smoke!"	1947	23

BOB WILLS & HIS TEXAS PLAYBOYS

"Smoke on the Water"	1945	15
"Stars and Stripes on Iwo Jima"	1945	11
"Silver Dew on the Blue Grass Tonight"	1945	14
"White Cross on Okinawa"	1945	5
"New Spanish Two Step"	1946	23
"Sugar Moon"	1947	6

SHEB WOLLEY

"That's My Pa"	1962	17

JOHNNY WRIGHT

"Hello Vietnam"	1965	21

TAMMY WYNETTE

"My Elusive Dreams"	1967	18
"I Don't Wanna Play House"	1967	20
"Take Me to Your World"	1968	17
"D-I-V-O-R-C-E"	1968	17
"Stand by Your Man"	1968	21
"Singing My Song"	1969	14
"The Ways to Love a Man"	1969	16
"He Loves Me All the Way"	1970	16
"Run, Woman, Run"	1970	15
"Good Lovin' (Makes It Right)"	1971	15
"Bedtime Story"	1971	15

"My Man"	1972	14
"Til I Get It Right"	1973	15
"Kids Say the Darndest Things"	1973	17
"Another Lonely Song"	1974	15
"'Til I Can Make It on My Own"	1976	15
"You and Me"	1976	16
"We're Gonna Hold On"		
(with George Jones)	1971	17
"Golden Ring" (with George Jones)	1976	15
"Near You"	1977	16

DWIGHT YOAKAM

"Streets of Bakersfield"		
(with Buck Owens)	1988	18
"I Sang Dixie"	1989	21

FARON YOUNG

"Live Fast, Love Hard, Die Young"	1955	22
"Alone with You"	1958	29
"Country Girl"	1959	32
"Hello Walls"	1961	23
"It's Four in the Morning"	1971	20

FOR THE SAKE OF THE CHILDREN

There are as many mamas and babies in country lyrics as there are car crashes in Burt Reynolds' films. There's probably no more parental love nor neglect among country singers than anybody else; they just know how to belt it out.

Roy Drusky	"You Better Sit Down Kids"
Michael Ballew	"Your Daddy Don't Live in Heaven (He's in Houston)"
Glenn Barber	"Daddy Number Two"
Bobby Bare	"Daddy, What If"
Sherry Brane	"Little Girls Need Daddies"
Dorsey Burnett	"Daddy Loves You, Honey"
Archie Campbell	"The Men in My Little Girl's Life"
Glen Campbell	"The Hand that Rocks the Cradle"
Johnny Paycheck	"I'm the Only Heel Mama Ever Raised"
Buzz Clifford	"Baby Sittin' Boogie"
Paul Evans	"Disneyland Daddy"

Charlie Louvin	"Little Reasons"
	"Here's a Toast to Mama"
Bonnie Owens	"Why Don't Daddy Live Here Anymore"
	"Consider the Children"
Loretta Lynn	"You're the Reason Our Kids Are Ugly"
	"The Pill"
Kentucky HeadHunters	"My Daddy Was a Milkman"
Johnny Cash	"Rosanna's Going Wild"
	"A Boy Named Sue"
	"Daddy Sang Bass"
Kitty Wells	"Anybody out There Wanna Be a Daddy"
Linda Martell	"Color Him Father"
Eddy Arnold	"My Daddy Is Only a Picture"
Claude Gray	"Eight Years and Two Children Later"
	"Daddy Stopped In"
Buck Owens	"Weekend Daddy"
Gail Davies	"Unwed Fathers"
Ferlin Husky	"A Room for a Boy...Never Used"
Waylon Jennings	"Only Daddy that'll Walk the Line"
The LeGardes	"Daddy's Making Records in Nashville"
Kenny Rogers	"I Don't Call Him Daddy"
Pattie West	"Mommy, Can I Still Call Him Daddy"
Hank Williams	"My Son Calls Another Man Daddy"
Hank Williams, Jr.	"Nobody's Child"
Tammy Wynette	"Kids Say the Darndest Things"
Ernest Tubb	"Daddy, When Is Mommy Coming Home"
Charlie Walker	"Daddy's Coming Home (Next Week)"

HEAR THAT WHISTLE BLOW

A train is more than an iron horse in country songs.

"Wabash Cannon Ball"
"Boxcar Willie"
"Desperados Waiting for a Train"
"Runaway Train"

"My Baby Thinks He's a Train"
"She Met a Stranger, I Met a Train"
"Georgia on a Fast Train"
"I Been to Georgia on a Fast Train"
"The Train Runs Through the Middle of the House"
"Freight Train Boogie"
"Big Train from Memphis"
"Train of Love"
"Steel Rail Blues"
"Canadian Pacific"
"Blue Train of the Heartbreak Line"
"New River Train"
"Yonder Comes a Freight Train"
"Train, Train (Carry Me Away)"
"Waiting for a Train (All Around the Watertank)"
"You Can't Blame the Train"
"Can't You Hear that Whistle Blow"

SONGS FOR LUVIN'

What is country music without lovers and liars and cheatin' hearts? These trenchant titles are just the tip of an iceberg.

"Love is a Warm Cowboy"
"Cigarettes and Whiskey and Wild, Wild Women"
"You Broke My Heart So Gently (It Almost Didn't Break)"
"It's Sad to Go to the Funeral"
"Dog Tired of Cattin' Around?"
"The One You Slip Around With"
"I Feel Better All Over More than Anywhere Else"
"Up Too Slow, Down Too Fast"
"If You're Waiting on Me, You're Backing Up"
"Your Heart Turned Left and I Was On the Right"
"It Takes All Day to Get Over Night"
"You Oughta Be Against the Law"
"Am I Going Crazy or Just Out of Her Mind"
"She's Not Really Cheatin', She's Just Gettin' Even"
"Now I Lay Me Down to Cheat"
"Old Flames Can't Hold a Candle to You"
"Livin' Like There's No Tomorrow Finally Got to Me Tonight"
"Cold and Lonely Is the Forecast for Tonight"
"She Took It Like a Man"
"I Love that Woman (Like the Devil Loves Sin)"
"Love Ain't Worth a Dime (Unless It's Free)"

"Walkin', Talkin', Cryin', Barely Beatin' Broken Heart"
"The Worst You Ever Gave Me Was the Best I Ever Had"
"She Can't Get My Love off the Bed"
"I Just Can't Turn My Habit into Love"
"She's Actin' Single (And I'm Drinkin' Doubles)"
"The Older the Violin, the Sweeter the Music"
"'Till My Getup Has Gotup and Gone"
"Guess My Eyes Were Bigger than My Heart"
"Red Neckin' Love Makin' Night"
"Eat, Drink and Be Merry (Tomorrow You'll Cry)"
"You're Out Doin' What I'm Here Doin' Without"
"Instead of Givin' Up (I'm Givin' In)"
"I'm Gonna Put You Back on the Rack"
"Leaving You is Easier than Wishing You Were Gone"
"In at Eight and Out at Ten"
"Don't Let That Doorknob Hit You"
"I'd Rather Loan You Out"
"From Now on All My Friends Are Gonna Be Strangers"
"She Put the Sad in All His Songs"
"Low Class Reunion"
"You Finally Said Something Good"
"You Just Stepped In (from Steppin' out on Me)"
"Common Colds and Broken Hearts"
"The Weeds Outlived the Roses"
"You're Gonna Ruin My Bad Reputation"
"Put Another Notch in Your Belt"
"You Changed Everything About Me but My Name"
"They Always Look Better When They're Leaving"
"I'd Rather Be Picked up Here (than Put Down at Home)"
"Slippin' up Slippin' Around"
"The King of Country Music Meets the
   Queen of Rock & Roll"
"Somebody Ought to Tell Him that She's Gone"
"Why Don't We Lie Down and Talk It Over"

SINGING MOVIE COWBOYS

Sound in the movies was a new and exciting innovation in the 1930s. For some fans of cowboy movies, that meant listening to the hero sing. Over the course of two decades, the following men, as adept with a guitar as with a gun, made hundreds of successful motion pictures:

Rex Allen   The last of the singing cowboys, Allen
                   made his first film in 1950, when popularity
                   of the genre was sinking. But he did star

in 32 films before moving on to a
singing career.

Gene Autry Autry was hired by Republic Studios when
John Wayne refused to sing in any more
films. He went on to star in more than
100 movies.

Bob Baker Baker had a brief career as a singing
cowboy in films that were box
office disappointments.

Dick Foran Born in 1910, Foran was educated at
Princeton, but he ended up in California.
Signed by Republic Studios in 1934, he
made more than two dozen westerns,
although he proved to be a better singer
than actor.

Monte Hale Born in 1921 in San Angelo, Texa, Hale
was one of the last of the singing cowboys,
starring in 19 films from 1946 to 1951.

Ken Maynard The star of many silent films, Maynard
became the first of the singing cowboys
after crooning "Cowboy's Lament" in the
1920 western *The Wagon Master*.

Jack Randall Randall was a fine actor whose career as a
singing cowboy was limited by the fact that
he couldn't sing.

Tex Ritter Ritter began his film career with *Song
of the Gringo* in 1936. He went on to
star in more than 60 films, usually with
his horse, White Flash.

Roy Rogers Roy Rogers was hired by Republic Pictures
in 1938, when Gene Autry was having a
contract dispute with the studio. His first
film, *Under Western Skies*, was a success,
and he made more than 100 pictures
1953. His horse, Trigger, and his co-star,
Dale Evans, became equally famous.

John Wayne Wayne appeared as Singin' Sandy in
Riders of Destiny. He sang three or four
songs in each following film—until
his contract expired.

Ray Whitley   Whitley made his first movie appearance in
               1936. He starred in 18 musical western
               shorts and appeared as the singing sidekick
               to George O'Brien and Tim Holt.

GRAMMY AWARDS TO COUNTRY SONGS AND PERFORMERS

AWARDS FOR 1964

Country & Western Single   Roger Miller,
                            "Dang Me"

Country & Western Album   Roger Miller,
                            Dang Me

Country & Western   Dottie West,
Vocal—Female   "Here Comes My Baby"

Country & Western   Roger Miller,
Vocal—Male   "Dang Me"

Country & Western (Songwriter)   Roger Miller,
                                  "Dang Me"

New Country & Western   Roger Miller
Artist

AWARDS FOR 1965

Contemporary (R&R) Single   Roger Miller,
                             "King of the Road"

Contemporary (R&R)   Roger Miller,
Vocal—Male   "King of the Road"

Contemporary (R&R)   The Statler Brothers,
Performance Group   "Flowers on the Wall"
(Vocal or Instrumental)

Country & Western Single   Roger Miller,
                             "King of the Road"

Country & Western Album   Roger Miller,
                             King of the Road

Country & Western Vocal—Male	Roger Miller, "King of the Road"
Country & Western Song (Songwriter)	Roger Miller, "King of the Road"
New Country & Western Artist	Statler Brothers

AWARDS FOR 1966

Sacred Recording (Musical)	Porter Wagoner & the Blackwood Brothers, *Grand Old Gospel*
Country & Western Recording	David Houston, "Almost Persuaded"
Country & Western Vocal—Female	Jeannie Seely, "Don't Touch Me"
Country & Western Vocal—Male	David Houston, "Almost Persuaded"
Country & Western Song (Tied)	Bill Sherrill, Glenn Sutton, "Almost Persuaded" and Hank Cochran, "Don't Touch Me"

AWARDS FOR 1967

Vocal—Female	Bobbie Gentry, "Ode to Billie Joe"
Vocal—Male	Glen Campbell, "By the Time I Get to Phoenix"
New Artist	Bobbie Gentry
Contemporary Female Solo—Vocal	Bobbie Gentry, "Ode to Billie Joe"
Contemporary Male Solo	Glen Campbell, "By the Time I Get to Phoenix"
Sacred Performance	Elvis Presley, *How Great Thou Art*

Gospel Performance	Porter Wagoner & The Blackwood Brothers Quartet, *More Grand Old Gospel*
Folk Performance	John Hartford, "Gentle on My Mind"
Country & Western Recording	Glen Campbell, "Gentle on My Mind"
Country & Western Solo Vocal-Female	Tammy Wynette, "I Don't Wanna Play House"
Country & Western Solo Vocal—Male	Glen Campbell, "Gentle on My Mind"
Country & Western Duet, Trio or Group (Vocal or Instrumental)	Johnny Cash & June Carter, "Jackson"
Country & Western (Songwriter)	John Hartford, "Gentle on My Mind"
Arrangement Accompanying Vocalist(s) or Instrumentalist(s)	"Ode to Billie Joe," arranged by Jimmie Haskell
Album Notes	John Loudermilk, *Suburban Attitudes in Country Verse*

AWARDS FOR 1968

Album of the Year	Glen Campbell, *By the Time I Get to Phoenix*
Song of the Year (Songwriter)	Bobby Russell, "Little Green Apples"
Best Engineered Recording (Other Than Classical)	"Wichita Lineman," engineered by Joe Polito

Album Notes	Johnny Cash, *At Folsom Prison*
Country Vocal—Female	Jeannie C. Riley, "Harper Valley P.T.A."
Country Vocal—Male	Johnny Cash, "Folsom Prison Blues"
Country-Duo or Group-Vocal or Instrumental	Flatt & Scruggs, "Foggy Mountain Breakdown"
Country Song (Songwriter)	Bobby Russell, "Little Green Apples"
Gospel Performance	The Happy Goodman Family, *The Happy Gospel of the Happy Goodmans*

AWARDS FOR 1969

Album Notes	Johnny Cash, Annotator, *Nashville Skyline* by Bob Dylan
Contemporary Vocal—Male	Harry Nilsson, "Everybody's Talkin'"
Country Vocal—Female	Tammy Wynette, "Stand By Your Man"
Country Vocal—Male	Johnny Cash, "A Boy Named Sue"
Country—Duo or Group	Waylon Jennings & the Kimberlys, "MacArthur Park"
Country Instrumental	Danny Davis & the Nashville Brass
Country Song (Songwriter)	Shel Silverstein, "A Boy Named Sue"
Sacred Performance	Jake Hess, "Ain't that Beautiful Singing"

Gospel Performance	Porter Wagoner & the Blackwood Brothers, *In Gospel Country*

AWARDS FOR 1970

Contemporary Vocal—Female	Bobbie Gentry, "Fancy"
Country Vocal—Female	Lynn Anderson, "Rose Garden"
Country Vocal—Male	Ray Price, "For the Good Times"
Country Vocal—Duo or Group	Johnny Cash & June Carter, "If I Were a Carpenter"
Country Instrumental	Chet Atkins & Jerry Reed, "Me & Jerry"
Country Song	Marty Robbins, "My Woman, My Woman, My Wife"
Sacred Performance—Musical	Jake Hess, "Everything is Beautiful"
Sacred Performance—Other than Soul Gospel	The Oak Ridge Boys, "Talk About the Good Times"

AWARDS FOR 1971

Country Vocal—Female	Sammi Smith, "Help Me Make it Through the Night"
Country Vocal—Male	Jerry Reed, "When You're Hot, You're Hot"
Country Vocal—Duo or Group	Conway Twitty & Loretta Lynn, "After the Fire is Gone"

Country Instrumental	Chet Atkins, "Snowbird"
Country Song (Songwriter)	Kris Kristofferson, "Help Me Make it Through the Night"
Sacred Performance (Musical)	Charley Pride, "Did You Think to Pray"
Gospel Performance— Other than Soul Gospel	Charley Pride, "Let Me Live"

AWARDS FOR 1972

Pop Vocal—Female	Helen Reddy, "I Am Woman"
Country Vocal—Female	Donna Fargo, "Happiest Girl in the Whole U.S.A."
Country Vocal—Male	Charley Pride, "Heart Songs"
Country Vocal— Duo or Group	Statler Brothers, "Class of '57"
Country Instrumental	Charlie McCoy, "The Real McCoy"
Country Song (Songwriter)	Ben Peters, "Kiss an Angel Good Mornin'"
Inspirational Performance	Elvis Presley, "He Touched Me"
Gospel Performance	Blackwood Brothers, "L-O-V-E"

AWARDS FOR 1973

Album Notes	Dan Morgenstern, *God is in the House*
Country Vocal—Female	Olivia Newton-John,

"Let Me Be There"

Country Vocal—Male	Charlie Rich, "Behind Closed Doors"
Country Vocal—Duo or Group	Kris Kristofferson & Rita Coolidge, "From the Bottle to the Bottom"
Country Instrumental	Eric Weissberg, Steve Mandell, "Dueling Banjos"
Country Song (Songwriter)	Kenny O'Dell, "Behind Closed Doors"
Inspirational Performance	Bill Gaither, "Let's Just Praise"
Gospel Performance (Other than Soul Gospel)	Blackwood Brothers, "Release Me From My Sin"

AWARDS FOR 1974

Album Notes	Charles R. Townsend, Annotator, *For the Last Time* by Bob Wills
Country Vocal—Female	Anne Murray, "Love Song"
Country Vocal—Male	Ronnie Milsap, "Please Don't Tell Me How the Story Ends"
Country Vocal—Duo or Group	Pointer Sisters, "Fairytale"
Country Instrumental	Chet Atkins & Merle Travis, "The Atkins/Travis Travelling Show"
Country Song (Songwriter)	Norris Wilson & Billy Sherrill, "A Very Special Love Song"
Inspirational Performance	Elvis Presley,

"How Great Thou Art"

Gospel Performance
(Other than Soul Gospel)

The Oak Ridge Boys,
"The Baptism of
Jesse Taylor"

AWARDS FOR 1975
Album of the Year

Linda Ronstadt,
Heart Like a Wheel

Song of the Year (Songwriter)

Larry Weiss,
"Rhinestone Cowboy"

Arrangement for Vocalist(s)

Ray Stevens, "Misty"

Country Vocal—Female

Linda Ronstadt,
"I Can't Help It if I'm
Still in Love With You"

Country Vocal—Male

Willie Nelson,
"Blue Eyes Crying
in the Rain"

Country Vocal—Duo or Group

Kris Kristofferson
& Rita Coolidge,
"Lover Please"

Country Instrumental

Chet Atkins,
"The Entertainer"

Country (Songwriter)

Chips Moman & Larry
Butler, "Hey, Won't You
Play Another Somebody
Done Somebody
Wrong Song"

Inspirational Performance

Bill Gaither Trio, "Jesus,
We Just Want to
Thank You"

Gospel Performance
(Other than Soul Gospel)

Imperials,
"No Shortage"

AWARDS FOR 1976
Country Vocal—Female

Emmylou Harris,
"Elite Hotel"

Country Vocal—Male	Ronnie Milsap, "I'm a Stand by My Woman Man"
Country Vocal—Duo or Group	Amazing Rhythm Aces, "The End Is Not in Sight"
Country Instrumental	Chet Atkins & Les Paul, "Chester & Lester"
Country Song (Songwriter)	Larry Gatlin, "Broken Lady"
Inspirational Performance	Gary S. Paxton, "The Astonishing, Incredible, Unbelievable, Different World of Gary S. Paxton"
Gospel Performance	Oak Ridge Boys, "Where the Soul Never Dies"

AWARDS FOR 1977

Album Package	Kosh, Art Director for *Simple Dreams* by Linda Ronstadt
Producer of the Year	Peter Asher for James Taylor, Linda Ronstadt, et al.
Country Vocal—Female	Crystal Gayle, "Don't it Make My Brown Eyes Blue"
Country Vocal—Male	Kenny Rogers, "Lucille"
Country Vocal—Duo or Group	The Kendalls, "Heaven's Just a Sin Away"
Country Instrumental	Hargus "Pig" Robbins, "Country Instrumentalist of the Year"

| Country Song (Songwriter) | Richard Leigh, "Don't it Make My Brown Eyes Blue" |

AWARDS FOR 1978

Pop Vocal—Female	Anne Murray, "You Needed Me"
Country Vocal—Female	Dolly Parton, "Here You Come Again"
Country Vocal—Male	Willie Nelson, "Georgia on My Mind"
Country Vocal—Duo or Group	Waylon Jennings, Willie Nelson, "Mamas, Don't Let Your Babies Grow Up to be Cowboys"
Country Instrumental	Asleep at the Wheel, "One O'Clock Jump"
Country Song (Songwriter)	Don Schlitz, "The Gambler"
Gospel Performance—Traditional	Happy Goodman Family, "Refreshing"
Inspirational Performance	B.J. Thomas, "Happy Man"

AWARDS FOR 1979

Country Vocal—Female	Emmylou Harris, "Blue Kentucky Girl"
Country Vocal—Male	Kenny Rogers, "The Gambler"
Country Vocal—Duo or Group	Charlie Daniels Band, "The Devil Went Down to Georgia"
Country Instrumental	Doc & Merle Watson, "Big Sandy"

Country Song (Songwriter)	Bob Morrison, Debbie Hupp, "You Decorated My Life"
Gospel Performance	The Blackwood Brothers, "Lift Up the Name of Jesus"
Inspirational Performance	B. J. Thomas, "You Gave Me Love"
Producer of the Year	Larry Butler for Kenny Rogers

AWARDS FOR 1980

Country Vocal—Female	Anne Murray, "Could I Have This Dance"
Country Vocal—Male	George Jones, "He Stopped Loving Her Today"
Country—Duo or Group	Roy Orbison, Emmylou Harris, "That Lovin' You Feelin' Again"
Country Instrumental	Gilley's Urban Cowboy Band, "Orange Blossom Special Hoedown"
Country Song (Songwriter)	Willie Nelson, "On the Road Again"
Gospel Performance— Traditional	The Blackwood Brothers, "We Come to Worship"

AWARDS FOR 1981

Country Vocal—Female	Dolly Parton, "9 to 5"
Country Vocal—Male	Ronnie Milsap, "No Gettin' Over Me"
Country Performance— Duo or Group	The Oak Ridge Boys, "Elvira"

Country Instrumental	Chet Atkins, "Country After All These Years"
Country Song (Songwriter)	Dolly Parton, "9 to 5"
Gospel Performance—Traditional	The Blackwood Brothers, "Masters"
Inspirational Performance	B. J. Thomas, "Amazing Grace"

AWARDS FOR 1982

Song of the Year (Songwriter)	Johnny Christopher, Mark James Wayne Thompson, "Always on My Mind"
Country Vocal—Female	Juice Newton, "Break It to Me Gently"
Country Vocal—Male	Willie Nelson, "Always on My Mind"
Country—Duo or Group	Alabama, "Mountain Music"
Country Song (Songwriter)	Johnny Christopher, Mark James, Wayne Thompson, "Always on My Mind"
Gospel Performance—Traditional	The Blackwood Brothers, "I'm Following You"
Inspirational Performance	Barbara Mandrell, "He Set My Life to Music"

AWARDS FOR 1983

Best Country Vocal—Female	Anne Murray, "A Little Good News"
Best Country Vocal—Male	Lee Greenwood, "I.O.U."
Best Country Performance by a Duo or Group	Alabama, "The Closer You Get"

Best Country Instrumental	The New South, "Fireball"
Best New Country Song	Mike Reid, "Stranger in My House"

AWARDS FOR 1984

Best Country Vocal—Female	Emmylou Harris, "In My Dreams"
Best Country Vocal—Male	Merle Haggard, "That's the Way Love Goes"
Best Country by Duo or Group	The Judds, "Mama, He's Crazy"
Best Country Instrumental	Ricky Skaggs, "Wheel Hoss"
Best Country Song (Songwriter)	Steve Goodman, "City of New Orleans"

AWARDS FOR 1985

Best Country Vocal—Female	Rosanne Cash, "I Don't Know Why You Don't Want Me"
Best Country Vocal—Male	Ronnie Milsap, "Lost in the Fifties Tonight"
Best Country Performance by Duo or Group	The Judds, *Why Not Me*
Best Country Instrumental	Chet Atkins, "Cosmic Square Dance
Best Country Song (Songwriter)	Jimmy L. Webb, "Highwayman"

AWARDS FOR 1986

Best Country Vocal—Female	Reba McEntire, "Whoever's in New England"
Best Country Vocal—Male	Ronnie Milsap, *Lost in the*

Fifties Tonight

Best Country Performance, Duo or Group	The Judds, "Grandpa (Tell Me About the Good Old Days)"
Best Country Instrumental	Ricky Skaggs, "Raisin' the Dickins"
Best Country Song (Songwriter)	Jamie O'Hara, "Grandpa (Tell Me About the Good Old Days)"
Best Spoken Word or Non-Musical Recording	*Interviews from the Class of '55 Recording Sessions* (Carl Perkins, Jerry Lee Lewis, Roy Orbison, Johnny Cash, et al)

AWARDS FOR 1987

Song of the Year (Songwriter)	Linda Ronstadt & James Ingram, "Somewhere Out There"
Best Country Vocal—Female	K. T. Oslin, "80's Ladies"
Best Country Vocal—Male	Randy Travis, "Always & Forever"
Best Country Vocal by Duo or Group	Dolly Parton, Linda Ronstadt, & Emmylou Harris, *Trio*
Best Country Vocal Performance, Duet	Ronnie Milsap & Kenny Rogers, "Make No Mistake, She's Mine"
Best Country Instrumental	Asleep at the Wheel, "String of Pars"
Best Country Song (Songwriter)	Randy Travis, Paul Overstreet, & Don Schlitz, "Forever and Ever, Amen"

Best Album Package	Bill Johnson, Art Director for *King's Record Shop* by Rosanne Cash

AWARDS FOR 1988

Best Country Vocal—Female	K. T. Oslin, "Hold Me"
Best Country Vocal—Male	Randy Travis, *Old 8 X 10*
Best Country Performance by a Duo or Group with Vocal	The Judds, "Give a Little Love"
Best Country Vocal Collaboration	Roy Orbison & k.d. lang, "Crying"
Best Country Instrumental	Asleep at the Wheel, "Sugarfoot Rag"
Best Country Song (Songwriter)	K. T. Oslin, "Hold Me"
Best Bluegrass Recording (Vocal or Instrumental)	Bill Monroe, "Southern Flavor"

AWARDS FOR 1989

Best Country Vocal—Female	k.d. lang, *Absolute Torch and Twang*
Best Country Vocal—Male	Lyle Lovett, *Lyle Lovett and His Large Band*
Best Country Vocal by a Duo or Group with Vocal	The Nitty Gritty Dirt Band, *Will the Circle Be Unbroken*
Best Country Vocal Collaboration	Hank Williams, Jr. and Hank Williams, Sr., "There's a Tear in My Beer"
Best Country Instrumental	Randy Scruggs, "Amazing Grace"
Best Bluegrass Recording	Bruce Hornsby & the Nitty Gritty Dirt

Band, "The Valley Road"

Best Country Song (Songwriter)   Rodney Crowell, "After All This Time"

AWARDS FOR 1990

Best Country Vocal—Female   Kathy Mattea, "Where've You Been"

Best Country Vocal—Male   Vince Gill, "When I Call Your Name"

Best Country Duo or Group   The Kentucky HeadHunters, *Pickin' on Nashville*

Best Country Vocal Collaboration   Chet Atkins & Mark Knopfler, "Poor Boy Blues"

Best Country Instrumental   Chet Atkins & Mark Knopfler, "So Soft Your Goodbye"

Best Bluegrass Recording   Alison Krauss, "I've Got That Old Feeling"

Best Country Song (Songwriter)   Kathy Mattea, "Where've You Been"

AWARDS FOR 1991

Best Country Vocal—Female   Mary Chapin Carpenter, "Down at the Twist and Shout"

Best Country Vocal—Male   Garth Brooks, *Ropin' the Wind*

Best Country Duo or Group   The Judds, "Love Can Build a Bridge"

Best Country Vocal Collaboration   Vince Gill, Ricky Skaggs, Steve Wariner, "Restless"

Best Bluegrass Album	Carl Jackson & John Starling, *Spring Training*
Best Country Instrumental	Mark O'Connor, *The New Nashville Cats*
Best Country Song (Songwriter)	Naomi Judd, John Jarvis, Paul Overstreet, "Love Can Build a Bridge"
Best Southern Gospel Album	The Gaither Vocal Band, *Homecoming*

THE COUNTRY MUSIC ASSOCIATION AWARDS

The Country Music Association was founded in Nashville in 1958 to promote country music. In 1961, the CMA founded the Country Music Hall of Fame and Museum; in 1967, the same year the Museum opened, it began its prestigious annual awards program.

ENTERTAINER OF THE YEAR		FEMALE VOCALIST OF THE YEAR	
1967	Eddy Arnold	1967	Loretta Lynn
1968	Glen Campbell	1968	Tammy Wynette
1969	Johnny Cash	1969	Tammy Wynette
1970	Merle Haggard	1970	Tammy Wynette
1971	Charley Pride	1971	Lynn Anderson
1972	Loretta Lynn	1972	Loretta Lynn
1973	Roy Clark	1973	Loretta Lynn
1974	Charlie Rich	1974	Olivia Newton-John
1975	John Denver	1975	Dolly Parton
1976	Mel Tillis	1976	Dolly Parton
1977	Ronnie Milsap	1977	Crystal Gayle
1978	Dolly Parton	1978	Crystal Gayle
1979	Willie Nelson	1979	Barbara Mandrell
1980	Barbara Mandrell	1980	Emmylou Harris
1981	Barbara Mandrell	1981	Barbara Mandrell
1982	Alabama	1982	Janie Frickie
1983	Alabama	1983	Janie Frickie

1984	Alabama	1984	Reba McEntire
1985	Ricky Skaggs	1985	Reba McEntire
1986	Reba McEntire	1986	Reba McEntire
1987	Hank Williams, Jr.	1987	Reba McEntire
1988	Hank Williams, Jr.	1988	K. T. Oslin
1989	George Strait	1989	Kathy Mattea
1990	George Strait	1990	Kathy Mattea
1991	Garth Brooks	1991	Tanya Tucker

MALE VOCALIST OF THE YEAR

MUSICIAN OF THE YEAR

(changed from instrumentalist of the year in 1988)

1967	Jack Greene	1967	Chet Atkins
1968	Glen Campbell	1968	Chet Atkins
1969	Johnny Cash	1969	Chet Atkins
1970	Merle Haggard	1970	Jerry Reed
1971	Charley Pride	1971	Charley Pride
1972	Charley Pride	1972	Charlie McCoy
1973	Charlie Rich	l973	Charlie Mccoy
1974	Ronnie Milsap	1974	Don Rich
1975	Waylon Jennings	1975	Johnny Gimble
1976	Ronnie Milsap	1976	Hargus "Pig" Robbins
1977	Ronnie Milsap	1977	Roy Clark
1978	Don Williams	1978	Roy Clark
1979	Kenny Rogers	1979	Charlie Daniels
1980	George Jones	1980	Roy Clark
1981	George Jones	1981	Chet Atkins
1982	Ricky Skaggs	1982	Chet Atkins
1983	Lee Greenwood	1983	Chet Atkins
1984	Lee Greenwood	1984	Chet Atkins
1985	George Strait	1985	Chet Atkins
1986	George Strait	1986	Johnny Gimble
1987	Randy Travis	1987	Johnny Gimble
1988	Randy Travis	1988	Chet Atkins
1989	Ricky Van Shelton	1989	Johnny Gimble
1990	Clint Black	1990	Johnny Gimble
1991	Garth Brooks	1991	Mark O'Connor

VOCAL GROUP OF THE YEAR

VOCAL DUO OF THE YEAR

(introduced in 1970)

| 1967 | The Stoneman Family |
| 1968 | Porter Wagoner & Dolly Parton |

1969	Johnny Cash & June Carter		
1970	The Glaser Brothers	1970	Porter Wagoner & Dolly Parton
1971	The Osborne Brothers	1971	Porter Wagoner & Dolly Parton
1972	The Statler Brothers	1972	Conway Twitty & Loretta Lynn
1973	The Statler Brothers	1973	Conway Twitty & Loretta Lynn
1974	The Statler Brothers	1974	Conway Twitty & Loretta Lynn
1975	The Statler Brothers	1975	Conway Twitty & Loretta Lynn
1976	The Statler Brothers	1976	Waylon Jennings & Willie Nelson
1977	The Statler Brothers	1977	Jim Ed Brown & Helen Cornelius
1978	The Oak Ridge Boys	1978	Kenny Rogers & Dottie West
1979	The Statler Brothers	1979	Kenny Rogers & Dottie West
1980	The Statler Brothers	1980	Moe Bandy & Joe Stampley
1981	Alabama	1981	David Frizzell & Shelly West
1982	Alabama	1982	David Frizzell & Shelly West
1983	Alabama	1983	Merle Haggard & Willie Nelson
1984	The Statler Brothers	1984	Willie Nelson & Julio Iglesias
1985	The Judds	1985	Anne Murray & Dave Loggins
1986	The Judds	1986	Dan Seals & Marie Osmond
1987	The Judds	1987	Ricky Skaggs & Sharon White
1988	Highway 101	1988	The Judds
1989	Highway 101	1989	The Judds
1990	Kentucky HeadHunters	1990	The Judds
1991	Kentucky HeadHunters	1991	The Judds

VOCAL EVENT OF THE YEAR (INTRODUCED IN 1988)

1988   *Trio* Dolly Parton, Emmylou Harris and
        Linda Ronstadt
1989   Hank Williams, Jr. and Hank Williams, Sr.
1990   Lorrie Morgan and Keith Whitley
1991   Mark O'Connor & the New Nashville Cats,
            featuring VinceGill, Ricky Skaggs and Steve
            Wariner

ALBUM OF THE YEAR

1967   *There Goes My Everything,* Jack Greene
1968   *Johnny Cash at Folsom Prison,* Johnny Cash
1969   *Johnny Cash at San Quentin Prison,* Johnny Cash
1970   *Okie from Muskogee,* Merle Haggard
1971   *I Won't Mention It Again,* Ray Price
1972   *Let Me Tell You About a Song,* Merle Haggard
1973   *Behind Closed Doors,* Charlie Rich
1974   *A Very Special Love Song,* Charlie Rich
1975   *A Legend in My Time,* Ronnie Milsap
1976   *Wanted—the Outlaws,* Waylon Jennings, Willie
            Nelson, Tompall Glaser, Jessi Colter
1977   *Ronnie Milsap Live,* Ronnie Milsap
1978   *It Was Almost Like a Song,* Ronnie Milsap
1979   *The Gambler,* Kenny Rogers
1980   *Coal Miner's Daughter,* Motion Picture Soundtrack
1981   *I Believe in You,* Don Williams
1982   *Always on My Mind,* Willie Nelson
1983   *The Closer You Get,* Alabama
1984   *A Little Good News,* Anne Murray
1985   *Does Fort Worth Ever Cross Your Mind,* George Strait
1986   *Lost in the Fifties Tonight,* Ronnie Milsap
1987   *Always and Forever,* Randy Travis
1988   *Born to Boogie,* Hank Williams, Jr.
1989   *Will the Circle Be Unbroken,* Nitty Gritty Dirt Band
1990   *Pickin' on Nashville,* Kentucky Head Hunters
1991   *No Fences,* Garth Brooks

SINGLE OF THE YEAR

1967   "There Goes My Everything," Jack Greene
1968   "Harper Valley P.T.A.," Jeannie C. Riley
1969   "A Boy Named Sue," Johnny Cash
1970   "Okie from Muskogee," Merle Haggard
1971   "Help Me Make It Through the Night,"
        Sammi Smith

1972	"The Happiest Girl in the Whole U.S.A.," Donna Fargo
1973	"Behind Closed Doors," Charlie Rich
1974	"Country Bumpkin," Cal Smith
1975	"Before the Next Teardrop Falls," Freddy Fender
1976	"Good Hearted Woman," Waylon Jennings & Willie Nelson
1977	"Lucille," Kenny Rogers
1978	"Heaven's Just a Sin Away," The Kendalls
1979	"The Devil Went Down to Georgia," Charlie Daniels Band
1980	"He Stopped Loving Her Today," George Jones
1981	"Elvira," The Oak Ridge Boys
1982	"Always on My Mind," Willie Nelson
1983	"Swingin'," John Anderson
1984	"A Little Good News," Anne Murray
1985	"Why Not Me," The Judds
1986	"Bop," Dan Seals
1987	"Forever and Ever, Amen," Randy Travis
1988	"Eighteen Wheels and a Dozen Roses," Kathy Mattea
1989	"I'm No Stranger to the Rain," Keith Whitley
1990	"When I Call Your Name," Vince Gill
1991	"Friends in Low Places," Garth Brooks

SONG OF THE YEAR (TO THE SONGWRITERS)

1967	"There Goes My Everything," Dallas Frazier
1968	"Honey," Bobby Russell
1969	"Carroll County Accident," Bob Ferguson
1970	"Sunday Morning Coming Down," Kris Kristofferson
1971	"Easy Loving," Freddie Hart
1972	"Easy Loving," Freddie Hart
1973	"Behind Closed Doors," Kenny O'Dell
1974	"Country Bumpkin," Don Wayne
1975	"Back Home Again," John Denver
1976	"Rhinestone Cowboy," Larry Weiss
1977	"Lucille," Roger Bowling & Hal Bynum
1978	"Don't It Make My Brown Eyes Blue," Richard Leigh
1979	"The Gambler," Don Schlitz
1980	"He Stopped Loving Her Today," Bobby Braddock & Curly Putman
1981	"He Stopped Loving Her Today," Bobby Braddock & Curly Putman
1982	"Always on My Mind," Johnny Christopher, Wayne Carson & Mark James

1983	"Always on My Mind," Johnny Christopher, Wayne Carson & Mark James
1984	"Wind Beneath My Wings," Larry Henley & Jeff Silbar
1985	"God Bless the USA," Lee Greenwood
1986	"On the Other Hand," Paul Overstreet & Don Schlitz
1987	"Forever and Ever, Amen," Paul Overstreet & Don Schlitz
1988	"80's Ladies," K. T. Oslin
1989	"Chiseled in Stone," Max D. Barnes & Vern Gosdin
1990	"Where've You Been," Jon Vezner & Don Henry
1991	"When I Call Your Name," Tim DuBois & Vince Gill

MUSIC VIDEO OF THE YEAR (INITIATED IN 1985)

1985	"All My Rowdy Friends Are Comin' Over Tonight," Hank Williams, Jr.
1986	"Who's Gonna Fill Their Shoes," George Jones
1987	"My Name is Bocephus," Hank Williams, Jr.
1988	(not awarded)
1989	"There's a Tear in My Beer," Hank Williams, Jr. & Hank Williams, Sr., directed by Ethan Russell
1990	"The Dance," Garth Brooks, directed by John Lloyd Miller
1991	"The Thunder Rolls," Garth Brooks, directed by Bud Schaetzle

HORIZON AWARD (INITIATED IN 1981)

1981	Terri Gibbs	1987	Holly Dunn
1982	Ricky Skaggs	1988	Ricky Van Shelton
1983	John Anderson	1989	Clint Black
1984	The Judds	1990	Garth Brooks
1985	Sawyer Brown	1991	Travis Tritt
1986	Randy Travis		

INDEX